# PRAISE FOR *USING SEMIOTICS IN RETAIL*

An essential guide for retailers and marketers looking to leverage the competitive advantage that comes from gaining a deeper understanding of customers and how they see your brand. Rachel provides some great insights, backed up by examples from her work with brands from across the globe, and provides a toolkit that allows you to apply the principles to your role right away.
**Gareth Lloyd, Head of Marketing, Pricing, Morrison Supermarkets**

What a fantastic read, full of thought-provoking insights for retailers, providing a great balance between theory and real-life application of semiotics in the commercial world. It was hard to put it down!
**Kamila Cedro, Insight Manager, Boots**

Rachel Lawes's book is as fascinating as ever in terms of her bottom-up semiotic analysis. What makes it vital though is the top-down cultural analysis. She details a cultural milieu riven by anxiety, loneliness and depersonalization but, critically, provides the thinking, tools and ideas for companies and brands to start to take remedial and ameliorative action. A vital read for the times we now live and work in.
**Richard Warren, Director of Marketing Communications, Lloyds Banking Group**

Finally, a book about semiotics in retailing by a semiotics veteran who lists Unilever, Procter and Gamble, Diageo, Boots, Morrisons and Mondelez among her present and former clients. Rachel Lawes knows the industry well! If you're a retailer, you need to read this book. If you're studying marketing, branding, retail UX and/or consumer behaviour, you need to read this book. In fact, if you're in any way, shape or form part of a digital ecosystem, you must read this book. Like, now! What are you waiting for? Add it into your basket and check out.
**Zubin Sethna, Professor of Entrepreneurial Marketing and Consumer Behaviour, Regent's University London, Co-author, *Consumer Behaviour***

Rachel Lawes takes us on a journey of semiotics, encouraging us to ask and address the killer consumer questions through this engaging read. Rachel propels our understanding of the consumer, enabling an improved retail experience with a revenue-driving focus at the root.

This book will help readers to use semiotic elements to connote free shipping, returns or hallmarks of quality that consumers are looking for to make a buying decision. This may play out in packaging and brand comms, or through building consumer trust to trigger the desired consumer response.

Rachel expertly intertwines real-world examples with theoretical concepts so we can better understand our consumers by simplifying complexity. Consumer memory structures and visual cues are critical as to whether you will win or be left behind in this fast-evolving retail landscape. If you want to authenticate your business and win with the consumer then I highly encourage you to read this book!

**Hugo Proffitt, Head of Ecommerce Singapore, adidas**

Whether you are a retailer, a retail marketer or a brand marketer who relies on consumers for brand engagement, affinity, advocacy and sales, Rachel Lawes has written the playbook to inform your future success. Lawes is not only a leading global authority on semiotics, but a futurist who shares her vision for the future of retail and shopper marketing. *Using Semiotics in Retail* is required reading for every executive who conducts business at the intersection of retail, shopping, consumers and marketing.

**Mark Beal, Assistant Professor of Professional Practice in Public Relations, Rutgers University, Author,** *Engaging Gen Z*

*Using Semiotics in Retail* is a potent cocktail of knowledge on retail and shopper behaviour. Offering a much-needed reality check, the book helps readers see the bigger picture and understand the power that semiotics can wield. Deep diving into digital ecosystems, behavioural futures markets, and decentralised economies, it is not only sensitive to emerging digital culture, diversity and inclusivity, it is an excellent follow up to Rachel Lawes' first book, *Using Semiotics in Marketing*.

**Muchaneta Kapfunde, Founder, FashNerd.com**

Humorous, thought-provoking and forward gazing! Another brilliant read by Rachel. This book reveals how the brand giants of this world apply semiotics, how you too can apply semiotics within your own work, as well as sharing manifestations of familiar cultural 'codes'. A particular highlight within this book for me is Rachel's documentary of human behaviour in the pandemic, the need states of shopping online! It's honest and refreshing to see these anecdotes in ink. An essential read for anyone working in marketing, design and branding. I am also pleased to hear that I am not the only one bulk buying Fruit of the Loom T-shirts!
**Caroline Brierley, Packaging Innovation Manager and semiotics enthusiast, Princes**

An insightful, surprising and highly enjoyable read. Rachel explains the theory and practice of semiotics with an energy that makes the pages turn themselves. But beyond that, it's also a brilliantly useful tool, because she never takes her eye off the end goal – how can all of this be used to create a competitive advantage?
**Ruth Chadwick, Head of Strategy, Lucky Generals**

Rachel is one of the most provocative and unique thinkers in the field of marketing I've ever encountered. Her approach to semiotics is weapons-grade insight for modern marketers. Her writing is not only clear and immediately helpful, it's also entertaining – something one rarely encounters in marketing literature.
**Bhavin Pabari, Strategy Director, Mother**

Wow! I loved her first book and this one is even better. I couldn't put it down. Entertaining, gripping and humorous – this book is all those things and still manages to be a serious, solid dive into the way shoppers shop, coupled to straightforward, practical advice that every marketeer can use. Rachel Lawes combines the literary style of a novelist with no-nonsense advice on actions every marketeer can do to improve sales, brought to life with real world examples. Learning about semiotics has never been more engaging for non-academics, nor more practically valuable for everyone.
**Andrew Cowen, Founder, Bluespark Commercial Strategy**

Semiotics can often feel daunting and inaccessible and this book will unlock understanding in how you can practically harness this methodology. I especially loved the case studies which really help to bring the theory to life – a must-read for anyone interested in how consumers assign meaning to colours, signs and symbols – then importantly, how you can harness this insight to create meaningful experiences.
**Hayley Ward, Director of User Research and Insight, Deliveroo**

Rachel Lawes' personal writing style is engaging, evocative, and enjoyable. It's like having an enthusiastic conversation with her about semiotics and its applications in society.

She guides you through what was and what is now retail and marketing and the total experience of shopping, as well as the rise of consumer activists. Rachel Lawes also provides a clear set of guides and shortcuts on how to arrive at the right signs to communicate the meaning of each element of a story effectively and evocatively. The example from Unilever helps explain the theory and practice to those new to the field.

More importantly, the book highlights the power of semiotics to influence individuals and society beyond consumerism towards responsible living. This resonates with current viewpoints in design practice and education, which is why I will be using this book to underpin learning and teaching in my undergraduate and postgraduate modules.
**Dr George Torrens, Senior Lecturer in Industrial Design and Assistive Products, Loughborough University**

I've had the pleasure of working directly with Rachel Lawes, collaborating on research projects conducted all around the world. Having the opportunity to not just tell a story about data, but instead tell a story about people, is what continues to drive me towards semiotics and collaborate with THE expert herself.
**Dana DiGregorio, Global Managing Director, MESH Experience**

This book will get you thinking differently about things you see every day. As someone who works in the creative side of advertising, this is the greatest gift I could ask for. Lawes' whirlwind tour through human behaviour, psychology and the shop aisle deepens your understanding of what it means to shop both in person and online. A must-read for everyone in marketing who wants to stay forever curious.
**Audrey Madden, Creative Strategist, Huel**

One of the original founders of commercial semiotics, Rachel Lawes, delivers again! Her new book helps you to look at the world from a semiotic perspective and understand how retail and shopping act like a cultural litmus test. *Using Semiotics in Retail* takes you on a journey from the present to the future, looking at how consumer culture may change. Filled with interesting examples, thought-provoking points and digestible activities throughout the text, Rachel Lawes also includes tools and questions for application. A plethora of resources to help you think critically about the versions of reality in which both consumers and businesses reside. Don't pass up the opportunity to take advantage of her decades of experience and clear articulation to make sense of your customers, whether online or offline, solve your marketing problems, design creative solutions and implement her top-down analysis to become a better semiotic practitioner and researcher. The future is yours; will you choose the light side or the dark side?
**Heidi L Dent, Assistant Professor of Marketing, Western Carolina University**

With 95% of purchase decisions being habitual, it is important to understand the rules your customer's brain is using to make a choice (so you can help them choose you). The subconscious buying brain is constantly looking for signs, symbols and other associations to help it make those decisions and *Using Semiotics in Retail* does a fantastic job of showcasing how to apply this skill to make it easier for the semiotics to work in your favour instead of against you. Everyone working for a retail brand needs to read this book so they can make it easier for customers to do business with them.
**Melina Palmer, Founder and CEO, The Brainy Business®, LLC**

Part semiotics bible, part personal diary, this is a fascinating account of all those delicate touches in malls and markets that subtly win us over. *Using Semiotics in Retail* will compel you to analyse every shelf, aisle and shop window in an attempt to uncover the layers of social intelligence that went into their design; whether it's the emotional impact of walking underneath arches, the nostalgic pull of jelly beans, the slickness of honeycomb structures or the power of creating actual magic in-store. This book has – quite literally – opened my eyes, and will probably make me money, thanks to all the new knowledge I have. No one knows the subject better than Rachel, and for the insider intel alone it's an absolute must for every communications student and marketer.
**Amy Charlotte Kean, Founder and CEO, Six Things Impossible**

# Using Semiotics in Retail

*Leverage consumer insight to engage shoppers and boost sales*

Rachel Lawes

KoganPage

**Publisher's note**

Every possible effort has been made to ensure that the information contained in this book is accurate at the time of going to press, and the publishers and authors cannot accept responsibility for any errors or omissions, however caused. No responsibility for loss or damage occasioned to any person acting, or refraining from action, as a result of the material in this publication can be accepted by the editor, the publisher or the author.

First published in Great Britain and the United States in 2022 by Kogan Page Limited

Apart from any fair dealing for the purposes of research or private study, or criticism or review, as permitted under the Copyright, Designs and Patents Act 1988, this publication may only be reproduced, stored or transmitted, in any form or by any means, with the prior permission in writing of the publishers, or in the case of reprographic reproduction in accordance with the terms and licences issued by the CLA. Enquiries concerning reproduction outside these terms should be sent to the publishers at the undermentioned addresses:

| 2nd Floor, 45 Gee Street | 8 W 38th Street, Suite 902 | 4737/23 Ansari Road |
| London | New York, NY 10018 | Daryaganj |
| EC1V 3RS | USA | New Delhi 110002 |
| United Kingdom | | India |
| www.koganpage.com | | |

Kogan Page books are printed on paper from sustainable forests.

© Rachel Lawes, 2022

The right of Rachel Lawes to be identified as the author of this work has been asserted by her in accordance with the Copyright, Designs and Patents Act 1988.

**ISBNs**

Hardback    978 1 3986 0384 4
Paperback   978 1 3986 0382 0
Ebook       978 1 3986 0383 7

**British Library Cataloguing-in-Publication Data**

A CIP record for this book is available from the British Library.

Typeset by Integra Software Services, Pondicherry
Print production managed by Jellyfish
Printed and bound by 4edge Limited, UK

# CONTENTS

*About the author* xiii
*Foreword by Unilever* xiv
*Dear Reader: a letter, from me to you* xv
*How this book is organized* xix

**PART ONE**
Case studies: semiotics in real-world retail 1

### 01 Semiotics will change your career in retail or retail marketing 3

A semiotic story about retail: jam of death 4
Activity: Where have I seen this before? 7
Prompt questions in semiotics 9
The overall approach of semiotics: big facts and key terms 10
How is semiotics used in retail marketing? 16
Is semiotics useful for designing customer experiences? 17
How is this book different from other books on shopper behaviour and psychology? 18
References 21

### 02 How Unilever uses semiotics 23

What's coming up 23
Introductions 24
What is semiotics? How is it applied within Unilever? 25
Business practice: tools for marketers 27
Global design and marketing 28
Category management, navigation and fixtures 31
E-commerce 33
The magic of semiotics 37
Marketing to specific cultures and regions 41
Endnotes 45
References 46

## PART TWO
The present day 47

### 03 Desire 49
What's coming up 49
How to excite shoppers: three big tips for retail marketers 50
Aesthetics, Instagram and the lifelong desire of the excluded 53
Pleasure and satisfaction: the immediate and the real 56
Romantic desire, imagination and longing 59
Rewards and disappointments of shopping 62
References 66

### 04 'Premium, natural, sensational!' How to create meaning 67
What's coming up 67
Premium 68
Value 70
Natural, healthy and sustainable 73
Authentic and traditional 75
Future-facing 77
Sensational and exciting 80
Power 82
Global and local 84
References 88

### 05 Shopper needs and behaviour 89
What's coming up 89
A shopper's story 89
Control, comfort and rewards 91
Shopper needs and missions 95
Stories: why they matter and what you should do about them 100
References 105

### 06 Shopping and identity 107
What's coming up 107
The Legend of GameStop and Wall Street Bets 108

Diversity and inclusivity 113
Conspicuous consumption: when more is more 119
Semiotic analysis: reality and representations of reality 120
Endnotes 124
References 125

**PART THREE**
The future 127

## 07 The future of business 129

What's coming up 129
The behavioural futures market 130
Double 11 134
Play-to-earn 139
Creator economies and decentralized economies 144
References 149

## 08 The future of consumers 150

What's coming up 150
Sicknesses of consumer culture 150
Relationships 157
Future objects of desire 163
References 168

## 09 The future of retail 171

What's coming up 171
Digital ecosystems 171
'I have a traditional grocery store or a small physical store' 176
'I am branching out with a digital presence' 180
'I want to design a fully integrated and innovative customer experience' 185
Endnotes 190
References 190

## 10 The future of everything 192

What's coming up 192
Talent 192

Smart cities 197
Future humans 203
Endnotes 212
References 213

**PART FOUR**

You can do semiotics: tools for retailers 217

## 11 Fast answers to everyday questions 219

What's coming up 219
1. Attention and attraction 220
2. Engagement 222
3. Selling 223
4. Merchandising and category management 225
5. Navigation 227
6. In-store experience, including pleasure 229
7. Communicating brand values 231
8. Communicating brand architecture and range 233
9. E-commerce 235
10. Global marketing 238
Endnotes 240
Reference 241

## 12 Tools for thinking: how to generate ideas using semiotics 242

What's coming up 243
Reality is in crisis 243
Reality is under construction 246
Everything is a group effort 249
How to decode stories 253
How to track power 257
Dear Reader: An end and a beginning 260
Endnote 261
References 261

*Acknowledgements* 262
*Index* 263

# ABOUT THE AUTHOR

Dr Rachel Lawes is a social psychologist specializing in the interface between individuals and consumer culture. She has supplied brand strategy and consumer insight, using social psychology, semiotics and discourse analysis, to brands in 20 countries via Lawes Consulting Ltd (established in 2002). The publication of *Using Semiotics in Retail* coincides with its 20th anniversary.

Rachel's academic career started with a PhD from Loughborough University's internationally renowned Discourse and Rhetoric Group (DARG), and recent academic positions include that of Principal Lecturer in Marketing at Regent's University London.

For 15 years she has convened the Advanced Qualitative Methods Masterclass for the Market Research Society in the UK. Her extensive publishing history includes her first book, *Using Semiotics in Marketing: How to achieve consumer insights for brand growth and profits* (Kogan Page, 2020). It is preceded by around 50 conference papers at the annual conferences of the Market Research Society, ESOMAR, IIEX, Qual360, the Social Research Association, the Association of Qualitative Researchers (UK), QRCA (USA), ASMRS (Australia), Social Intelligence World and many more. Her writing spans marketing industry trade journals, academic publishing in psychology and market research, and journalism.

Rachel is recognized as one of the founders of British commercial semiotics and is known for her engaging style and ability to make difficult concepts and theory accessible to non-academic audiences. She is a Fellow of the Market Research Society.

# FOREWORD

I first met Rachel when she was giving a debrief to a confectionery manufacturer on how we could bring emotion to the fixtures to reflect the joy that people felt in the consumption of the products, which was lacking from the shelves. I was amazed at the depth of understanding that Rachel was able to demonstrate through semiotics to make the shopping of the category simpler and easier.

Over the subsequent 13 years, I have worked directly and indirectly with Rachel on a number of projects and each time I have learnt more.

I have worked in Shopping Insight since the late 1990s and the insight that semiotics brings to this area is very valuable. Whether we talk about 'System 1' and 'System 2' or 'the Elephant and the Rider' the amount of information that our brains process below the conscious level is remarkable, the various decisions weighing up brands, price, environment, context all have an impact on what is finally bought, and some would not be articulated if we asked someone about their motivations. Yet semiotics, the unwritten rules, the understanding of signs and symbols help us to understand these influences of our behaviour, some of which seem amazingly obvious when Rachel draws them to our attention but were hidden in plain sight before we have the benefit of her expertise in semiotics.

This book brings together a wealth of examples that help us to understand how semiotics can be used to improve retail and shopping performance. I can see real benefit for both retailers and suppliers, in-store and online, in the application of these findings, helping to better apply a richer appreciation of how much we can impact how people feel about where and how they are shopping by activation through the lens of semiotics.

Keith Sleight
CMI Director, global Shopping Insights
Unilever
October 2021

# DEAR READER: A LETTER, FROM ME TO YOU

Dear Reader, you have in your hands a big, sexy, ambitious book about retail and shopping. It builds on my first book, *Using Semiotics in Marketing*, while breaking new ground with original insights about the semiotics of retail and shopper behaviour, which appear in print for the first time. I am pleased with it and I hope you love it, but I will admit to you now that it is not what I first expected. Events panned out a little differently. Here is the true story of what happened to me when I was writing this book.

At the beginning, I envisaged a book that was practical and tightly focused, because we marketers like practical advice and economical writing. It would tell people what kinds of signs and symbols to include in stores, at fixtures and in packaging and it would make sure to include e-commerce platforms. I knew such a book would be useful for readers, and indeed *all of these elements are fully present*. I thought the book would be straightforward to write, because I've had a 20-year commercial career in which I have been required to research and explain these topics many times.

About halfway through the writing process, a lot of things changed.

## My view of shopping changed

I no longer regard shopping as largely consisting of 'person buys socks in a supermarket' or 'person buys children's toys online', nor is it about ordering pizza at dinner time. I came to realize that purchasing may be the number-one way that most people obtain 'things' or 'stuff' and that this is anthropologically interesting, because there was a time in human history before retail dominated, in which people hunted and gathered, made things, and bartered, or exchanged gifts. Our relationship to our food, daily necessities and possessions is, to a vast extent, mediated by retail.

Why does this matter? It matters because the 'stuff' does more than feed, clothe and entertain us. It tells us who we are, it reassures us of our identity. It broadcasts messages to others. Your belongings grant you access to places and social circles; you must bring your swimming costume to the city pool; the right tie or handbag might help you acquire certain friends. What's more, accumulating possessions makes many people feel safe. That might seem misguided or naïve, but I write this in the UK, where historically and culturally, people are very set on owning their own homes. Not being able to get on the housing ladder is a source of widespread distress. Moreover, during the COVID-19 pandemic, people in my country, and perhaps yours too, stockpiled items from toilet paper to alcohol. There's security in owning things – and retail is the mechanism through which that security is obtained. That's a big opportunity for retailers and marketers, but it's also a heavy responsibility. It led me to a different level of insight, beyond 'brands have meanings' and being able to say what they are.

## Retail changed

Of course, retail changes all the time, but until I slowed down my daily work for several months so I could write this book, I was too occupied with the details of individual client projects to be able to see the big picture. It is one thing to be able to answer questions about what makes a good unboxing video or product photo on a digital platform. It is another thing to 'know' in a simple and factual way what new products Google is developing, what Facebook's ambitions are and how emerging Chinese business models differ from their Western counterparts. But it is something else altogether to invest time in seeing how these insights and facts fit *together* to reveal a dramatic and brilliantly coloured landscape of global, human and technological evolution.

What's more, semiotics goes far beyond collecting and joining jigsaw pieces. Once you can see the big picture, the work has barely begun. The challenge at this point is to test that picture and push it to its limits by asking a uniquely semiotic set of questions (jump to Chapter 12 if you would like to see some right now). These questions encourage the researcher to refuse to accept without criticism the dominant narratives and popular versions of the truth, no matter how large and attractive they are. They oblige the researcher to ask penetrating questions about what other versions of reality exist, their relative costs and benefits to the public, and who has a stake in either driving change or keeping things the way they are now.

It was eye-opening and it led me to new ideas about marketing. This book is packed with them. But change was still happening. It kept growing, getting better and, in some ways, worse.

## I changed

I once worked with a company that makes homewares and giftware. One of my contacts there was someone whose entire job, all year round, was

Christmas decorations. I wondered how she coped. She didn't seem wild about Christmas, if I'm honest. At the very start of this book, I was a bit like her. I knew a lot about shopping from spending 20 years researching shoppers and helping brands and retailers with branding and point-of-sale marketing. Perhaps because of this, I did not shop for fun. It was work. It wasn't my thing. Or at least, that was what I told myself.

By the time I was halfway through writing this book, I was no longer the same person. To begin with, I was no longer able to hide from myself. It became clear that I was shopping rather enthusiastically and with all sorts of complicated psychological justifications and excuses. It became clear that the old version of me, who said *and believed* that they didn't much like shopping, was achieving this through a bit of mental gymnastics in which 'shopping' meant going into physical stores and buying low-engagement necessities, such as detergent. I was conveniently excluding the behaviour of going on Amazon (or AliExpress, Cass Art, Jackson's Art Supplies) and indulging slight whims relating to pens, notebooks, sketchbooks and office supplies. I was aided in shielding this behaviour from my conscious awareness by the seductive and easy omnipresence of online shopping. There is no need to 'go to the shops'. Nor can I thwart my own shopper impulses by not 'going on Amazon'. Opportunities to shop, in the form of Instagram 'shop now' buttons, links on Twitter bios and product recommendations on Reddit coalesced into a lingering haze that surrounded me at all times, matching my thoughts of the next desirable acquisition.

I wish I could say that this rather embarrassing revelation concerning my own psychology and behaviour resulted in more rational shopping choices. Unfortunately, it didn't. I continued to write, to serve my clients, to wait out the pandemic and to sit at my desk, trying not to think about the human suffering caused by a disease that was beyond my control, and about the life I had before COVID, when there were days out in the summer and friends whom one could hug. By the end of the book, I was a compulsive shopper. I see now that it will not desist until my daily routine is reset.

As a result of all these factors, one more thing was altered.

## This book changed

The book fulfils the original brief of equipping marketers and retailers with dozens of practical tips and tools to implement for any brand, across multiple categories and in markets around the world. Indeed, I thought about these issues, on which I have advised brand-owning clients so many times, more comprehensively than perhaps on any other occasion in the last 20 years. And yet, as I wrote, it became clear that there was much more at hand than the book I initially thought I was going to write, which in retrospect would have been too slight.

I knew I was writing about professional marketing communications, which are made by businesses, and also about consumers. I then came to realize that I was simultaneously writing about the present day and the future. Have you ever heard a marketer say that the problem with market research is that consumers are forever looking in the rear-view mirror? It's not that market research respondents are inherently bad at imagining the future – thanks to the availability of information, they are much better at it than they used to be. Yet there remains a big difference between your average member of the public and the giants of business and technology who are ushering in the future as we speak. The difference is power and money. Joe Public might be capable of imagining electrifying versions of the future, but he has only a small audience and lacks billions of USD or RMB to make his dreams come true. Because of this, the parts of this book that I thought would divide into chapters about consumers and about business, revealed a second, deeper structure. I realized that, usually, when I was writing about consumers, I was simultaneously writing about the present day, because that's where they live – due to a lack, not of imagination but of resources. When I was writing about business, I was often simultaneously writing about the future, because business is driving us humans into the future as well as making fast and far-reaching decisions about what the future will be.

Having the rare luxury of time, I looked deeply into these questions. As the scope of the book expanded, I was able to see how retail and shopping act like a barometer of our culture, revealing a great deal about how people think and behave, and how our lives are changing. Quite a number of surprising people and events crossed my path as I hurtled into the future, in hot pursuit of the semiotics of retail and shopping. In the pages of this book, you will meet people who love being told they can't have things, a man who destroyed all his possessions, people who pretend *to themselves* that they are like Mark Zuckerberg, people who cause havoc on the stock market, technologically augmented soldiers, and people who no longer believe that other people are real. All of that is not the reason why I set out to write this book, but in the end, it was the reason why I couldn't stop.

And now, let's get down to business. Immediately following is a tour and preview of the contents of this book, set out to show how semiotics is going to solve your real-world retail-marketing problems and improve the bottom-line profits of your business.

# HOW THIS BOOK IS ORGANIZED

This book has 12 chapters, in a sequence that will take you on an adventurous expedition through the wilds of retail marketing and shopping. At the end of the journey, you will be ready to keep on noticing new marketing opportunities and having creative ideas for retailing, because this book passes on skills. Whether you are a retailer, a marketer, a brand owner or a market researcher, semiotics offers you a refreshing point of view of shopping and retail that you can make truly your own, and that gets better the more you use it. The book is divided into sections and covers some big topics. Here's a preview.

### Part One: Case studies: semiotics in real-world retail

The first two chapters make the business case for semiotics. Chapter 1 introduces you to the exciting and colourful world of semiotics and shows how marketers use it to win people's hearts. It avoids difficult theory, supplying just enough in the way of key terms and concepts for you to begin with confidence. It explains how semiotics as a professional service fits in to the marketing industry and answers some common questions.

Chapter 2 considers the changing shape of retail and presents a client case study and an interview, both of which show how semiotics affects the bottom line, resulting in a sales uplift. These chapters are not just about transmitting facts; they are an invitation to begin your own project in semiotic analysis. Semiotics is something that you can learn to do and get paid for, whether that's in the form of improved sales in store or providing creative ideas and retail marketing strategy to others.

### Part Two: The present day

In this part, we dive into the everyday lives and experiences of consumers: rich ones, poor ones, people who like to collect things, people who adore tragedy, people who form intimate friendships with strangers on the internet, and people who can expertly critique drawings of women's bottoms. All these people are your customers.

Chapter 3 concerns **desire**, a tremendously interesting topic that lives with many consumers like a member of the family and flourished during the 2020 pandemic and its many lockdowns. Desire drives late-night shopping on Amazon and it leads groups of shoppers to consume voraciously in specific categories.

Chapter 4 is about the ways that consumers recognize a range of **meanings** that stores and brands are often very keen to offer them. What does it take to persuade a shopper that they have encountered something 'premium', 'natural' or 'artisanal'? How would they know when they encounter 'value for money'?

Chapter 5 explores shopper **needs**. Marketing has established its own system of knowledge concerning shoppers, so that speaking in terms of shopper missions and purchase decision trees becomes second nature. This chapter takes a fresh look at shopper needs and behaviour from the point of view of semiotics because valuable insights await discovery.

Chapter 6 investigates shopping and **identity**. This is a fascinating aspect of shopper psychology that is changing rapidly and is no longer solely about consumers displaying their wealth to each other with designer labels. Retail spending can be a form of activism in its own right and consumers are looking for reassurance that brands and stores are inclusive.

## Part Three: The future

Part Three concerns matters that are clearly within the control of the business community, rather than the consumer. Here we will explore the immediate future, which unfolds moment by moment, and we'll also bravely peer as far ahead into the future as this book's lens of retail and shopping enables us to do, which is a pretty long way.

Chapter 7 explores the future of **business**, which includes, but is larger than, retail. We'll take a view of the behavioural futures market, the Chinese shopping event Double 11 and a new business model called play-to-earn. If you think you have encountered these topics before, please know that I am not simply recounting a few facts. At every stage in the chapters of Part Three, I apply and reapply semiotic tools for thinking to these products of human invention, because applying this type of pressure causes new insights to emerge.

Chapter 8 is about the future of **consumers,** or about the tools that we put into the hands of consumers and how society is changed as a result. We'll explore the unconventional yet real relationships among consumers that technology has facilitated, as well as looking at how the same tech is connected to human suffering. The chapter concludes with a list of ten things that shoppers of the future will want to pay for, plus four different kinds of escape that people are eager to buy.

Chapter 9 is about the future of **retail,** and here you will find practical advice for retail businesses of all sizes. In fact, throughout this book, I'll suggest marketing actions that are within reach even for smaller businesses. This is the chapter for you if you like non-judgemental marketing advice concerning your small traditional store, your plan of taking a traditional business online, and your ambition of designing an innovative customer experience.

Chapter 10 modestly aims for 'the future of **everything**'. Here you will find the future of work, including jobs in retail. We'll also explore smart cities. Are the cities where your business operates becoming smart? Do you ask consumers to use smart devices to access your services? Have you ever considered how smart cities vary around the world? Lastly, we'll consider the future of humanity, and what happens to your brand or business when everything is finally connected to everything else, in what we will soon learn to call the metaverse.

## Part Four: You can do semiotics: tools for retail marketers

The final two chapters of this book are about your future in retailing and retail marketing. Chapter 11 provides 'fast answers to everyday questions'. If you have very specific questions about how to attract and engage shoppers, make sales, manage categories and handle the tricky business of communicating brand architecture, *and* you need to take action today, this chapter is ideal for you.

Chapter 12 equips you with a set of powerful, heavy-duty tools for mining insights from the coal face of consumer culture. If you love semiotics, or have fallen in love by the end of this book, and you want to start having new ideas on your own, here are 15 of my most-used prompts, hypotheses and questions. They can be applied to any aspect of marketing, shopping and any innovation in retail. As you will see, semiotic investigation delivers rewards every time you use it. It offers dozens of ways to engage and stimulate shoppers, but even more importantly, it will empower you to make new discoveries that are yours alone. You will be able to solve new marketing problems as they arise and think ahead about how to plan for changes in business and society.

This book, like its predecessor, *Using Semiotics in Marketing*, is the latest stage in a long journey. As a young adult, I spent years in higher education, emerging with a PhD in psychology. I then started a business that solves marketing problems for brands around the world. Its 20th anniversary coincides with the publication of this new book. If it's not obvious already from my personal letter to you at the beginning of this book, semiotics changes a person. It will demolish the familiar beliefs on which one used to rely and supply a fresh, exhilarating and only occasionally disturbing view of that which remains. It will change your career and eventually it will change your life.

Ready? Let's dive into the semiotics of retail.

**PART ONE**

# Case studies: semiotics in real-world retail

# 01

# Semiotics will change your career in retail or retail marketing

This is a book with big ambitions. If you are a retailer or a retail marketer and you want fast, actionable ideas that sell products, then this book has lots, all ready to use. That's not the main reason for this book's existence, though. Its larger purpose is to equip you with the ability to generate creative and timely solutions to retail marketing problems yourself, even in challenging and stressful situations.

There's a set of tools that I use every day as a marketer, which I share with you here. It is sometimes thought of as a research method but in fact it is an entire *point of view*. It is a particular way of looking at the world around us, including physical stores, apps and everywhere that retailing and shopping take place. Because it is a distinct and complete point of view, it reliably generates original and refreshing insights, and this is something that can be passed on to you within these pages. Its name is **semiotics,** and it is how I get paid. I boost footfall, customer engagement, sales and profits for retailers and their marketers, and I do this by thinking up ready-to-use marketing actions that chime with the needs of consumers, and more importantly by passing on transferrable and reusable skills to the people who work with me.

In this book, I invite you to join me in an experience that I regularly share with my clients, who are the owners of the world's largest brands. They are usually senior people and they work with me because I have provocative ideas that the next marketer or market researcher might not have. Often, they are very interested in the thought processes that lead to these ideas but, because they are busy, they want to get straight to the strategic-level thinking and not become bogged down in the technical details of semiotic method. This book is for them and also for you. In this type of situation, I will usually say to my client, '*Let me show you what I can see when I look at shopping'* – or a specific category such as groceries or whatever the topic du jour happens to be. Using persuasive words and images, I show them a new vision of their place of business, brand or category. By doing this, they not only benefit immediately from insights, but they are also able to grasp what it means to look at the world from *a semiotic perspective*. From there, they can begin to adopt that stance themselves, so they can see what I see, first-hand. I can do this for you as well and we do not need to get too caught up in the machinery of semiotics to make it happen.

Here is the plan. In the chapters of this book, I will show you what I can see when I look at shoppers, customer experiences and the everyday practice of retailing. I'll tell you some stories of the kind that stick in my clients' memories and I'll suggest activities and prompts that you can use to develop your own uniquely semiotic point of view, which you can apply to your own brand or retail outlet, now and in the future.

If you fall in love with semiotics along the way and you want the kind of technical instruction that will equip you to run structured research projects, using semiotics, there's a book for that too. *Using Semiotics in Marketing* (Kogan Page, 2020) has everything you need to become a confident, independent researcher. In the meantime, I expect you want to cut to the chase. I promised you stories and a new world view, so let us begin right away with a rather shocking story that is about jam and also about death.

## A semiotic story about retail: jam of death

Once upon a time, not too long ago, I was hired by a company that makes traditional and luxurious fruit jam, or preserve, to give it its proper name. The product was dense and rich; it had an exciting range of flavour variants, and the company had a very attractive brand story to go with the product, which concerned elegance and European history. The company had invested quite a lot of money in renting a shop. It was only a small shop, but it was in the picturesque Old Town that every historical European city offers its visitors. Then the company spent some more money designing the store interior. They knew they were going for classical elegance, so they made restrained design decisions. They used a lot of black on the walls and shelving, with the brand name picked out in delicate gold lettering, not too large. Black was used at the top of the walls to give the illusion of a gracefully vaulted ceiling. The floors were creamy stone tiles. The counters and cabinets were made of a pale wood with small brass details. Even the sales assistants were tastefully attired in black, giving them an air of dignity. Outside the store, an unusual arrangement in a window at the side showed the lovely jars of jam erected on plinths, flanked by curtains, softly lit and presided over by an antique portrait of someone who might have been the company's founder.

It was all very careful. The problem was that the store simply was not succeeding as well as expected. People liked the product, and brand awareness was good. The brand story was working. But there was something about this shop that people didn't like. The company called me, and I went with my camera to take a look. One of the central questions or prompts in semiotics, which is used in every project is '*Where have I seen this before?*', because this is the question that customers ask themselves, consciously or unconsciously, when they encounter a new brand, store or customer experience. On examining the store, I had a pretty good idea where I had seen all of it before, and when I returned to my desk, I did not have much difficulty finding the visual evidence that confirmed my hunches.

As I compared two sets of photos side by side – those I took myself, and those which I gathered from visual research online – the answer to the question 'Where have I seen this before?' was staring me in the face. Unfortunately for the fruit jam company, it was the funeral parlour, the crematorium, the crypt and the columbarium. The store reeked of death.

## Signs and symbols

In semiotics, there's a lot of talk about **signs and symbols**: units of communication that mean something. Here are some of the semiotic signs that the jam company accidentally used in trying to create a place to sell luxury food:

- Funeral parlours, specifically the room where funeral services take place, are commonly arranged so that thick, pleated or gathered floor-length curtains in muted colours are the dominant feature of the room (to hide or reveal a casket at the right moments). The lighting is soft, and natural daylight rarely penetrates.
- Crematoria, as you can verify by going to Google Images now and searching for 'cremation', rely on two semiotic signs. The first is the urn, which happened to be exactly the same shape as the jars of jam. In the curtained window display of the store exterior, these urn-shaped jars were placed

on pedestals under protective glass domes. Between them sat the other key semiotic sign of cremation: a large portrait of the deceased person.

- Stepping into the shop – if anyone were brave enough to get past the exterior, which suggested that the funeral of the man in the portrait might be in full swing – the customer entered what could accurately be described as a crypt. Crypts usually have stone floors and low, vaulted ceilings (because they are built underground). They rely on a colour scheme of mainly black and white, interrupted by natural stone and wood.
- You may know that funeral caskets tend towards a similar appearance. In the country where this shop was located, caskets are nearly always made of light-coloured pine or poplar. They have small brass fittings and are minimally decorated with grooves that make up simple square or shield shapes. These were the characteristics of the counter and cabinets in the exclusive jam shop.
- A columbarium is a room where funerary caskets are stored on shelves. The urn-shaped jars, with their minimalist, undecorated labels, and the sombre shelving, perfectly recreated a columbarium in the store.

You can perhaps see why the company wasn't selling as much food as it hoped. Luckily, by asking 'Where have I seen this before?' and following up with research to find out, I quickly found some practical solutions to get the brand back on its feet. I returned to the brand story, which featured elegant European designs of history and found that the brand's own country and specific time period offered a wealth of design options that were elegant and dignified but also joyful, celebratory and appetizing. Recommendations included:

- A specific palette of colours in which black was used *sparingly* to contrast with rich jewel tones and sugary pastels.
- Pictorial designs for counters, cabinets and tables. In the time period being referenced, furniture makers loved to decorate wooden surfaces with painted scenes, often depicting the countryside.
- Designs for staff uniforms. The outfits of rural people and the serving classes were simple compared with those of the aristocracy, but used fresh colours, floral patterns and flowing shapes. They did not dress like modern-day funeral directors.
- A range of ways to display food. Apart from the jars of jam themselves, food was conspicuously absent from this store, yet the historical period at hand is remembered for its elaborate and decorative work with pastry and other foods.

- A visual library of patterns, motifs, decorative objects and dressings for shop doors and windows that were all on-brand to make the store appear premium and at the same time charming and inviting.

The company found these recommendations straightforward to activate. Uniform rows of shelving that made up the columbarium were removed and replaced with wooden fixtures in creamy colours, decorated with romantic and bucolic illustrations. The fixtures were designed to include open spaces, allowing daylight to pass through, brightening the interior of the store and removing the feeling of being in an underground crypt. At the same time, unnecessary furniture was removed, creating a more welcoming space for customers, with room to move around. Packaging started to appear in pastel colours appropriate to the historical period and for contemporary audiences in that location. The shop even started to sell a limited range of charming homeware items, all made in natural materials and extending the countryside theme seen in the new fixtures. Footfall improved and in-store sales went up. All was happy and well.

Then, in the fullness of time, a pandemic came to town. A new set of problems arose for retailers, requiring even more resourcefulness and imagination to solve, and demand for semiotic thinking within the marketing industry continued to grow.

'Jam of death' was a simple project, as semiotic projects go. It concerned just one store, in one city, which is why it is possible to compress the whole story into a few paragraphs here. It also used only one or two aspects of semiotic thinking, which is an astonishingly large and diverse resource. Because of its simplicity, it is a great place to begin practising our skills in semiotics, so here is an activity for you, which you can apply to your own brand or place of work.

### ACTIVITY: WHERE HAVE I SEEN THIS BEFORE?

*'Where have I seen this before?'* is a foundational question in semiotics.

You don't have to begin right away with your own brand or your own store and indeed you will find semiotics easier to pick up if you start with an example of retailing that you did not make yourself. Start by analysing your competitors, then, when you know you have good insights, you'll be able to look at your own brand more objectively.

Pick a category and a retail outlet that are interesting to you. Collect photos or screenshots. Ideally, aim to find a range of shots of the store exterior, the interior and the details of the fixtures. Try to include a few photos that show floors, ceiling, lighting and in-store signage, if there is any.

> Consider all the photos in light of the question, 'Where have I seen this before?' Don't store the answers in your head. Externalize your answers by recording them. Then look for evidence. If your hunch is right, evidence will easily come to hand, as was the case with the funeral parlours and crematoria of the jam shop. If the evidence is not readily available, or if your interpretation is so rarefied that consumers are likely to be oblivious to it, go back to your photos and ask the question again. There's nothing new in this world (as semiologists, among others, are fond of saying). If something exists, then something like it already existed: it has points of reference, otherwise it couldn't have been invented.
>
> Below are some examples of ways that you could answer this foundational question, *'Where have I seen this before?'*

*Item:* **Balloons at the entrance to a store**.
*Where have I seen this before?* Parties, celebrations, especially children's parties. Good for communicating seasonal events, special promotions or just a general air of festivity.

*Item:* **Yellow and black signage**.
*Where have I seen this before?* The combination of yellow-and-black is often used to convey warnings. Signs in these colours alert the public to chemical hazards, radioactivity, hot surfaces, magnetic fields and so on. It's not mere coincidence that these are also the colours of certain animals that are irritating or dangerous to us, such as wasps and some snakes. Humans often give this relationship between colour and negative experience an evolutionary explanation; that is, we explain to ourselves that we have evolved to pay attention to things that are yellow and black because they are dangerous, so that's why we like the colour scheme for warnings of other dangers. If yellow and black are the core colours in the environment of the brand or store, then that's something to consider. Did you intend to issue a warning or imply situations of danger? It could be good if you sell equipment for mountaineering and adventure sports, not so good if you are selling groceries. We'll return to this example later.

*Item:* **Piped music**.
*Where have I heard this before?* Ask this question if you can detect any sounds in the physical or digital store. I was once in a very respectable mid-range toy shop in Belgium. It sold quality toys and books for babies and children. As I

> examined the cuddly toys in the peaceful environment of the lower floor, I suddenly noticed the piped music that played softly in the background. It was a song I recognized but I couldn't place it at first, so I pulled out my phone and the Shazam app immediately identified the song as 'It was a Good Day' by US artist Ice Cube. It was released in 1992, which is more than enough time for the track to have been re-released on various compilation albums, one of which the store was playing.
>
> *Where had I heard this before?* Ice Cube is an American R&B artist, actor and film-maker. In 1992, he was at the forefront of the musical genre known to some as 'gangsta rap'. The song appeared on his third album, *The Predator*. In line with the rap genre, the album is a protest against poverty, racism, state brutality and the systematic oppression of African-Americans. It is a rallying cry, and as such, it is angry. The lyrics of 'It was a Good Day' include references to none of his friends having been killed that day, and the pleasure of not having to use his AK-47 assault rifle. An unusual choice for a children's toy shop. It was the first time in my life that I'd had cause to think about assault rifles while examining a display of fluffy animals.

A related prompt that I like to use when doing this type of semiotic thinking is: '*Are all the semiotic signs pointing in the same direction?*' Do they support each other by conveying similar or harmonious meanings, or is there discord? Are any semiotic signs pointing in another direction? In the Belgian toy store – a well-made haven of middle-class parenting – one semiotic sign was pointing urgently in another direction. In the upmarket jam store, nearly all the signs were strongly and coherently pointing in the same direction, just not the one that the owner intended and not one that's good for food retail.

You can perhaps see why semiotics is a useful line of enquiry for brand owners, retailers and marketers. It helps us quickly to identify problems and solve them to create a better, more profitable shopping experience.

## Prompt questions in semiotics

This book contains a set of prompts, questions and hypotheses that are central to the larger project of semiotics – a project that I see as a global effort, spanning businesses and academia. When you ask these questions, you are not alone but are instead joining a host of other people, now and in history, and we learn from each other's efforts. The best thing about these foundational questions is that you can start using them right away: you don't need a degree in semiotics to start exploring. Here are the two we've met so far; there are more to follow, and several sets of them in Chapter 12.

> Here are two foundational questions in semiotics, to start off your collection.
>
> - **Where have I seen or heard this before?**
>   When you show consumers your new brand or open your store to customers, this is the first question they will ask themselves in order to make sense of what you are showing them. Whatever it is you have for them is going to evoke memories something of else, whether that's romantic depictions in novels, films and TV of Old Europe or the violent protests in South Central LA in the 1990s, a precursor to the Black Lives Matter movement.
>
> - **Are all the semiotic signs pointing in the same direction?**
>   When you look at your brand, fixture or shopping platform, do all the constituent elements such as colours, shapes and materials seem as though they 'go together', or are some out of place? Assuming that most go together, and you aren't looking at something completely random, what customer experience or version of reality are they working to create? Is it exciting or soothing? Childlike or distinctly adult? Do you have the feeling of having wandered into an enchanted forest or is it more like being inside a machine? Was that intentional?

## The overall approach of semiotics: big facts and key terms

In this chapter, we've made a quick start with semiotics by immediately getting involved with the sort of semiotic thinking that occupies every day of my working life as a professional supplier, consultant and marketer. There is, of course, much more to semiotics than wandering around asking what things remind you of and whether any aspects of brands and retail environments look out of place. There is something called *The Semiotic Challenge* (also the name of a book by luminary semiologist Roland Barthes), which is the whole and complete line of enquiry that all these individual questions belong to. The purpose of this book is to enable and encourage you to discover that challenge and enjoy the eye-opening and profitable results. But in order to go on this quest, you need some basic equipment, in much the same way that Frodo Baggins receives donations of magical swords and armour in the opening chapters of Tolkien's *Lord of the Rings*. With that happy image in mind, here are a few items you can bring along as we embark on a journey to achieve a view of retail marketing that you've never seen before.

### Semiotics studies culture, not individual consumers

Semiotics took off in marketing as a form of market research, and has since bloomed into something larger, as both suppliers and buyers discover its explanatory power, problem-solving ability and seemingly endless supply of strategic thinking. Despite this large scope, returning to the world of market research to see how semiotics fits in alongside other methods is helpful for the reader who is trying to get a quick view of what semiotics is and how it works.

Figure 1.1 shows market research methods divided into two groups, according to the way that they conceive of the consumer. For most of its history, market research relied on methods, tools and theories that were born in academic psychology. Psychology, though a large science, is primarily about the individual human and the contents of their mind. It leans towards the view that people are all different from each other, they all have their individual personalities and they all have a lot of hidden *stuff* inside their heads that is useful to market researchers – such as attitudes, prejudices,

**FIGURE 1.1** Inside-out vs outside-in approaches to market research

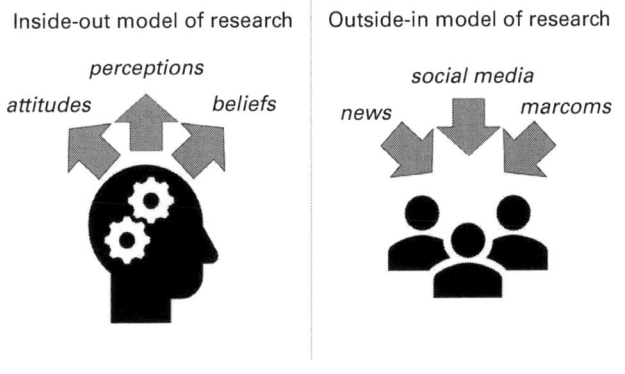

needs and motivations. This view of the human is acceptable to market research respondents as well as researchers themselves, who use a range of psychological instruments, such as survey questionnaires, finely crafted interview discussion guides and projective techniques, to excavate the psychological stuff from the depths of people's heads and make it externally visible. This has become known as **the inside-out approach to research** (a term I first used in 'Demystifying Semiotics', one of the earliest papers on semiotics for marketers, back in 2002).

An alternative family of methods has grown up alongside this approach and has brought significant change to the market research industry. Here, instead of trying to extract hidden psychological matter out of people's heads, we ask how it got in there in the first place. Where did all these attitudes and beliefs come from? In this paradigm, the answer is taken to be that they come from the surrounding culture of which each consumer is a part – and in fact cannot escape. In these methods, of which the three biggest are semiotics, ethnography and discourse analysis, culture is the object of study. All three include large amounts of anthropology, which you have run into before if you've ever seen a really good ethnographic debrief that revealed the magical rituals that people use when cleaning their homes, starting their cars and trying to get their computers to work. Within this group, semiotics distinguishes itself with its ability to decode signs and symbols, just as we did with the jam shop example earlier. This family of methods represents **the outside-in approach to research.**

## Semiotics studies culture, not social trends

If you have any background in sociology or if your work requires you to regularly analyse trends data, at this point you probably have some questions about what semiologists mean by 'culture' and how that is different from 'society', which is perhaps easier to understand and certainly easier to quantify. Here's a short and handy distinction:

> **Society** is found wherever people live in groups, in proximity to each other. Societies can vary in size, and often these groups will develop institutions that are reflected around the world: marriage, family, the law, education systems and so on.

> **Culture** is what makes societies different from one another. In the practical, daily business of semiotics, 'culture' means something like 'all the communicative output of a society'.

I'm defining communicative output very broadly because it needs to include everything that humans have invented for themselves that makes their cultures similar yet different from each other: yellow school buses; wine on the table at lunch; how much snow may fall before people regard it as a problem.

The reason why, at the start of this chapter, we were very concerned with the question 'Where have I seen this before?' is because we ask it on behalf of the consumer. When you present the consumer with your new product, packaging, in-store promotion or shopping platform, they will use all of their cultural experiences to interpret it and form a view of how it succeeds or fails in being appealing or meeting their needs. Jam shops need to be instantly recognizable as the sort of place where jam should be sold. Local culture is what sets the standards when consumers are making this type of decision.

## Semiotics identifies signs and symbols and says what they mean

This is the easiest possible definition of semiotics and you will run into it a lot in marketing. It explains what semiologists do: they look at things, especially visual communications like ads, packaging and in-store signage, and they pick out elements that mean something. They can tell you if your brand should be red rather than blue; they can make your fixtures easier to navigate and your store more inviting.

This activity of picking out signs and decoding them is the best-known and probably the most distinctive element of semiotics. It is known as **bottom-up analysis** because it begins with the observation of a small unit of communication, such as a supermarket fixture or a single item of packaging, and tries to work out what it means to the consumer and as a competitor to other brands. We start from the *ground*, with a small detail, like the piped music in a store, and we work *up* to meaning, which is linked to both the consumer's own culture and the ambitions of the business owner.

Bottom-up analysis is an easy point of access to semiotics. It is not the whole package, but we could say that it is the first half.

## Semiotics provides new and revelatory visions by holding a mirror to society and culture

This is where the focus of our analysis becomes much larger in scope. We become more capable of envisioning new strategies, innovating with products and platforms and seeing off competitors. It is called **top-down analysis**. As its name suggests, it identifies interesting topics or data points at a macro level rather than a micro level.

While bottom-up analysis might begin by noticing a brilliant spotlight in a grocery store, going on to decide what that means and how it impacts the brand or retailer, top-down analysis starts at the level of society, cross-cultural differences and big numbers. Social trends and big data certainly do play a role here, but they are a starting point for analysis, not the end point. They are prompts, not conclusions.

For example, top-down analysis might begin by considering the changing patterns of consumer behaviour as events like pandemics come and go, elections are won and lost and the public mood shifts. The point is to explain these objectively measurable events in terms of the culture that guides consumers in interpreting those events. COVID-19 is an event. Collected statistics on hand washing are useful and reasonably objective data. But culture is found in choices such as a refusal to wear a face covering, and in fears that the virus is a biological weapon or is somehow spread by telecoms technology. Culture is found in behaviour such as displaying children's paintings of rainbows in windows, as an expression of gratitude, hope and perhaps faith. Culture is found when people stand outside those homes and bang their pots and pans to express their support of doctors and nurses, as they did in the UK in 2020.

FIGURE 1.2 Bottom-up and top-down analysis in semiotics

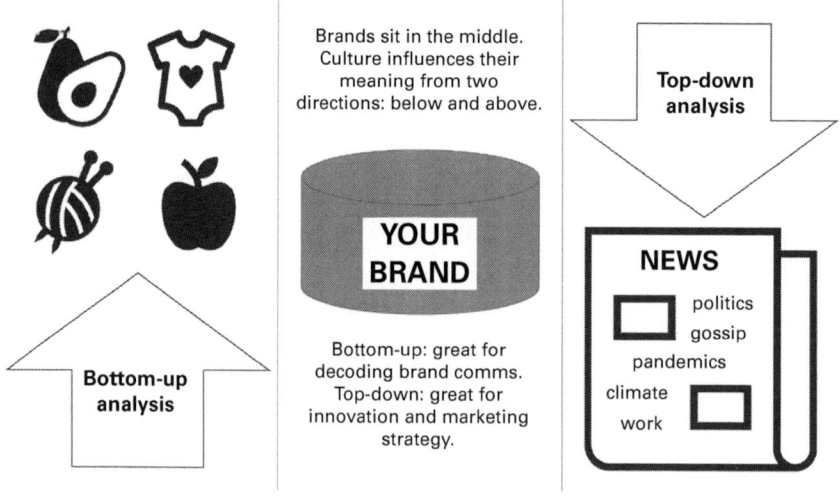

This is top-down semiotics. Having started at the *topmost* level of granularity in semiotic thought, it then works *down* the ladder and settles on marketing actions for individual brands and retailers as its outcome.

For our purposes in this book, we do not need to get too hung up on this distinction. The important part for you as a retail marketer, and the reason I'm telling you this, is because top-down thinking might be a challenge in terms of stretching your imagination and vision of the future, but once you've grasped the overall perspective, top-down analysis is a very liberating activity that will encourage thoughts that are genuinely different and even provocative in your brand, sector or category.

Top-down analysis is not most people's point of access to semiotics, but only because there hasn't been much clear instruction until now. This exciting activity is the second half of semiotics. Figure 1.2 shows the complementary relationship between the two approaches.

*Semiotics can refer to collecting samples of culture and formally decoding them, or it can mean simply thinking about an issue using key semiotic questions*

In my previous book, I supplied a detailed, step-by-step guide to the procedures of semiotic research. This type of thing is immensely welcomed by agency and client-side market researchers, who run discrete projects. In this book, we are doing something different. I'm operating on the assumption that you want to have good ideas, fast. So that's why I'll avoid setting you tasks such as writing a brief or a presentation. I'll also try to avoid giving you too many market-research-type of activities that involve collecting a lot of primary data. Instead, we'll focus on this latter part of semiotics, and I will hand you a series of penetrating questions throughout this book which you can use right away without leaving your desk.

The types of questions and prompts we will encounter are:

- Where have I seen this before?
- Is anything here a simulation of reality?
- Where there is choice, there is meaning. If something could have been expressed or implemented in any other way, the fact that it was done in this particular way means something.

- How is the topic at hand shaped by assumptions of gender, race or sexuality? This is important even if you are a rather traditional brand with conservative values and customers – you want to communicate with those customers in the right way and describe a world that makes sense to them.
- If something is true, the opposite of that thing is probably also true. Note that this is a hypothesis, not a statement of fact.
- There is nothing outside the text (hypothetically, as above).
- For every story, there's another story just behind it that is trying to break through. That is to say, where at first glance you see a jam shop, a second look might reveal a funeral parlour.
- … And many more, throughout this book and especially in Chapter 12.

## How is semiotics used in retail marketing?

The following chapter explores this question in detail, but here's a short answer. As a professional semiologist, I work with brand owners and their marketers and also with retailers and the owners of retail space, including small stores, department stores, shopping centres, digital stores and many more. We work together to solve a wide range of problems, including all the items on the list below. A spread of these problems and solutions is reflected in the chapters of this book.

- How to get a competitive edge in e-commerce. How to design websites, choose photos and make videos that users respond to.
- How to predict the future impact of technological and social revolutions on consumers' use of everyday categories such as household care.
- How to design brands and marketing communications that stimulate emotions.
- How to get shoppers to notice and engage when they encounter a new brand in store.
- How to help shoppers navigate stores and categories. How to help them understand brand architecture and provide cues about product use and occasions of consumption.
- How to display prices, create interest at the fixture and encourage experimentation.

- How to create exciting shopper experiences in physical stores and on digital platforms.
- How to stimulate desire and maximize the pleasure of shopping.
- How to convey specific messages in store environments, such as 'premium', 'value' and 'natural'.
- How to serve and occasionally disrupt shopper missions.
- How to respond to hot topics, political conflicts and social justice movements.

## Is semiotics useful for designing customer experiences?

Customer experience, and its sibling, user experience, keep growing in popularity as marketing concepts. These terms to some extent obscure their own history. Customer experience was once imagined in a more limited and functional way as customer service. User experience grew out of human-computer interaction, a highly rational discipline that prioritized things like ergonomic design and the practical usability of computer systems. In both cases, the introduction of the experience component is a shift towards engaging consumers more deeply, building trust and loyalty, and going out of our way to create positive experiences and emotions before things can go wrong, not just being good at handling customer complaints or reducing the risk of repetitive strain injury.

This shift away from a problem-solving approach and towards a creative, constructive approach to giving consumers positive experiences is part of the larger shift in marketing; the movement away from selling and towards relationship marketing, content marketing, helping and authenticity. Semiotics is the right method for this cultural shift because it has always been focused on the whole package of the consumer's daily, lived experience and the cultural resources they bring with them to occasions and places of shopping.

In Chapter 4, I give instructions for creating different flavours of meaningful experience in stores. In Chapter 9, 'The future of retail', I have quite a bit to say about the relationship between 'shopping' and 'experience', and what should be the order of priorities. I discuss it in the context of the future, because most retail experts and futurists agree that experience is going to be ever more important as an aspect of shopping, as the retail landscape changes. The subject of customer experience comes up again in

Chapter 11, where I provide a list of actions that you can implement in store, even on a modest budget.

## How is this book different from other books on shopper behaviour and psychology?

This is an important question, especially for people who don't have time to read everything and, added to that, there are other books on semiotics as well. In fact, there are at least three kinds of published literature which this book connects to. Here's an overview of the kinds of resources you and I will draw on as we progress through this book, all the while developing a uniquely semiotic perspective on the things we know about retailing and shopping.

### Business books about shoppers and shopper behaviour

- *Why We Buy* (Paco Underhill, 1999, 2008)
- *Inside the Mind of the Shopper* (Herb Sorensen, 2009, 2016)

There are lots of these, for and mostly by people with a background in business. A few classics rise to the top, such as *Why We Buy* and *Inside the Mind of the Shopper*. Both these volumes contain immensely practical advice, which is grounded in first-hand observations of shoppers moving around stores as well as real-world business experience. For example, Sorensen will tell you, in no-nonsense terms, that the retailer needs to help the shopper locate the items they came in for, because that shopper has an itch to scratch. These items are the biggest-selling items that shoppers have top-of-mind when they start their mission. In a complementary manner, Underhill reveals that most people aren't looking at in-store signage, even though many stores are festooned with it. He uses the example of McDonald's restaurants, where the only signs that people appear to engage with are the ones pointing towards the counter and the toilets. Elaborate menus are on display in McDonald's, but people don't read them until after they've placed their order. They complete their mission first, then they have the time and headspace for looking at non-essential information.

These books are successful because they are rational and empirical and they focus on visible behaviours that lend themselves to quantification. We can tell that the authors have spent time on the ground, in the aisles of supermarkets. Surprisingly, they don't include a lot about shopper psychology, if one defines that as something more than physical behaviour. Both books focus on traditional, physical stores and Underhill endured harsh complaints about his neglect of e-commerce before adding a new chapter on the internet in the revised edition of his book.

In the book you are reading now, we will take a different approach. We are just as interested in e-commerce as in bricks-and-mortar stores, and we don't need multiple different kinds of semiotics to explain them. Semiotics has always taken an omnichannel point of view on retailing. And even though this book is primarily about culture, which is outside of and bigger than consumers, we'll get a surprisingly good look at the living, beating heart of consumer psychology, because shopping provokes and facilitates certain kinds of emotions, as when someone who made it through a difficult business meeting self-rewards with a lipstick, or a person who has suffered romantic disappointment runs out to buy a container of ice cream.

### Business books on semiotics, and books at the border of business and academia

- *Using Semiotics in Marketing* (Rachel Lawes, 2020)
- *Semiotics, Marketing and Communication* (Jean-Marie Floch, 2001)
- *Creating Value* (Laura Oswald, 2012)

A few of these exist. Of course the one I am going to recommend first is *Using Semiotics in Marketing*, which contains considerable instruction on decoding physical environments and revealing the implicit brand values that reside in cafés, convenience stores and even office buildings. I'm also pleased to highlight Jean-Marie Floch's early work *Semiotics, Marketing and Communication*, which has a chapter on hypermarkets. Another highlight is *Creating Value*, which has a valuable chapter on the design of service spaces such as pizza restaurants.

All these books offer good insights, but because they are concerned with the whole of marketing, they need to limit their discussion of retail to one chapter in a book that mostly concerns other topics. Retail marketing is a big subject and a single chapter here and there or even a recurring theme simply isn't enough to fully empower those for whom retail and retail marketing is a full-time job. Inevitably, most aspects of retail marketing are left unaddressed. But here, in *Using Semiotics in Retail* we have the luxury of 12 chapters in which we can cover a host of interesting topics for retail marketers that have not previously been given much dedicated space.

## Academic books on the semiotics of shopping and consumerism

### *Distinction: A social critique of the judgement of taste* (Pierre Bourdieu, 1979, 1984)

There are a surprising number of these and some of them are a joy, bursting with memorable and lasting insights. They are mostly overlooked by the business community because of their academic language, but they are full of gems if you know how to look for them and polish them up. Here is just one of my favourites – there are more to come.

Pierre Bourdieu, the French philosopher and leading light of semiotic thought, published extensively on the subject of taste and social class in France in the 1960s and 1970s. Even though it was a long time ago, the power of his insights means that they have barely tarnished with age. For example, he diagnoses a certain *immediacy* in the taste of working-class people. By this he means bright colours, bold flavours, high alcohol and/or calorie content, gifts in large packages, music that gets better as it gets louder and so on. He explains this with reference to the constraints of money and work on working-class lives. Specifically, and in a nutshell, he says that people who do manual work have very immediate and physical experiences during the day, so it's not a surprise if they wish to be soothed and comforted with equal immediacy and sensuous pleasure. What's more, when a person's life is economically fragile and does not rest on a bed of inherited wealth, that also explains why they desire and value tangible objects and exciting experiences.

In contrast, says Bourdieu, the comfortable lives of wealthier people, where work is more likely to involve mental effort than physical pain, and who have been trained through systems of education and professional advancement to respect deferred gratification, are more patient. They also, he says, have a lot invested in preventing people below them on the social ladder from becoming like them and joining their social circles. So, their tastes are more remote, distant and formal. They have learned to value subdued colours, abstract ideas, clever and thoughtful design. The conditions of their lives, which have taught them to study for exams and use their indoor voices, have a powerful normalizing effect on individual taste.

The strength of Bourdieu's analysis is that it is still useful today, in other countries and half a century later. We can see it in the things people shop for and how they shop. In my country, as in so many countries around the world, people know what kinds of products, stores and shopping experiences they are supposed to feel drawn to, in line with their demographic and local culture. Working-class women mitigate the drudgery of housework with products that offer a variety of powerful fragrances and that perform interesting, sensory actions such as foaming. Their middle-class counterparts buy products that are eco-friendly, look tasteful in the carefully designed kitchen and are used by the professional cleaner who visits twice a week, while the owner retires to another room to throw out her possessions in line with the instructions in a book on minimalism. When you have everything you need, and perhaps only then, less is more.

If you are a retailer or if you are a marketer with some influence in how things are sold, I hope that Bourdieu is already firing your imagination. Whatever it is you have to sell, from laundry detergent to entertainment, Bourdieu's ideas about the immediacy and the remoteness of pleasures in consumers' lives generate all kinds of practical suggestions for packaging, signage, fixture design, promotions, app development and the interior design of stores. Lots of this type of insight is coming up in this book, translated from academic dialects into the more everyday and business-focused language of marketing.

In the next chapter, we'll take a closer look at how semiotics fits into the rapidly changing world of retail marketing, and you'll hear from one of my biggest clients about how semiotics is used to make their business more successful.

## References

Barthes, R (1994) *The Semiotic Challenge*, University of California Press, Berkeley

Bourdieu, P (1979, 1984) *Distinction: A social critique of the judgement of taste*, Routledge, Abingdon

Floch, J-M (2001) *Semiotics, Marketing and Communication*, Palgrave Macmillan, London

Lawes, R (2002) Demystifying Semiotics: Some key questions answered, *International Journal of Market Research*, **44**, 3, pp 1–10
Lawes, R (2020) *Using Semiotics in Marketing,* Kogan Page, London
Oswald, L (2012) *Creating Value*, Oxford University Press, Oxford
Sorensen, H (2009, 2016) *Inside the Mind of the Shopper*, Pearson FT Press, Upper Saddle River
Underhill, P (1999) *Why We Buy*, Orion, London

# 02

# How Unilever uses semiotics

Let me begin this chapter by thanking Unilever. I'm thankful and honoured to have had seven years of serving Unilever's Consumer Market Insights (CMI) team as a preferred supplier of semiotic consultancy. I'm also extremely grateful for Unilever's kind support of this book, which you can read more about in Keith Sleight's Foreword and in the Acknowledgements. This chapter is organized around an interview with Iris Cremers, CMI Global Shopping Insight Manager, based at Unilever's head office in the Netherlands, and Corinne Trentadue, CMI Shopping and Commerce Insight Manager, France.

Our conversation ranges across a number of topics, which I use to structure this chapter. Between the interview segments, I'll give real-world examples to support the descriptions from Iris and Corinne, so you can see what we do when we work together and how I help Unilever brands achieve their success.

The images in Figures 2.1, 2.3, 2.4 and 2.6 are owned by Unilever and used with permission. Images should not be reproduced, copied or stored without Unilever's written permission.

> **WHAT'S COMING UP**
>
> By the end of this chapter, you will be able to:
>
> - see how a large FMCG business uses semiotics to design brands, packaging and point of sale materials;
> - envisage a toolkit of shopper insights, to which semiotics makes original and valued contributions;
> - recognize and use several semiotic principles that result in designs with global appeal, across categories and markets;

- apply simple techniques with lighting and in-store signage to give shoppers an easier, happier experience;
- make social media graphics that are informative without being demanding or overwhelming;
- design brands and marketing communications with a recognizable provenance;
- explain and interpret your own reactions when you like or dislike a design.

## Introductions

I've had the privilege of working on shopping insight with Iris Cremers in the Netherlands for around five years, and she came to know me because of some groundbreaking semiotic projects on shoppers and retailing that I delivered previously for Unilever teams in South Africa, the United States and Mexico. Corinne and I met this year and have just completed a project together.

**Iris:** My role is shopping insight and our purpose or aim is to make shopping easier for everyone. We want shoppers to have an easier time making selections and a more pleasant shopping experience. We aim to make life easier for retailers, by bringing them insights. And internally at Unilever, we work to make shopping easier to understand for people within the business. Corinne is an expert on some tools we have developed and make available throughout the business. These tools now include many original semiotic insights, but we also find that semiotic advice supports, and is supported by, our other kinds of research within Unilever.

Shopping Insights is a part of Unilever that is heavily based in psychology. A lot of colleagues are very data driven and very keen on understanding the brain. We have a number of in-house tools and checklists that people can apply in a few minutes that were developed from these other methods.

When we look at these closely, we can see how closely linked it is to semiotics. A lot of things ultimately come back to semiotics. I see it as kind of a foundational layer in a lot of psychology or social science.

## What is semiotics? How is it applied within Unilever?

**We use semiotics to help us design our brands, their packaging and point of sale.**

**Iris:** Internally, we use semiotics to help us design our brands, their packaging, and point of sale materials. Semiotics helps you design the key visuals that communicate the right messages and get attention.

**Corinne:** Semiotics is always very interesting, from a human point of view, and a futures point of view. It's a big subject. But the essential questions are about how to convey messages through things like packaging, logo designs and branded displays. It's about colours, shapes, human faces, words and all these different elements of design which all convey certain messages to the shopper or consumers. It's a simple example, but if you think of Axe [deodorant], it's black. If I suddenly decide to use green or yellow, the shopper might be completely lost.

**RL:** It's about brand recognition and being able to find their brand, but it's also about what those colours mean. Black is a reliable sign for masculinity but yellow and green don't have these well-established meanings in men's deodorant. It's going to be a lot harder for people to understand what you are trying to tell them.

Packaging is the number one point of access to semiotics, for my clients and my friends and colleagues in the market research community. It's immediately obvious *how* packaging is made up of visual and verbal signs (images and words), in contrast to abstract concepts like 'family mealtime' or emotions such as 'feeling like a kid in a sweet shop', which require a bigger, more nuanced appreciation of what semiotic signs are and how they work.

In 2021, Unilever unveiled a rebrand of Magnum ice cream, with the creative work done by the talented agency Sunhouse. The final selection from Sunhouse's various designs was made by a small team of in-house and agency branding and comms experts, of which I was honoured to be a member. Unilever wanted the brand to communicate pleasure and quality as strongly as possible, and the new packaging improves on the old in lots of ways.[1] Here, I'll concentrate on just one element, the brand mark, but if you compare the old and new packs, you'll be able to spot lots of meaningful changes – and where there is meaning in communications, there is semiotics.

In Figure 2.1 you see the old (left) and new (right) brand marks side by side. The rebranding team agreed that the new version is 'better', as did consumers in qualitative research. Semiotics has a particular way of viewing brands and their communications (which I share as thoroughly as possible throughout this book) with the result that it supplies very specific reasons *why* some marketing and design decisions are better than others. It sheds light on what 'better' means. Here are a couple of key elements that make a difference: a small one, then a larger one.

On the new pack, the gold hue has softened considerably. It glows gently rather than harshly reflecting brilliant light. While the older brand mark looked good at the time, the new version reveals the old as perhaps rather brassy. The new version is more subtle and more luxurious, suggesting the depth of real gold rather than the surface gleam of brass.

However, there's more going on than a softer gold, which I will try to explain. Making products look more premium by adding gold is not a new trick in marketing – all sorts of brands do it. The thing is, there's nothing to *stop* anyone from doing it, with the result that there are plenty of bad examples out there. Also, it doesn't cost much to achieve. Where once it might have meant applying aluminium foil to a pack, the invention and take-up of metallized plastics in food packaging meant that gold was available to all. Light plastic flow-wrap packaging, the kind you might find on a cheap chocolate bar or bag of potato crisps, became easy to polish up with a metallic finish, and, to this day, there are lots of quite downmarket foods wrapped in loud, shiny, metallic wrap in various colours. Gold is not what it once was.

FIGURE 2.1   Magnum rebrand by Sunhouse for Unilever

Reproduced with kind permission of Unilever

I'm telling you this because it's important to Unilever for Magnum to be seen as premium and also indulgent. As time passed, it was getting increasingly difficult for the old brand mark to do this work when any less prestigious competitor could slap a shiny gold logo on a pack or even cover the whole wrapper in high-gloss gold. What we see in this new brand mark is a more subtle design that puts Magnum ahead of cheaper brands, at least for the time being.

The main thing I want you to notice is the rather literal approach to design seen in the old brand mark. If you asked a member of the public who has no design training to make you a brand mark, it's quite possible that they might draw a circle, write your name in the middle and add some fancy effects such as metallics *to the brand name* because it's the obvious thing to do. Sunhouse's clever move was to retain the circle device and apply (softer, more elegant) gold to everything within it *except for* the brand name. The effect is similar to engraving and, combined with the circular shape, is reminiscent of the metal stamps and sealing wax that are no longer used for everyday correspondence but which today's consumers still recognize as prestigious and as conferring particular importance on anything that the seal is applied to. It's an elegant design decision that upgrades the brand mark and differentiates the brand, while still being a recognizable Magnum asset.

## Business practice: tools for marketers

**RL**: Tell me some more about your checklist. I developed a number of semiotic insights for you, which apply globally, that anyone in Unilever can understand and use. And you include this list as part of a formal set of tools, is that right?

**Iris**: Yes, so every time we do semiotics studies with you, we learn something. Sometimes these are global principles that describe best practice and they apply everywhere. So, it is our job to then turn these principles into free tools for our teams throughout Unilever, and Corinne is an expert in that.

**Corinne**: We have in-house tools and we ask people, 'OK, before you go to any expensive research, check these basics,' and in the end all of it is to do with semiotics. We also say, 'This is important for our category – do you have it in place? Please optimize it before you go to testing, because we know for sure that testing goes better when we already have all these basics right.'

I love to work with Unilever because they are so organized and invest resources in making sure that no valuable insight goes to waste. When I start a project with a new-to-me Unilever colleague who is working on some aspect of branding or shopper marketing, they regularly show familiarity with semiotic research that I've delivered previously, even though this is our first meeting. Aside from being flattering, this really helps us to hit the ground running, because they can tell me what they already know about the semiotics of food, personal care or household care and they can envisage what semiotics could tell them that is not yet known.

If you are a marketer, then the more you gather experience with semiotics, the more you will get out of it. Semiotic knowledge accumulates and rarely expires. A semiotic research project that you do now may uncover insights that keep delivering value to you and your brand 10 or 20 years down the line.

## Global design and marketing

**Semiotics points out global design principles that are essential knowledge.**

Iris and Corinne are pleased when we uncover principles that apply globally – across all categories or specifically within categories. I know you want examples, so I will briefly describe a few of the more universal insights here. Some are recurring themes in this book and enjoy more detailed discussion later. This is a sample, very far from an exhaustive list.

- **Images outrank words**. As much as I love words, global consumer culture becomes more visual over time. People like visual demonstrations and visible evidence. Signage without words works particularly well in the fresh produce area of stores and supermarkets. You don't need to say 'apples' when you can show an apple.
- **Use negative space**. Negative space is any unfilled space that surrounds a product or fixture, in a two-dimensional image or in a physical store. Negative space will occur naturally unless you make a point of eliminating it. My advice is to keep it, but use it intentionally. Intentional use of negative space is what you see when a circular fixture on a shop floor can be approached on all sides. The space and the movement of shoppers through space is an intentional part of the fixture's design. Unintentional

negative space is what surrounds the last remaining package of toilet paper on an otherwise empty supermarket shelf.
- **Depict authentic emotions.** I collect examples of in-store signage and graphics. These regularly feature stock images in which models grimace while holding a family-size bar of chocolate near their face or smelling their laundry. I know these images are convenient and inoffensive, but they are so inauthentic that they undermine the pleasant fantasies your customer is trying to enjoy concerning eating sweets and having a supply of clean clothes. Naturalistic photography by professional and semi-professional artists and models is more widely available than it used to be and is a place to find real smiles.
- **Nature is celebrated by cultures around the world.** Variation in how it is represented and celebrated can be surprising and sometimes subtle. Think of the differences between the French formal garden as seen at the Palace of Versailles; the immense scale and power of nature in American landscape painting and colonial architecture; and the delicate, fluid trees and birds of centuries-old Chinese ink painting. Despite these variations, you can count on it that nature in general is a welcome feature of branding and marketing.

**Iris:** Another piece of semiotic insight that has been useful for Unilever concerns curves and arches. It's another example of something that you can see when semiotics points it out, and it works globally. I feel it's essential knowledge that my colleagues within the business should know – that curves work better than sharp angles. It's just a global human truth that is relevant each time we have to decide on a display or work with key visuals.

**RL:** Indeed, I have certainly found this to be true globally, that people like curves. For example, they feel special if you give them the chance to walk under an arch – it instantly feels as though you are stepping through a portal into some magical place. It creates this feeling of a special occasion.

One thing I like about this particular insight is that it can be used even in small stores on small budgets. For instance, when I worked with Unilever in South Africa, I found a great example of a modest supermarket in Durban where the owner had placed a balloon arch near the entrance of the store, to draw attention to a promotion. It was exactly the type of balloon arch that is popular at children's parties. So, all arches are good. You don't have to spend a million dollars to make things feel a bit special.

Iris is speaking with me from Unilever's headquarters in Rotterdam. It's a place I love to visit because it's a chance to visit the Markthal in the historic Laurenskwartier of the city. Coming in at the extreme other end of the budget from a balloon arch, this landmark building designed by MVRDV[2] comprises above-ground and below-ground retail space, including market stalls, supermarkets and restaurants. The outer layer of the building includes residential dwellings. Photos of this spectacular building show off its pleasing breaks with conventional architecture. While other modern buildings are rectangular, this one has the corners rounded off. While other buildings are completely filled with rooms, walls and doors, this one has a curvy hollow space at the centre, rather like a conch shell. But the most showstopping aspect of the Markthal has to be the vast mural of fruit and flowers that begins on one wall, soars over the shopper's head across the arched ceiling and cascades down the other side. You can see photos at www.markthal.nl.

By including the example of Markthal, I don't mean to imply that every reader has millions of euros to invest in building a mighty cathedral. I include it because I assume that most people's budgets will find a balloon arch easier to accommodate and therefore you want to make it as good as it can be. I collect brilliant examples of semiotics in action and share them with clients and readers, so that we know what we are aiming for.

What does Markthal tell us about balloon arches? First, it is a useful reminder that consumers appreciate things based on what they *signify*, not what they *are*. It's not the case that people like balloon arches because they are excited by inflated sacks of rubber with a knot in one end. They like *balloons* because they are used everywhere to denote celebration. They have reliably achieved this meaning, which is why you see them at parties and on birthday cards.

People like *arches* because they are an architectural accomplishment that most people will have seen in physical buildings that are sacred or precious, such as large churches, mosques and palaces, and also in symbolic arches that are part of rituals. In military weddings, it's quite common for officers to form an arch using their swords, which the couple passes under. The sabre arch is a way of honouring the couple. All these various bits of knowledge and experience come together when a shopper encounters an arch in a retail setting.

This information is not of mere incidental interest. If what I'm saying makes sense to you, you can see why the one change I would have made to the balloon arch I encountered in Durban is placing it more exactly at the door so that people can walk under it. That said, it was not in a bad spot: it was clearly in view by shoppers entering the store and drew the eye upwards to a large, hanging banner informing visitors of a store-wide promotion.

## Category management, navigation and fixtures

**Corinne:** Retailers are not focused on only one problem. They are not focused on one single brand, but they are very interested in category management and in how people use stores.

> Semiotics helps us understand how shoppers see the category.

**Iris:** Yes, when you [RL] did semiotics research for us on retail and shopping in the Netherlands, there's that part in your report where you say we expose people to a sea of products. It's as though we are saying to people, 'Good luck finding what you want, you will need it.' Sometimes I feel sorry for people. But semiotics helps us understand how shoppers see the category and how we and the retailer can make the store easier to shop. Ease of shopping is the most important thing. If all the categories are easy to shop, then it's more pleasant for the shopper, it's good for everyone.

In retail, there's a tendency to be hyper-rational. Retailers understandably want to get as much value out of their space as possible as well as being able to keep track of where everything is, so they have every reason to fill it with rectangular fixtures, arranged in straight aisles. In turn, this engenders boxy, shelf-ready packaging. Brands are often dressed in shouty colours, designed to drown out competitors, while being overwhelmingly similar in their size, shape and packaging materials. Then on top of that, there is signage. There's solid research evidence that shoppers become frustrated when they can't find what they want. A shopper who can find what they are looking for is a happy shopper. This contributes to highly rational overhead signage that simply directs people to 'bread' and 'cereal', as though the reasons why people want those items are nobody else's business.

There's nothing wrong with giving people simple information, but the typical warehouse-like grocery store is not a place where imagination comes to life. It's a pity, because when we look at places like markets, vendors often use signage that shows they understand the pleasant emotions that shoppers link to categories, and they manage it on a small budget. Elsewhere in this chapter, I argue for well-chosen graphics, but if all you have is a chalk board with room for a single line of text, there's still plenty you can do.

I visited Neighbourgoods Market in Johannesburg, which had a variety of examples of what to do, and a few to avoid. 'Nostalgic Cocoa Bar' is better than simply 'cocoa' because of the semiotic meaning ascribed to cocoa: just like balloons, the idea is worth more than the object. Cakes were sold under the banner 'Made with love' because who doesn't want to feel loved while eating cake? A less good example was 'Flavoured Cheese'. You can see how, compared with love and nostalgia, 'flavoured cheese' is a factually true, unemotional message that is capable of working with all the other semiotics of a typical supermarket to make people feel they are inside a giant machine.

**Semiotics makes stores and fixtures easier to shop and more appealing.**

Iris: Semiotics helps us predict the impact of making changes at the level of the category, shelf and fixture. It answers a lot of questions. For example, if we move a product or display to a different part of the store, how does that change its meaning or accessibility for shoppers? How is the shelf organized? Many fixtures are hard to read and semiotics helps to simplify matters so that people can understand what's on offer and how to find what they want. Then there are specials and promotions – they only become appealing when they are visible and offering something that shoppers actually want. Lastly, is the fixture or shelf a pleasant place to be? Semiotics has given us a lot of useful ideas about small changes that are easy to apply but do a lot to help customers feel more cared for.

Here's the type of thing Iris is talking about; another small change that you can make in-store to help shoppers find what they want and keep them in a happy mood.

Light and lighting are semiotic signs, just like everything else. Light is a neglected aspect of many retail environments, yet it is able to convey a great deal of meaning. I was shopping for food in the Netherlands when I encountered a display of prepared fruit that exemplified this perfectly. All the ready-to-eat prepared fruit was gathered in one part of the store, as you'd expect, and was packaged in disposable plastic tubs that implied immediate consumption. Here's where things get interesting: the shiny, black plastic

FIGURE 2.2  Prepared fruit: melon and pineapple; grocery store, Netherlands

Fieldwork photo, 2017

tubs had clear lids, which allowed the beauty of the fruit inside to make an impression, rather than hiding it with a label or band. Directly above the display, brilliant spotlights pointed at the tubs of melon and pineapple. The result was electrifying. I've rarely seen watermelon that was redder, or pineapple that was more exactly the colour of pineapple. It's easy enough to grasp that spotlights add to a sense of theatre in store, but here the combination of lighting and packaging worked together to help shoppers find the fresh fruit (in fact, it was unavoidable) and show off the arresting beauty of the product. It was like an augmented version of reality, achievable by careful choice of packaging and the installation of light bulbs.

## E-commerce

At Unilever, we have proved how important it is to use the right semiotic signs.

**Iris:** Semiotics has a lot to say about signs and symbols and their meaning, such as the meaning of different colours. At Unilever, we know and have proved how important it is to use the right semiotic signs. This is even more important when shopping happens online. If you track the eye movements of shoppers both online and offline, you can see people focusing on visual cues.

**Corinne**: There are so many ways that shoppers benefit when shopping online is made easier. They might be struggling to navigate the category or store; they might be doing the whole shopping experience on their phone.

**Iris**: Yes, and people also get confused about pack sizes. So, there are some extra considerations when people are shopping online compared with when they are offline. But underlying that, are humans trying to deal with complexity, and semiotics is good at introducing simplicity.

A report (Delacour, 2021) on the website of the Institute of Grocery Distribution (IGD.com) sets out five of 'Unilever's strategic choices', of which two are especially relevant here. The first points to Unilever's growth in markets outside Europe: the company already has a strong position in the US and India, is building relationships with Chinese retail giants and recognizes markets such as Brazil, the Philippines and Mexico as valuable for the future. The second insight concerns e-commerce specifically: *'Unilever ecommerce sales grew by 61% and now make up 9% of Unilever's total turnover.'* This is the business context of Iris's and Corinne's remarks. The issues they bring up are not isolated or trivial, but are central to Unilever's present success and future growth.

By now, Unilever has developed so much confidence with semiotics that I am asked 'quick questions' about e-commerce just as often as I'm asked to conduct more in-depth pieces of research that focus on specific markets, brands or categories in the e-commerce space. The kinds of topics I'm asked about are the following.

**Big topics:**

- What do online retailers in different parts of the world do to convince shoppers of their trustworthiness?
- How do leading e-commerce retailers manage and guide customer journeys around virtual stores?
- Do shoppers' expectations of e-commerce vary in different parts of the world? How do they align with culturally-specific expectations of brands and retail more generally?

**Quick questions:**

- What kind of language evokes positive emotions and enhances online shopping experiences? Are there any words to avoid?
- What's the difference between a good (appealing, compelling) unboxing video and a terrible one?
- In the context of e-commerce, where the main forms of visual representation are photos and video, why do some brands and platforms use illustration? What does it mean and what is it good for?

As you are already beginning to detect, semiotics is a big subject. Its capacious view of the world around us as being made almost entirely from human communications means that it has answers to all these questions, and many more. Without giving away all the secrets I share with Unilever, here are some examples of the kinds of things I normally tell them about e-commerce, with visual aids.

In our conversation, Iris particularly highlights confusion about pack sizes as a problem for online shoppers. One common solution in markets like the Philippines (for example, on Lazada's website) is to clearly print the size or volume of the pack in numbers, and to show how many items are included in a multipack. So, for example, you might see a thumbnail that shows three bottles of shampoo and a text bar within the thumbnail that says, 'shampoo x3, 350ml'. This isn't a bad solution, but still, it's possible for shoppers to be entirely confused about what 350ml looks like in real life. How long will 350ml of shampoo last? Will the bottle fit in a gym bag? It's not as obvious as one might think. I examined the products in my own bathroom and found that a 250ml pack is not half the size of a 500ml pack, nor are all 250ml packs the same size across different brands. Envisaging a 350ml bottle of shampoo can be unexpectedly difficult.

As I write these words, I'm looking at an image that Instagram used in 2017 to promote its then-new shoppable photos (see Ong, 2017). The image includes a face mask product in a tub, a decorative box and a couple of applicator brushes. Placing these products next to each other helps to establish the scale of the items. Other brands will sometimes include a person's hand in shot, a reliable guide to size, if not always the most elegant solution.

Before we move on, I want to discuss another couple of items, from Sunsilk India. They are a still image, shown in Figure 2.3, and an Instagram post from April 2021, promoting the same product. Sunsilk is of course another Unilever brand. The product is a variant called Black Shine, which adds gloss to black hair.

I'm taking the opportunity to draw these to your attention because I'm often asked about branded video for social media. With the rise of digital culture, video is very important and we'll explore the reasons for that in later chapters where we talk about e-commerce in the context of creator economies. However, you do not need action-packed video sequences 100 per cent of the time.

FIGURE 2.3  Sunsilk India promotional image, 2021

Reproduced with kind permission of Unilever

In Figure 2.3, a halo of light surrounds the products. It appears to be spinning even when viewed as a still image. This is just the kind of single design element that can be animated in order to catch viewers' attention on digital platforms. It is enough to draw attention to the product without overwhelming or confusing a viewer who is scrolling and skim-reading.

In its Instagram post of 19 April 2021, Sunsilk India created a very short animation – only five seconds. This is such a short time that it makes a traditional TV ad look like a feature film. It is too short for characters, dialogue or a plot. It is thoughtfully designed so that, rather than having everything move around, as with video, only selected items move so as to catch attention. The shampoo bottle wobbles and bounces, while the amla berries, the hero ingredient, look about to explode but suddenly coalesce and morph into a shampoo bottle.

People don't need to be overwhelmed with action-packed videos just because you have video capability. Animation of selected elements can be just as good at getting your point across and can deliver a message in five seconds rather than 15 or 30.

## The magic of semiotics

**The most fascinating part of semiotics is that it explains our own experience.**

**Corinne:** You can apply semiotics to anything. Any aspect of your branding; it has so many applications. But the most interesting part is where it explains our own experience. You know, sometimes when you see a font or a packaging and it really resonates with you, and you don't know why. It's because it reminds you of something you know from your culture. It's fascinating.

**Iris:** Yes, that's the fascinating part of semiotics, because you can have that experience any time. You could enter a house or you could look at a brand visual and you know straight away that you like it or you don't like it, but you can't tell why. Semiotics shows you why. I think that's really the secret of semiotics.

There's one question that everyone asks themselves when they encounter a new object: 'Where have I seen this before?' If you've ever observed market research in which respondents are presented with a new product or brand, you will have noticed people trying to understand the new item by comparing it with things with which they are already familiar. People draw on their experience. 'Experience' consists of their whole lives so far, including every ad and brand they've ever been exposed to, along with every TV show they've ever watched, every fashion choice they've ever made, every social media meme they've ever seen, and so on, going right back to people's earliest memories.

Ben & Jerry's ice cream is one of Unilever's best-loved brands. Probably its most distinctive brand asset is its typeface – or, in fact, two typefaces if you look carefully. They were handmade by award-winning designer Lyn Severance.[3]

FIGURE 2.4　Ben & Jerry's pack with Severance and Chunk Style typefaces

Reproduced with kind permission of Unilever

There's a great deal to be said in favour of brands using custom-made typefaces that they can fully own. Once consumers have learned to recognize it, it becomes a powerful brand asset. But if consumers are viewing something like a typeface that they haven't seen before, how do they decide what it means?

In this situation, the consumer or shopper draws meaning from individual design characteristics of the typeface and also from its overall appearance. To begin with the details, if you look at a pack of Ben & Jerry's you will see that all the letters in the brand mark and the flavour name are quite fat and chunky. Apart from hinting at large, chunky inclusions in the ice cream, this also helps to convey an innocent, even naïve, appeal – thick, rounded letters are often used in children's reading books. However, this isn't for kids: the letters have serifs, and some characters, such as 'g' and the ampersand, have elaborate flourishes. It's childlike fun, but for grown-ups.

But this isn't the whole story. Although these are original typefaces and key brand assets, with their unusual combination of wide, rounded letters, serifs and flourishes, they also bear somewhat of a resemblance to a font that consumers know very well and which connotes 'cool' retro style: Cooper Black.[4] You can see a visual demonstration of the culturally acquired meaning of Cooper Black in Figure 2.5. It may seem to you that Cooper Black has a light-hearted feel that is well suited to the subjects 'pop art', 'cookies' and 'psychedelia', but seems to undermine the seriousness of 'tax office', 'surgery' and 'prison'. Let's explore why.

Cooper Black was first designed in 1922, but many consumers will have encountered it in the context of the youth culture of the 1960s and 1970s, a time in Western history when there was a revolution among young people, a celebration of ideals such as uninhibited love, and rebellion against the social and moral constraints of previous decades. Cooper Black appeared on the album covers of cutting-edge musicians such as David Bowie and the

FIGURE 2.5 Uses of the typeface Cooper Black

| **Pop art** | **Tax office** |
|---|---|
| **Cookies** | **Surgery** |
| **Psychedelia** | **Prison** |

Beach Boys, and you can see it in visual arts such as the poster used by Tate Museums in the UK to promote the Andy Warhol exhibition of 1971.[5]

Cooper Black became so firmly welded to ideas of youthful rebellion and pop art that it never lost the connection. Young and hip brands used and reused it, benefiting from and simultaneously reinforcing the message of the swinging 60s and the saucy 70s. In fact, since most consumers who are under retirement age will have had little or no first-hand experience of that era, what they remember is memories of the era, rather than the era itself. They may never have seen an album cover by Bowie or the Beach Boys, yet they have been trained, by creatives and designers who do remember, to recognize it and know that it means cool, fashionable youth lifestyles. One good example is French fashion brand the Kooples, which allowed Cooper

FIGURE 2.6 Ben and Jerry

Reproduced with kind permission of Unilever

Black to do quite a lot of the work in helping consumers understand its iconic portraits of couples, some shot in black and white for extra retro appeal. You can see lots of examples online.[6]

I mention all this detail, about Cooper Black, David Bowie, Andy Warhol and the Kooples, not because Cooper Black is the same as the bespoke Ben & Jerry's typefaces. Those are unique assets. However, Cooper Black is used all over the world, has a stronger meaning than most fonts, and is similar enough to the Ben & Jerry's typefaces that it helps the consumer to answer the question 'Where have I seen this before?'

Knowing 'where have I seen it before' helps the consumer work out what this brand is all about – it is cheeky, fun-loving and full of retro cool. If you look up images of Ben and Jerry, you'll see the photos too often conform to these values, as do most or all of the other design decisions that make up this brand.

To summarize: if you see a new brand with a new, custom-made typeface or brand mark that you've never seen before, yet you like it, or dislike it, and can attach meaning to it, it's because you asked, 'Where have I seen this before?' That's why the same question is at the centre of semiotic analysis, and where we can help brands find the answers.

## Marketing to specific cultures and regions

**RL**: If I remember correctly, one aspect of semiotics that Unilever has found especially useful is understanding the meaning of semiotic signs like colours, shapes and words, at the level of specific geographies and regions. Design in China is not the same as in India. The Netherlands is different from the US, and so on. So, when we are choosing semiotic signs for packs and fixtures, we want to achieve cut-through and help people navigate, but beyond that we want to choose visual cues and signs that are right for that culture, *and* right for marketing those brand origins in other parts of the world.

This morning I was looking at Italian fashions and noticing a divergence. On the one hand, Italian fashion is quite sombre and classic: a black dress, a man in a black suit with a tie. On the other hand you have Versace and all these splashy colours and elaborate decorations. Inspecting the decorations more closely soon led me to pictures of the Vatican, the palace with its amazing tiling in the walls and ceilings. There you can see the classical motifs which are then repeated in Italian style and in design, right down to the level of FMCG packaging. So, for me, it's a rewarding journey of discovery, finding out which semiotic signs in brands hold clues to different regions and cultures.

Bertolli was founded 150 years ago in Italy. Originally a brand of olive oil, it expanded over time to include a range of other Italian foods and was a part of Unilever's portfolio for several years in the 2010s. Its current packaging was designed by a UK agency, Stranger & Stranger, in 2018, not by an Italian monk in the 18th century.[7] I point this out because it's a very common example of a brand with regionally specific ties which needs to succeed at home and abroad. If you go too authentically Italian (or Chinese, or whatever), you risk producing something that looks great at home but is less suited to global taste. The trick is to include just enough of the right semiotic signs without overwhelming the shopper. If you look very closely at the Bertolli labels, you'll see all sorts of subtle details that make the brand 'feel' more Italian while simultaneously conforming to contemporary design conventions that allow the viewer some breathing space in between motifs – the negative space that I spoke of earlier. For instance, here and there you'll spot delicately drawn scrolls and curlicues, which are classical Italian motifs.

**Semiotics reveals new insights even in cultures we know well.**

RL: When I did that research for you on shopping in the Netherlands, I recall that I wrote quite a lot about a particular shade of yellow that is very popular there. I saw it everywhere, often contrasted against a neutral ground, which helped me trace it to the De Stijl art movement.

Iris: Yes, this was really interesting to me because I live here, this is our culture, and of course Unilever knows a lot about Netherlands culture. Despite this, there are always more observations that semiotics invites you to notice. When I saw all those pictures that you collected on your field trips, I was like, 'Oh my goodness, yellow is very important here, yes, it's so true!' When we can see it, then we can use it. The semiotic understanding makes something we knew implicitly, explicit.

I want to share with you one of my favourite photos of all the thousands I've ever taken. Figure 2.7 shows part of a kitchen in an apartment, in a small town in the Netherlands. The resident of the property was making us coffee and that's what I was trying to photograph. When I was back in London and had time to sort through all the photos I took on my field trip, I found that the gentleman had stepped out of shot just as I took the photo and I'd accidentally captured an image of the wall behind him. It's a tiled wall. The tiles are square, uniform and grey. In the centre of my photograph, but not quite in the centre of the wall, is a single yellow tile, in this shade that I now think of as Netherlands yellow.

FIGURE 2.7   A single yellow tile in a grey wall

Fieldwork photo, Netherlands, 2017

I'm telling you about this because I want to share something important. In another culture, that wall would have looked different. A reason to use one yellow tile would have been a reason to use several. What's more, they would have formed a pattern such as a chess board, or would have clustered together to represent flower shapes, or some further element of design would have been added. The Netherlands is one of the only world cultures I can think of that is capable of looking at one yellow tile and recognizing it as enough. It's not simply that people like bright colours in small amounts, but also a sense that you need 160 grey tiles for the beauty and impact of that one yellow tile to be fully revealed.

These insights are useful in one very obvious sense: they offer design tips that please shoppers at home as well as those overseas who want to buy authentic-looking Dutch products. If this were all semiotics could do, it might be enough. But there's a second, deeper, more anthropological layer of insight. The culture of the Netherlands values orderliness, as a general rule and a default to which occasional exceptions may be made. There is a culturally based sense of restraint that says that pleasures are best appreciated within delimiting boundaries. Cake tastes better if you *don't* eat it every day. A stamppot, a traditional dish in the Netherlands, tastes better and does not seem to lack anything *because* it incorporates only two or three vegetables. This type of insight keeps on delivering beyond packaging design and helps my clients to deepen their understanding of what shoppers want from everyday products and how they plan to enjoy them.

Let me draw your attention to one last brand before we leave this chapter. Seepje is an interesting Netherlands company that manufactures soap and detergent from fruit shells. If you have a look at their website[8] you may be able to see the package that I found in a local store. The product is called 'Seepje supershells' and it arrives in a brown card pack with the slogan 'Let nature wash all laundry' or 'Laat de natuur je was doen'. It attracted me because I could see how its use of semiotic signs conformed to the taste of the Netherlands, meaning that it would likely appeal to local shoppers. I could also see how those semiotic signs belonged to a set, which in semiotics is called a **code**, which marketers use to tell people that things are eco-friendly and natural. Here are some highlights.

The pack makes excellent use of negative space. The tiled kitchen wall in the apartment also makes fantastic use of negative space and hints at the way it is specially appreciated in the Netherlands. In the Seepje pack, there's plenty of undecorated space which makes the design restful to look at, in line with the expectations of today's consumers (like the discreet, not overdecorated Bertolli packs). The 'empty' space is not actually empty but is there to showcase the restrained and natural-looking brown card of the outer wrapper. Then there's the hole cut in the centre. Simple illustrations with clean lines and only just enough detail reveal a washing machine. The hole is a door through which we peep to see the soap shells inside. This is a thoughtful and imaginative use of negative space, and that's especially valued in this part of the world.

Overall, the design shows a policy of 'less is more'. This pack is not crowded with information. It says just enough. Nature. Laundry. Not too much text. No screaming colours. Please note the decision to dress this pack using a palette of only three, rather subdued, colours, a bit like a stamppot with three everyday vegetables. It's very Netherlands, and of course it also supports the brand message about being eco-friendly and reducing waste.

*Code* is a useful concept in semiotics because it helps marketers recognize when an individual semiotic sign such as a word, colour or use of space is capable of delivering more than one meaning. In fact, it's quite common for semiotic signs to do this: blue can mean health *and* 'blue sky thinking'; red can mean good luck *and* dominance or urgency. The versatility and applications of semiotic signs are explored in much more detail in the rest of this book.

This chapter concludes the introductory part of this book. In the next part, we'll take a deep dive into the semiotics of retail marketing in the present day and then the wild, thrilling future. Come and see – I have something to show you.

## Endnotes

1 Illustrated discussion of the rebrand can be seen at: https://www.creativebloq.com/news/magnum-rebrand (archived at https://perma.cc/CSZ6-HHGH)
2 See the Markthal in MVRDV's projects at: https://www.mvrdv.nl/projects/115/markthal (archived at https://perma.cc/UR8Y-T5DF)
3 Look at: http://www.harveyseverance.com/ben-and-jerrys.html (archived at https://perma.cc/Y55K-5BVG)
4 A popular choice among brands, some great examples of Cooper Black can be seen at: https://cooperblacklogos.tumblr.com/ (archived at https://perma.cc/YN84-2KQ4)
5 For example, see: https://www.artsy.net/artwork/andy-warhol-marilyn-tate-gallery-london-1971-signed-poster (archived at https://perma.cc/FB9A-KL3T)

6   For example, see: https://www.thefashionisto.com/kooples-fallwinter-2014-ad-campaign/ (archived at https://perma.cc/Q556-WE59)
7   See the oil bottles, for example, at: https://www.strangerandstranger.com/work/bertolli-olive-oil (archived at https://perma.cc/26D7-AY9D)
8   See: https://www.seepje.com/seepje-shop/#cat-individual-shells (archived at https://perma.cc/27WB-UUHR)

## References

Delacour, M (2021) Supplier insights: Unilever's five future-facing strategic choices, *Retail Analysis*, https://retailanalysis.igd.com/news/news-article/t/supplier-insights-unilevers-five-future-facing-strategic-choices/i/27657 (archived at https://perma.cc/GT7Y-RP3N)

Ong, T (2017) Instagram is expanding shoppable photos to thousands of merchants, *The Verge*, https://www.theverge.com/2017/10/5/16418776/instagram-shopify-shopping (archived at https://perma.cc/8UAJ-A8X9)

**PART TWO**

# The present day

# 03

# Desire

Welcome to Chapter 3, the first in a set of four chapters which all concern topics that begin and end with the consumer: desire, meaning, needs and identity. The things people want and the ways in which they want them are the subject of this chapter. Wanting and desire reside in the consumer's mind, in their imagination and emotions and their culturally acquired beliefs about where pleasure is found. They don't originate in your brand, store or marketing. However, there are lots of things you can do at the level of retail marketing that give pleasure and desire their best possible chance to flourish.

Chapter 4 is about meaning: the types of meaning that brand and store owners are very keen to impress upon customers, like 'premium', 'value' and 'organic'. I have some specific techniques for you, even though a business can never fully own these meanings: they are out in the wild, where they grow. Chapter 5 concerns shopper missions and moral economies. Chapter 6 is about identity.

Of these four vital aspects of consuming and shopping, the most foundational is wanting and desire, so this is where we begin.

> **WHAT'S COMING UP**
>
> What does it mean to want things? Where does desire come from? How is it ignited and how should it be satisfied, if at all? By the end of this chapter, you will be able to:
>
> - excite shoppers with three powerful triggers of wanting and desire;
> - recognize different kinds of pleasure and desire and know how to respond to them;
> - see how the pleasures and disappointments of shopping go hand-in-hand – how to increase one and reduce the other;
> - understand why shoppers 'zone out' and 'go on autopilot' while shopping and learn some techniques to wake them up.

## How to excite shoppers: three big tips for retail marketers

*Desire* is a word with a lot of meaning packed into it. We'll unpack it much more thoroughly later in this chapter. Right now, if you are looking to get a quick handle on how to excite shoppers, all you need to know is that desire can be very motivating; whether it's an intricate fantasy of luxury or an urgent compulsion to drive to the bargain store to complete a set of fragranced cleaning products. The following are three big principles that you can use right away.

### Nostalgia

In your physical or digital store, or in your product range and brand architecture, offer people cues and triggers that take them back to their youth or even further back, to an imaginary 'golden age' that might have existed before they were born. People like revisiting past times and can become sentimental about them. Here is a practical example of how to activate nostalgia at the level of retail marketing.

IN STORES, PLACE OUTSIZED OBJECTS THAT MAKE ADULTS FEEL LIKE CHILDREN.
When upmarket department store Selfridges opened a branch in the industrial city of Birmingham, UK, in its newly redesigned Bull Ring shopping centre, there was rejoicing among the city's residents. Occupying a large part of the Bull Ring and as one of its flagship stores, Selfridges was spread over three floors. In the basement was an impressive confectionery department. In a rather moving tribute to the city that was so pleased to welcome Selfridges, the store recreated a large statue of a bull entirely from jellybeans, placed it on a giant pedestal and made it the centrepiece of the department.

The bull is the city's much-loved symbol and mascot. This particular bull was a life-size (or even larger-than-life) replica of the bronze bull statue that sits directly outside the Bull Ring at street level, where it is much petted, climbed on and photographed. This colossal jellybean bull was quite a spectacle when viewed from the descending escalator that passed alongside it. In fact, it was equally spectacular when looking directly up at it from the shop floor. In Birmingham, a common childhood experience is visiting the city museum, where there is a life-size replica of a T-Rex. Generations of children have gazed up at the creature and experienced the delicious thrill of being overshadowed by what might as well be a mythical beast.

In this way, the jellybean bull tugged at people's memories and heartstrings two or three times over. It brought back childhood memories. It recreated the excitement of being a kid in a sweet shop. And it forged a strong link between the Selfridges brand and the Bull Ring market, which has been trading on that spot since the 12th century.

## Projection

Desiring things can be very much about predicting the future. I don't just mean being in a grocery store and thinking that the bread you have at home will soon go out of date. More than that, a big chunk of consumer desire is about people expressing a hope and belief that tomorrow is going to happen and happiness is within reach. For example, lots of people spend money buying 'stuff' for hobbies that they do not have time to pursue. It's an act of hope and a refusal to give up on a valued identity, even though the responsibilities of real life threaten to drown it.

People desire and acquire stuff when they envision better versions of themselves or their lives. This could be buying exercise equipment, with a vision of oneself in mind that does not just focus on better abs but in fact is a constellation of fantasies about a healthy daily routine, mindful eating and early mornings. They may also fantasize about solving problems – for example, 'If I get this language-learning package, I will finally master Portuguese', after years of self-teaching that hasn't quite succeeded. Or they buy wrecks of cars and furniture, envisioning both the final state of the restored item and the happy hours of productive activity restoring the thing. Planned or imagined creative activity has belief in the future built right into it and often revolves around one or two things:

1 The person has seen a **spectacular example** of something and they believe they can emulate it.
2 When they look at a crafted object, they can see how it embodies a **process**, which they want to experience. This could be, but need not always be, something like working with particular types of material, such as pastry, or it could be about experiencing a design process, as when people build Lego kits.

You can encourage projection in store rather easily by showing people spectacular yet achievable objects, bundles and kits that bring them closer to a desired lifestyle, and novel experiences, such as trying out new creative processes. Cooking videos on Instagram are often good at this – they are short, the finished product is alluring and the process looks novel and enjoyable.

## Collection

Collecting is a very interesting behaviour, psychologically, having to do with control, imposing order, gathering and completing. Collections can happen in specific categories to which the shopper habitually returns over a lifetime, and in categories that are intensely but only briefly interesting. Anything can become a collection, as when the UK saw something of a craze for Zoflora disinfectant, with consumers avidly trying to collect all the fragrances. In fact, this is an impossible task, as Zoflora regularly mixes up its offering with limited editions and seasonal editions, while retailers replenish their stock with varying frequency.

Collections can be about the *future*, as with a library of books or video games that one hopes to use. But the traditional type of collection, where people search for, assemble and keep groups of similar items, is simultaneously about the immediate *past*, where something in the wild has been rounded up and brought into the fold. Nineteenth-century Europeans were obsessive collectors and cataloguers, and this was because they were building a system, not just of objects but of knowledge. To be a collector is to have the chance to achieve mastery over something.

The impulse to collect can be a powerful motivator for shopping and there are quite a few things you can do with retail marketing to help it along:

- Within a product range, offer varieties and keep changing them.
- Discontinue products or variants when sales start to drop off, before they completely lose their allure. Sell off the remaining stock at a reduced price. Doing this at the right time can stimulate last-minute demand and even prompt consumers to begin a search for discontinued items. I've seen this happen with Benefit Cosmetics, for example, which makes good use of a 'recently discontinued' section of its website.
- At the level of the fixture or store, make as much as you can of seasons and festivals. These can be local festivals, imported festivals or even events that you make up yourself.
- In the store or on your digital shopping platform, give people items to collect as they move around or over more than one visit. This could be a mechanism such as points on a loyalty card, or discount codes and vouchers that are placed strategically and increase in value as more are collected.

## Aesthetics, Instagram and the lifelong desire of the excluded

*Beauty*

Perhaps you've noticed people and everyday things around you growing progressively more *crafted, cultivated and photographable* over the years. Sociologists such as Mike Featherstone started commenting on and predicting it back in the early 1990s, and even then could detect historical precedents. For example, at the same time as observing the state of consumer culture in 1991, in what was then the present day, Featherstone finds early markers of what he calls *the aestheticization of everyday life* in the art of the surrealist movement (circa 1920s). Among other objectives, these artists were very interested in the banal objects of everyday life, revealing clocks, hats, pipes and many more ordinary items as worthy of artistic depiction, worth looking at, worth exhibiting, and full of inherent interest and meaning. Now here we are 100 years later, in the 2020s, and Instagram is full of selfies and photos of people's dinners and portraits of tiny details of their belongings and daily experiences. People do this because it can sometimes be monetized, but also because it is fun – as long as you can afford to keep playing.

The word 'aesthetic' has noticeably passed into everyday conversation. Only about ten years ago, its use would have been much more restricted to the art world, the fashion industry and academia. Now the general public largely accepts that it has a meaning. We're out of the realms of art theory now, so the meaning is broadly 'look harmonious, present a pleasing appearance'. And people accept that the meaning expressed by 'aesthetic' is important. There is a push to make ourselves and our everyday lives more viewable, more interesting and fuller of vitality. Here are some of the ways that people pay attention to aestheticization in the 2020s:

- Instagram posts, already a well-developed art form, do not succeed or fail purely on their individual merits. Content-makers and consumers also consider and view them as a set. The rule is that individual posts, usually photos, need to harmonize with each other. That is, the social media output of private individuals is becoming increasingly clever about coherent branding and is curated in the way that artists curate their portfolios. Everything needs to hang together.
- Domestic interiors. People have always decorated their homes, but 'aesthetic' is more of an organizing principle, with great attention paid to the overall effect or mood. This is why some homes develop an increasingly retail-like aesthetic. They eventually become a reflection of the

- stores in which the items were purchased, almost like a showroom. It's not just domestic interior design trends that people are using as guidance and inspiration, it's shops and hotels.
- Teeth, hair, skin should all be highly aesthetic, according to advanced consumer culture. Cosmetic and aesthetic surgery is undeniably popular, profitable and a growth industry around the world. Every aspect of the body, for men now as well as women, has an idealized look, a beauty standard that real-life bodies either meet or miss.
- Outdoor space. Yesterday I learned that Gen Z users of TikTok are buying packets of flower seeds to throw on neglected ground. This is a really positive aspect of aestheticization, which cultural commentators normally regard as somewhat bad news. It represents a decision that the environment shouldn't be ugly, bleak or neglected. Flowers should grow. Places should be beautiful. Expectations are raised. Global mass culture and consumer culture seem to show agreement.

### Poverty

The obvious problem with all of this for the consumer is that not everyone finds aestheticization easy to afford. If you are one of the millions of consumers that has a social media account and uses their own everyday life as (possibly revenue-generating) content, you may know that this activity is capable of becoming an expensive investment, in money as well as time. This applies especially and particularly if you started out poor. If you live in public housing, as I did as a young adult, then achieving an aesthetic for one's home might depend on substantial and perhaps impossible improvements, repairs or even moving house.

Adding to these problems, the growing assumption in consumer culture that 'everyone' wants physical features, such as manicures and bright white teeth, eventually becomes *normative*. Normative is a social-science term that means people will pay a social cost, usually in the form of other people's disapproval, if they don't comply. Thus, teeth that diverge from the new standard become stigmatized, *even though* the wall between imperfect and perfect is made of history, culture and money and not of individual moral failing.

The pain of not being able to afford things can be chronic. It's part of a constellation of problems, curtailed life opportunities, humiliations and social exclusions. Some consumers, especially in adulthood, cope by turning away from categories that they cannot afford. But over time, being excluded from having nice things leaves a scar, especially when the visible niceness of things – that is, aesthetics – becomes more important with every passing year.

When people are economically hard-up, consumer culture offers them very few opportunities to feel special, or important, or even that they exist. Pampers are good for most people's babies, but not for your baby. People in stores are nice to you if you dress in your best and most conservative clothes, but if you show up in attire that is appropriate for your daily responsibilities and within your daily limitations, like workwear, or the clothing of someone who cleans all day or does unpaid childcare, then you may be ignored or even monitored.

> EXERCISE
>
> These are hard topics, I know, whether or not you've ever been poor. Here are some **actions** that we can take at the level of stores, promotions and packaging that make shopping more pleasant and rewarding for everyone.
>
> - If you're a large brand owner, note that the small **stores** in developing neighbourhoods, where low-income consumers make everyday purchases, are often struggling with difficult circumstances themselves; they might have modest premises that are in need of repair and not much money for features such as lighting. There's so much that larger brands can do in this respect. Some stores welcome exterior decorations that brighten up worn walls. Some tiny stores are dark and could be illuminated by a branded sign or cabinet. Branded seating outside serves the community if it is a spot where people meet and exchange news.
> - People with precarious, low-income jobs have experience that makes them suspicious when an organization assures them that 'we are all on the same team'. People with low incomes are often, however, great at teamwork, out of necessity. I've seen women in particular behave very strategically around BOGOF **promotions**. Where there are many of these in the same store, shoppers will buy two of everything, split the purchases into separate bags and take the duplicates to a relative or neighbour. People take opportunities to buy things in groups, so look for promotional mechanisms that reward their resourcefulness and teamwork skills.
> - **Packaging**. As with product design, people on limited incomes don't want worse versions of the things that wealthier people have. They want products

> that are affordable *and* functional *and* attractive. This is a reasonable expectation and a known challenge for product designers. But at the level of packaging, it is fairly straightforward. Consumers will thank you if you take the attitude that *all* of that is a reasonable expectation. Affordable shouldn't have to mean ugly. The effort of making fast-moving consumer goods (FMCG) and household essentials more aesthetic is appreciated when people who don't have a lot of money take these objects into their homes.

## Pleasure and satisfaction: the immediate and the real

Some consumers, often people of average or modest income, as well as those of more restricted means, are very focused on immediate and sensual pleasures when it comes to taste. As immediacy is so important in this *habitus* (a mix of habit, lifestyle, taste, consumer choices – Bourdieu's word and a concept that I simplify here), let's begin this section by saying immediately what retailers can do to arouse this kind of excitement among consumers, then we'll look at the rationale.

Here are some in-store activations that appeal to this habitus; they can be applied across multiple categories, such as snacking, laundry, beauty and personal care, alcohol, fresh produce and digital products, and for retailers who are marketing their own stores.

1 **Lots of choice, variety.** A brand that does this well is Shopkins: children's toys consisting of miniature grocery products, each one containing a small character mascot. Shopkins are released in seasons: Season 12 includes around 60 characters and there are hundreds all together. It has seemingly infinite variety, it is cute, collectible and affordable. Other brands that do well at this: Bath & Body Works and Starbucks, both of which add seasonal variants to their usual product range.

2 **Glitter and metallics.** Sparkles, surfaces and materials that are shiny silver, gold and rose gold, things that look like gems. In the habitus of the Immediate and the Real, there is no need for modesty, it's fine to enjoy glamour at any time of the day. Glitter can be incorporated into mugs, pens, nail polish, shoes, cupcakes and Prosecco, as well as used to create eye-catching displays in store.

3 **Colours** don't always need to be vivid. Some consumer groups in this habitus enjoy neutrals, such as white and silver, which are good at showing

off shine and sparkle. They also like pastels, especially pink. But with these caveats, the colours this habitus is best known for are rich, bright and saturated. A tip for marketers is to look at street art for colour inspiration. (There's more on street art in Chapter 4.)

4 **Animation.** I mentioned animation earlier, in connection with digital stores. But animation also works in traditional stores. Where free-standing structures can be placed, there are opportunities for things to rotate, tilt and wave. Time spent on shop floors tells me that people will stop to look at moving installations. It makes them feel special, because someone has tried to entertain them, and distracts from the warehouse aesthetic of many stores.

5 **Gifts and samples.** A lot of independent online retailers are good at this. Etsy vendors who sell personal items and homewares in letterbox-sized packages routinely incorporate tiny extras such as a sweet, a sticker or something like a decorative paper clip, depending on what they are selling. This is a major point of distinction from the shopping experience offered by larger, corporate retailers.

6 **Many items for not much money.** If you've never watched a shopping-haul video, there are plenty on YouTube. Haul videos are different from influencer videos, which are more professional and often feature premium brands. A haul video can mean going to a discount store and unpacking your purchases on camera. The point is that there should be lots of items to unpack.

7 **Packaging that is satisfying to open.** Satisfying packaging need not be limited to costly items. People love peeling the wax off Babybel cheese. Peeling the foil off a tube of Pringles is also fun (perhaps because it releases a burst of aroma). The deeply semiotic act of untying ribbon or string that is wrapped around packaging and tied in a bow is a special moment in miniature.

8 **Fragrance.** There are many reasons why fragrance matters in this habitus. For example:
   a. people on modest incomes do their own cleaning and domestic labour, which needs all the help it can get to become enjoyable;
   b. fragrance delivers an instant hit, you don't have to wait for it to cook, or lose weight to fit into it;
   c. fragrance easily evokes good feelings, especially when linked to seasons and festivals.

9  **Something to celebrate.** Speaking of festivals, these present constant opportunities for retailers. There are always things to celebrate in store, like International Women's Day, the World Cup and World Children's Day, as well as local festivals. Moreover, consumers of this habitus have enthusiastically adopted celebrations such as bridal showers and gender-reveal parties.

10  **Things that are charming and cute.** Cuteness has a variety of visual styles that vary regionally. In China, Japan and Korea, cuteness is more adult, elegant and cleanly designed than is seen in the West, which drives many Western consumers to buy imported beauty products. In Mexico, cuteness is found in cartoon characters and brand mascots on everyday products, which bring extra decoration, personality and warmth to stores and to consumers' homes.

What makes all these things work well together? Why are Immediate and Real pleasures so important? Recall that I spoke in Chapter 1 about Bourdieu's analysis of habitual taste in terms of social class and the material conditions of people's lives. When people's daily routines are physically and emotionally effortful, it's not a surprise if they appreciate rewards and comforts that deliver fast hits of specific pleasures. This is an insight that has stood the test of time, even though Bourdieu was writing in the 1970s.

In fact, there is a great amount of useful insight like this in academic sociology, anthropology and cultural studies. But my goal in this book is to keep things simple in a situation where it's all too easy to disappear down a rabbit hole of interesting theory. So here is just one more big idea that qualifies for discussion here because of its practical implications.

## *Immediate pleasures*

In his 1987 book, *The Romantic Ethic and the Spirit of Modern Consumerism*, Colin Campbell paints a historical portrait of two kinds of pleasure. Up until about the first half of the 18th century (at least in the regions that Campbell studied), pleasure was directly connected to satisfaction. Pleasures like food and sex were discrete and linked to specific activities and occasions. They were uncomplicated and delivered an instant hit. You can see all of this reflected in the list above, and, as marketers, we know that working- to middle-class consumers are particularly keen on this type of pleasure. An alcohol-soaked holiday in Ibiza is an immediate pleasure. The British homemakers who follow local influencer Mrs Hinch are like early 18th-century hedonists when they avidly seek out the whole range of cleaning products within a particular brand and clean their toilets and basins with products that burst into luxurious foam. This is the first kind of pleasure in Campbell's story.

Then, a new way to experience pleasurable sensations emerged, in the middle of the 18th century, for reasons which had to do with both religion and capitalism. This was a very interesting turn of events that shaped the tastes of more affluent consumers and is the subject of the next section.

## Romantic desire, imagination and longing

This new kind of pleasure that seemed to emerge around the mid-18th century was favoured by more affluent consumers and is still around today. Their cultivated tastes may seem subdued, remote and distant, compared with the flamboyant alternatives discussed above. Why are consumers who are rich in both money and life chances so interested in things that are less obviously *fun*? Where is the appeal?

The answer is *desire*, which is a different animal from pre-18th-century hedonism, and which keeps people spending in discretionary and high-end categories. Desire is a kind of unfulfilled longing; a yearning for something perpetually out of reach; a fantasy that lives in the imagination. Think of poets and the heroes and heroines of romantic novels, swooning, experiencing the exquisite pain of unrequited love.

There are various historical reasons for the emergence of desire. For our purposes, it is enough to say that the global economy changed and so did religion, which made a virtue out of *having and expressing emotions* such as pity for the poor. Although it was a long time ago, you may be able to detect a similarity to cultures of the present day, in which feelings and their expression are assigned great importance.

All of this helps us to see what the tastes of a more privileged habitus is delivering, beyond giving affluent consumers a way to distance themselves from other social strata. Emotion and the heightened sensation of desire are the main attractions. These are things we can offer through retailing and marketing. Here are some key things to know about romantic desire:

- **Fantasy is central to desire**. People want what they can't have. This is the difference between a shopping-haul video and an influencer video. The shopping-haul video is typically about attainable, immediate pleasures, as when a woman dashes to Home Bargains and comes out with 15 brightly coloured cleaning products for £15, which she paid for with her own money. The pleasure is immediate and attainable. The influencer video often strays into other realms. It is often about unattainable fantasies and pleasures of the imagination, as when an admiring audience watches a young woman unwrap mountains of gifts that have been bestowed on her by companies that compete for her attention. 'Imagine being her!' is not simply envy, it is an invitation to imagine that it could happen to you; a pleasurable fantasy.

- **Fantasy can concern travel as well as wealth.** A popular trope in the world of stationery and crafting is a young American woman inviting YouTube to come with her on a trip to somewhere like 'Japan's largest stationery store', where she scoops up cute staplers and sticky notes with the fervour of a 19th-century botanist on a once-in-a-lifetime trip to the Amazon rainforest. Hopping on a plane to Japan just to purchase desk toys is out of reach of most, even wealthy, consumers, and this is exactly where it gets its allure.

- **A little tragedy adds flavour and depth to the fantasy.** One of the reasons people enjoy nostalgia is because memories seem all the more precious when we have reason to think that whatever it is has gone for ever. Think of separated lovers. Children who grow up too quickly. Your own lost innocence. Traditions and rituals that have nearly vanished. Feelings of nostalgia and loss fuel all kind of purchases. This is why certain demographics of parents buy their children traditional wooden toys such as spinning tops, hobby horses and toy trains, even though much shinier and more 'modern' products exist.

- **The product itself may be entirely imaginary.** In Chapter 6, we discuss the online community Wall Street Bets, which at the time of writing was causing havoc on the stock market. This loosely organized collective of retail investors is, from one point of view (not necessarily my own), investing in nothing, in so-called 'meme stocks', which are popular simply for being popular, like reality TV stars. WSB's investments raise shares in selected companies to astronomical prices that cannot be predicted or controlled through any kind of rational calculation. What are investors paying for? It is not certain that they are paying for anything tangible. A good feeling. Pride. Community. A dream of making the world change.

*How to activate desire*

Desire can be used to market just about anything, but especially premium brands and lifestyle products and services.

1. **Stock limited supplies.** PlayStation released its latest console, the PS5, in November 2020. Stock immediately sold out and remained in short supply several months later. It was and is a sought-after item. Reserve this technique for non-essentials; nobody enjoys the anticipation in queuing for toilet paper.

2. **Build up anticipation.** Announce things before they happen. Cosmetics brand Clinique has done well for years out of 'Clinique Bonus Time'. Bonus Time is a gift-with-purchase promotion that is highly co-ordinated across retailers who carry the brand, with their individual Bonus Times happening on various dates, spread throughout the year.

3. **Tertiary colours.** Desire loves things that are mysterious and rare, and these consumers love colours that don't have short names and are hard to find on the colour wheel. They offer a needed change from Millennial Pink and neutral grey. Use this knowledge to refresh packaging, build colour into brand architecture and give stores a feeling of being up to the minute.

4. **Maximalism** means rich colours, intricate patterns and ornate decoration. It is an emerging trend in the West because minimalism is starting to feel repetitive and dull to consumers who have the privilege of being able to care about these things. Trends are slow to change; you need not abandon minimalism today if it is working for your organic skincare or food brand. However, maximalism will make a bigger impression on consumers if you do it now rather than waiting until every company is doing it in ten years.

5. In marketing, use ideas of **the past, the future or the exotic** to encourage fantasy:
   - The **past**. In the desire habitus, people will pay extra for history. Techniques could range from decorating a store's Christmas tree in 19th-century reds and golds to selling 'palaeolithic' diet plans and the beauty products of Hollywood's Golden Age.
   - The **future**. This isn't just about selling people the latest iPhone. Recall the photo of prepared fruit in Chapter 2, in which a grocery store creates a highly futuristic atmosphere around tubs of fruit salad, using

- The **exotic** is somewhere that is far away from the consumer, too far to easily visit or even access online. Any aspirational travel destination can be exotic, whether it's Scotland or the Dead Sea. If you plan to activate the exotic with your brand or in store, take care to avoid colonialist imagery, which we will discuss in Chapter 6. You could also take a look at the discussion of Haitian art in Chapter 4 to see the difference between 'authentic' images and those that are manufactured for tourists.

## Rewards and disappointments of shopping

For consumers, purchasing items and becoming their owner (or, increasingly, becoming a subscribed member) has rewards but also disappointments. Let's consider the disappointments first, so that we can finish on a happier topic.

### Disappointments

#### IN THE STORE

It is a source of concern to brand owners in many categories that shoppers frequently seem to zone out and go on autopilot when they are inside stores. This is especially the case with supermarkets because without a lot of interior decoration, they reveal themselves as warehouses. Writers with a more or less behaviourist approach to shopping, such as Sorensen (2016), observe that supermarket shoppers traverse only about 20 per cent of the store on a single visit, and 85 per cent of time on the shop floor is spent looking for items that they already knew they wanted before they entered. This means that if you are trying to get shoppers to notice or try something new, the odds are already stacked against you. Only a small amount of their time is available to you, so you need to reach out to them in store with visual cues that attract them to the laundry aisle (or whatever it is) and then clearly flag up the item at fixture level so that people know where they are supposed to direct their gaze. Use those flags to trigger emotional responses, by designing in elements such as nostalgia, collectibles and visions of the future.

## AFTER PURCHASE

'Buyer's remorse' is a phrase that has passed into common parlance because of the regularity of post-shopping regrets and disappointments. It is sometimes linked to the regret of spending more money than one could afford but includes more than that. Shoppers may be disappointed by:

- Products that are smaller than expected, sometimes due to misleading photography or packaging. People have an idea of the sizes that homewares and personal items are supposed to be, and not delivering that can be a source of disappointment, especially if they stretched their budget to achieve the purchase.
- Products that decay quickly: fragrances that evaporate and become undetectable in minutes; items with a shorter sell-by or use-by date than expected.
- Products that become dull when opened. In many countries, consumers like to eat chocolate eggs around Easter time. Today, the way the big mass-market confectionery brands respond to that is by selling a foil-wrapped egg and two units of their signature chocolate bar placed alongside the wrapped egg, and the whole thing is encased in plastic. When opened, the egg retains its semiotic value. Because people who celebrate this tradition tend not to eat chocolate eggs all year round, everything that is unusual about the egg makes it feel special: its shape, its foil wrapping, the (usually fruitless) hope of there being something inside. But the chocolate bars, once removed from the plastic casing and separated from the egg, are revealed to be exactly the same items that are on sale every day of the year, wherever food is sold. They only retain whatever magic they possess as long as they are still in the unopened box, rather like collectible toys.

As a marketer, my first instinct is to agree with the common-sense view that we should strive to avoid disappointing our customers. In fact, there is an alternative point of view which comes out of academia. In her helpful review of Colin Campbell's work, Celia Lury (2011) highlights an important insight concerning disappointment as part of the romantic experience described earlier in this chapter. In this view, disappointment or incomplete satisfaction is an important part of the process.

The title of this chapter is 'Desire', an emotive word that describes a condition of pleasurable yearning and longing. If you can think of a time when you have yearned or longed for something, and succeeded in getting it, you may remember experiencing momentary joy and triumph, followed by a sense of anti-climax. For romantic consumers, if not necessarily all consumers, wanting something is often much more exciting and pleasurable than owning it. The marketing implication is that consumers like being teased. Whether you have in mind an in-store event, a promotion, a range of new products, new content or an expansion of a digital product, build up the anticipation and release it in small pieces ahead of the main event. When it has launched, don't hesitate to let people know when even more content is expected.

> **IN-STORE ACTIVATIONS: MANAGING DISAPPOINTMENT**
>
> - Shoppers want to have a pleasant experience in store, yet traditional supermarkets often feel like thinly disguised warehouses. Even a little decoration, such as some bunting or a few balloons can help to make the store visit feel warmer and more special.
> - Items that look special need to be special. US consumers expect Halloween candy to arrive in limited-edition flavours, not be their everyday candy in a different wrapper.
> - Think of romantic, desiring segments of shoppers as being in love. They are caught up in the allure of whatever the desired object is. Build up anticipation, make it available slowly and have something ready to hint at to consumers when they immediately want to know what your *next* move is going to be.

## Rewards

In this chapter, I've already said quite a lot about the different kinds of rewards and pleasures that people are able to access through shopping. These have included:

- nostalgia – a bittersweet experience;
- projection – an expression of hope and belief in the future;
- collection – a very pleasurable activity that is a way of taking control and is a route to mastery of some topic or skill;
- feeling socially included (and not actively excluded);
- immediate, real and sensory pleasures;
- longed-for, imaginary and remote pleasures, symbolic and imaginary products;
- products that retain their 'specialness' when opened;

- stores that have some aesthetically pleasing aspects and do not feel like forbidding or indifferent warehouses;
- waiting for things, and then immediately waiting for the next thing.

We don't need to cover all these items again in this last section on the rewards of shopping, but I will use this space to bring up one more insight concerning the Immediate and Real shopper versus the Romantic, Desiring shopper, which I think you'll find useful. Remember that, like the hedonists and libertines of the 17th and early 18th centuries, shoppers who like immediate and real pleasures will often link those pleasures to specific experiences. Food is its own pleasure, so is alcohol, so is sex.

But for the more Romantic, Desiring shoppers, who enjoy being seduced by their own imaginations, pleasure can be taken anywhere. It exists at the level of **emotions** – their experience and expression. It is not limited to one product category, one occasion, one store, one shopping mission or one consumer need. It is therefore enormously flexible, which is good news for marketers. If you encourage fantasy and imagination, you can trigger emotion, and now we have the potential for desire. This is how Apple sells iPhones, but it can also be implemented at smaller scales. For example, if you think about the luxury jam shop in Chapter 1, it benefited when it began to help shoppers invest in the fantasies they wanted to have, about historical elegance and refinement (a romantic, desiring fantasy indeed), which were the very fantasies that the brand itself wanted to evoke but could not deliver as an in-store experience until semiotics got involved.

> ### EXERCISE
>
> This chapter has a lot of information packed into it. If you need a break before tackling Chapter 4, take a fresh look at your store, digital shopfront or packaged product. Ask yourself where sensory pleasure and romantic desire are located and which of this chapter's tips you can use to increase them. Even quite masculine and prosaic items such as barbecue sets and shaving kits can be imbued with pleasure if we choose. If they are absent from our store or brand, there should be a reason why.
>
> When you've identified at least one immediate and sensory pleasure, one source of romantic desire and one way to manage disappointment, let's move on to Chapter 4, where we'll consider the serious business of conveying complex meanings, such as 'premium', 'value' and 'natural', at the level of retail.

## References

Campbell, C (1987) *The Romantic Ethic and the Spirit of Modern Consumerism*, Blackwell, Oxford

Lury, C (2011) *Consumer Culture*, Rutgers University Press, New Brunswick

Sorensen (2016) *Inside the Mind of the Shopper*, Pearson FT Press, Upper Saddle River

# 04

# 'Premium, natural, sensational!' How to create meaning

Welcome to Chapter 4, the second in a set of four chapters on the thoughts, imaginations and everyday lives of consumers. Your customers are going about their lives with a set of ideas already installed about what value for money looks like, or what seems healthy, or what seems like it would be fun. Businesses cannot aspire to entirely control consumers' thoughts about these topics, but there is certainly a lot we can do to encourage and stimulate these ideas and link them to our stores and brands.

> **WHAT'S COMING UP**
>
> This is a reference chapter that you can use as a dictionary of semiotic signs. You can return to it after you have finished the book, to solve marketing and design problems on the fly.
>
> By the end of this chapter, you will know where to look for semiotic signs, how to combine them, and how to apply them in a range of retail marketing settings. Doing this will help you to communicate key messages to the shopper, such as:
>
> - premium – worth paying more for;
> - value for money, economy;
> - natural, healthy and sustainable;
> - authentic and traditional;
> - future-facing, modern;
> - sensational and exciting.
> - powerful and effective;
> - global and local.

Throughout this book, we will explore various marketing actions that can be implemented when we are designing stores, fixtures, packaging, shopping apps and e-commerce sites. These actions are provided in the context of solving some big challenges for marketers, principally including:

- how to create better *shopper experiences* in physical and digital stores;
- how to get shoppers' *attention* and aid *navigation* at the level of the physical or digital fixture.

This is very important because retail is evolving in the direction of providing better and more interesting experiences (partly as a survival mechanism), and also because studies of shopper behaviour show that attention is limited and navigation is difficult. However, this chapter is about something different. No matter how seriously we take these conceptual opportunities and practical constraints, there are still very many occasions when a brand or retailer needs to **convey some specific message in store**. For example, it's urgently necessary to convey 'premium' or 'tasty' as reliably as possible.

In 20 years of working with brands and retailers, I have found that the same topics regularly appear in the specific messages they want to convey. In this chapter, I have identified eight of these big topics, which we could regard as impressions or meanings that the brand is trying to create in the mind of the customer. For each topic, I provide a variety of semiotic signs that can be used together to create this meaning and be applied across multiple channels and platforms. Providing a completely exhaustive list in each section would need a book of its own, so I will selectively point out some suggestions for activation in each section and try to show the overall theme so that you can extrapolate it to other retail marketing decisions.

## Premium

Just about anything can be made to seem premium, whether it is simply a variant of some mass-market product, an event, an e-commerce store or a huge department store. Let me reveal the secret right away: the key thing that people want, across all different styles of premium, is Signs of Care. This applies equally whether you are selling some comfortingly rustic item, or going for traditional classic luxury or some upmarket version of futurism. Signs of Care can apply to store exteriors and interiors, marketing communications, product and packaging design and customer service. The point is that, on some level, people are aware that when they pass through a store they are being processed through a machine. Signs of Care are creative, human interventions that supply evidence that someone cared about the shopper or consumer enough to try to improve their experience and make it less machine-like.

### Store furniture, category management and merchandising

Where possible, give things their own special spaces, like the switch to wooden shelves and softer lighting in Waitrose wines and spirits. If you have something special to promote, pick some detail of the product or offer and develop it into a theme. I saw an attractive example in Fortnum & Mason in London where the item being promoted was champagne. The bottles were stacked in a pyramid shape on a free-standing structure in the middle of the shop floor – the pyramid is a tried and tested Sign of Care that works even in stores with small budgets. The theme was 'bubbles'. 'Bubbly' is a metonym for champagne (a small part of the item describes the whole thing), and a cluster of large, clear baubles was suspended on strings above the fixture. This thoughtful gesture added to the overall aesthetic appeal of the display, enhancing the shopping experience, and at the same time conveying the frivolous and fun aspects of the product and its usage occasions.

### Pack formats

If 'value' and 'economy' products usually come in large packs, you can make things seem more premium by putting them in smaller packs; things often feel more precious as they become smaller. Shoppers experience Signs of Care where a lot of design effort has been expended per square inch of packaging. You can also communicate Care by avoiding industrial elements in packaging unless they are an intentional aspect of branding. I've seen luxurious hand soaps where the product colour, on-pack text and bottle design are thoughtful and elegant, but the effect is spoiled by a plastic pump dispenser, suitable for a garage or hospital, as though the consumer shouldn't mind, or should be willing to pretend they can't see it. Brands ask shoppers to perform this act of polite, accommodating, social blindness more often than you would think. Signs of Care relieve them of the burden.

*Colours*

Dark colours are good for communicating sophistication because of the dual connotations of night-time and adulthood (in contrast to the primary colours and pastels of children's products). Black is reliable as long as you are using it intentionally and not simply defaulting to it. Dark shades that can be used to suggest a conservative or classic style of premium include dark purples (aubergine, raisin), navy blue, burgundy and racing green. If you want to use metallics, gold is still luxurious, but use it sparingly and consider alternatives such as pewter. If you are designing for a market that likes a lot of gold, such as India or the Middle East, then use it thoughtfully – create intricate patterns, don't just splash it around.

*Typefaces*

Times New Roman is a reliable go-to for premium, because of its 'classic' look, and 'premium' typefaces are often, but not always, with serifs. Tall, skinny typefaces convey elegance and are often, but not always, upper-case. Cursive script can work to convey delicacy, although it is very overused in mass-market brands and settings.

The way we see this play out with different versions of premium is that a traditional port or sherry will use Times New Roman or similar, perhaps all in upper case. A tech brand will stick with a skinny typeface because it looks elegant but switch to sans-serif for extra modernism. A rustic brand might go for a cursive script that looks carefully handwritten. Remember, the demonstration of Care is paramount, so as long as your design decisions and execution are intentional and thoughtful, you have a lot of flexibility in which typefaces you use.

## Value

Value for money (VFM) will always be interesting to shoppers, and messages that promise VFM have been around since the dawn of retail. Because of this, you already know a lot of the semiotic signs! This makes VFM relatively easy to implement at the level of retail. Despite this, we still need to use signs for VFM judiciously. While Signs of Care make things seem more premium, we shouldn't automatically conclude that the way to communicate value for money is carelessness. Deploying too many semiotic signs for VFM can result in making your store seem at risk of going out of business.

To see an example of VFM messaging dragging an offering downmarket, search online for the artwork *Closing Down Sale* (1992, 2016), a series of installations by British artist Michael Landy (who later became famous for destroying all his possessions). *Closing Down Sale* is an astute collection of signs for VFM.

---

EXAMPLE: *CLOSING DOWN SALE* BY MICHAEL LANDY

- The installation is set in a large supermarket trolley. This is a clue that the trolley (itself a metonym for the supermarket) is a semiotic sign that shoppers treat as a cue to look for VFM.
- The trolley contains items such as oversized novelty toys, large gadgets and utilitarian household items. If they have a common theme, it is that they are mostly made of garishly coloured plastic.
- The items are nearly obscured by a proliferation of cardboard notices. The notices are stuck to the products and also to the trolley. Their colours are fluorescent yellow, pink, orange and green. They bear captions that might have been handwritten with a marker pen: 'EVERYTHING MUST GO!', '50% EXTRA FREE', '1/2 PRICE', 'LIQUIDATION CLEARANCE' and (ironically) 'OUR REPUTATION IS YOUR GUARANTEE'. All the text is upper-case, here giving the impression of shouting, and the neon colours appear to be shouting as well.

---

Landy is conducting semiotic analysis on our behalf – this is quite common in contemporary art, so it's useful to be acquainted with it. What Landy is showing us is carelessness. None of the signs, considered individually, is wrong, but here they appear in excess. They are crowded together, one heaped on top of another, the products themselves almost buried beneath the promotional offers. The impression is that the store manager needs to shout and make their voice heard more urgently than the shopper needs the goods.

Avoid the effect of a closing-down sale by using the following semiotic signs selectively. Two or three will do. You don't need them all. Consider limiting them to certain parts of the store.

### Fixtures

Shoppers everywhere understand the concept of the bargain bin. In my opinion, the bargain bin achieves its best expression when its contents are relatively valuable, for example, bottles of wine. Sorting through a bin, looking for a bargain, can be fun. You can also see shoppers enjoying this type of behaviour when supermarkets place a mix of fresh bakery items in a trolley near the checkouts, to achieve last-minute sales at the end of the day.

### Signage, price notifications, words and text

VFM messaging is more appealing when it is celebratory (in contrast to the rather desperate tone of Landy's *Closing Down Sale*). In recent years, digital retailers have led the way in making value for money sexy. Here, achieving VFM is a sport, not a compromise. Retailers such as Amazon, eBay, Tmall and Taobao make the most of Black Friday and Singles Day, engaging shoppers in time-sensitive and elaborate games to snare a bargain before someone else snaps it up. Timers count down, prizes appear and then disappear. There's a sustained atmosphere of excitement and animation. A McKinsey report of 2019 states that during the previous Singles Day event in China, half of all Tmall vendors used live streaming to sell their products. Price notifications are always prominent but the new standard for VFM retail marketing also includes a large element of entertainment.

### Colours

The classic colours for promotions are red, white and yellow. Notices that say 'SALE' or 'OFFER' may be round, rectangular or occasionally banner shaped. Text dominates the space within the frame and may be red on a white ground, or reversed-out white on a red ground. Yellow may be used for details and highlights. Notices that indicate the price of specific items for sale are usually, but not always, black and white: a combination used to communicate hard facts and simplicity.

### Pack formats

Help the shopper achieve VFM with family-size packs, multipacks and other large-pack formats where they can achieve an economy of scale.

## Natural, healthy and sustainable

Natural, Healthy and Sustainable are big topics for both consumers and businesses. They manifest in a wide range of categories, including but not limited to food, personal care and home care. In this section, I'm treating these ideas in a group because they all derive their persuasive power from an idea of some original state of nature, pure and unspoiled, before humans interfered with it.

Messages about nature are especially appealing to people who feel that they don't get enough of it. Many people around the world spend their lives working indoors, in office and factories. They may be in highly urbanized environments that are crowded with people, ads and products. Their ability to work long hours may rely on remote services. A pizza is delivered because there is no opportunity to cook. A doctor's appointment takes place remotely, by video link, and the patient is glad not to have to attend the clinic. Holidays and even outdoor physical exercise are out of reach. These people, some of whom are well-paid consumers, can be left craving nature and cherish the idea of it, even as they are deprived of the reality. Here is a small selection of the dozens of semiotic signs for nature that can be applied in retail.

### Store furniture, category management and merchandising

Wooden crates, pallets, wooden tables. Wicker baskets and white chalk letters on a blackboard communicate the wholesome simplicity of a farmer's market. Hot areas of the store are fresh produce, bakery, delicatessen, coffee.

### Pack formats

Packages with windows through which you can view the contents are displays of honesty. Packaging that is simple and not fussy is appealing, such as brown paper bags. (See also 'Materials', below.)

### Colours

Green and also 'natural' neutrals such as wheat, stone and charcoal. If you want to make this premium, note the need for subdued colours: this is the difference between a pack of organic porridge or chia seeds that comes in more reserved or neutrally coloured packaging, and depictions of nature on a box of mass-market family cereal featuring a bright yellow sun, a brilliant blue sky, a dazzling yellow-white corn field, and so on.

## Materials

Brown paper and string. Recycled paper, handmade paper, corrugated card, fabric, especially hessian. Straw. Anything that is woven, braided or plaited. Resistant materials, such as wooden blocks, brick and tiles can be used to suggest a traditional butcher or dairy.

## Images and icons

Include objects from nature, such as fruits and vegetables, of course, but also animals, birds, trees, fields, mountains and the sun. Rivers and waterfalls. Flowers and blossoms. Pastoral scenes: lambs in the fields; snowy forests. There's also room to enhance Nature messaging with signs for Authentic and Traditional, found in the next section.

## Typefaces

Letters that are imperfectly aligned convey the idea of something handmade. Some brands use fat, rounded, easy-to-read typefaces to communicate nature and the idea of things being unspoiled. This meaning is achieved by appealing to semiotic codes of childhood: the item is so innocent that a child could understand it, and its gentleness, purity and closeness to nature are that of a child's.

## Digital, e-commerce and social media marketing

Use photos or videos to show off the natural origins of whatever you are selling. Some influencers are great at this. For example, jewellery maker, photographer and musician Jonna Jinton sells her own products through her social media presence. Her marketing is so thoroughly anchored to the physical geography and unspoiled landscapes of rural northern Sweden that she also effectively markets the whole country as a place of purity and escape.

## Tone of voice

This is where your design decisions will vary according to the exact message that you want to get across.

- **Natural.** An atmosphere of tender emotions, comprised of a mix of elements such as 'loving care' (loving humanity, the Earth), wide-eyed innocence, nostalgia, longing for a return to nature, appreciation of the beauty and purity of nature.
- **Healthy.** Depictions of human smiles. Sunshine. Energy and vitality: for example, a typeface that shows the letters as sheaves of corn, springing up towards the sun. **Wellbeing** is more contemplative, where product use is part of being 'in the moment'.
- **Sustainability.** Flatter the consumer that their actions are moral ones and their purchases make a difference. This can be a very feel-good message but needs a backstory in which the business itself makes an ongoing commitment to building a better world. Look at the discussion of smart cities in Chapter 10 for more about what 'a better world' could consist of.

## Authentic and traditional

The same overworked, time-poor consumer who dreams of nature and will pay a little extra for it when retail makes it available, may also hunger for authenticity. The fantasy of pure, raw nature is often mixed with nostalgia for real or imagined times past, in which people had genuine relationships with each other, had meaningful connections to the place where they lived and worked, food took a long time to cook, and things were done properly. As participants in advanced capitalism and consumer culture, we are victims of our own success. We invented Facebook and Twitter and now they mediate our relationships. We invented call centres and now people have to work in them. Authenticity has been a buzzword in recent years because, like nature, it can be in short supply.

Brands and retailers know very well how compelling a longing for authenticity and tradition can be. These are similar to nature in representing simplicity and purity but are firmly located in the realm of the human: human activities, creative processes and rituals. As I wrote these words, a Twitter user called Conor Lynch (@ConorLynchEsq) posted a photograph of Victoria Street in London. It is a photograph of dramatic contrast, in which skyscrapers of steel and glass overwhelm a tiny scrap of a street that once existed, in the form of the Albert pub, built in 1862. In this photograph, the pub is the last, fragile vestige of history, like the last natural tooth in an old head. The building is distinguished as traditional (historical and therefore authentic) by its much smaller proportions than the surrounding towers, but also by being much more decorative. The arched, latticed windows and white-painted shutters stand out against the warm, yellow brick. Shrubs and hanging baskets of flowers adorn the exterior of the building at street level and even hang from balconies on the floors above. At ground level, the windows are dressed with long curtains and are flanked by pillars with flourishes such as decorative cornices. These architectural features are conspicuously absent in the sleek, shiny, angular and emphatically modernist towers that are the Albert's neighbours. This contrast marks the Albert as small, precious and fragile and simultaneously rather majestic. Above all, it is authentic. It doesn't look machine-made. It has human craftsmanship and artistry all over it.

Here are a few easy semiotic signs of the authentic that you can incorporate into stores and retail marketing. After that, I'll say a few words about how to be traditional yet modern.

## Store furniture, category management and merchandising

If you consider the grid-like aesthetic of most supermarkets, and the shiny uniformity of modernism, you can perhaps see how consumers feel that they have encountered authenticity when a little imperfection and spontaneity are allowed to creep in. Break away from traditional shelving and pile things on distressed wooden tables. Create the opportunity for discovery; try grouping unexpected items together.

## Materials

As well as the natural materials listed previously, consider textiles such as wool, silk and cotton. If you operate in a packaged-goods category where things come wrapped in plastic, consider the allure of older packaging materials such as waxed paper and even foil.

## Images and icons

As well as signs for Nature, given above, consider depicting objects that represent traditional, more 'natural' and less 'spoiled' processes: a kettle that heats on the stove rather than plugging into the wall; an old-fashioned bathtub made like a barrel, from wood and steel hoops; a stone pestle and mortar for grinding herbs and spices.

## Typefaces

Painted signs, or signs that look as though they have been painted, are an underused alternative to signs that look like chalk on a blackboard.

## Traditional, yet modern

In just the same way that you can drag a brand down by using too many signs for Value for Money, history can eventually become too much of a good thing. You can attach a halo of authenticity or tradition to your contemporary brand without overwhelming it by being selective about how many signs you use. For example, if you look at historical packaging you will see that it is frequently crammed with text and fine print. Don't simply copy this design decision – today's consumers want cleaner design with more unfilled space. Find a balance by leaning towards modern design while incorporating a few key elements that refer to the past, such as decorative scrolls and columns. We met both negative space and decorative scrolls in Chapter 2, in the context of talking about Dutch restraint and Italian flourishes.

# Future-facing

The Future is a big topic that can be expressed by brands and business owners in a few different ways. One is to publicly embrace future-facing values such as inclusivity. (This is discussed in detail in Chapter 6.) Another way is to deploy simple semiotic signs of futurism at the level of packaging and in store displays: this is where we would expect to see 'space age' design choices such as shiny surfaces, white, silver and chrome, and adventures in minimalism. I'll expand on these details below. Then there is the future in the sense of technological innovation. If your customers can use tech to try on clothing, redecorate their home, test drive a car, explore a holiday resort or climb a mountain, they are likely to agree that they are having a future-facing experience. If you are going to take the technological innovation route to the future, the guiding principle is that the innovations should satisfy a genuine consumer need or add value to the shopper's experience in the form of genuinely improved ease of shopping, or else entertainment. Too many physical stores have created apps because they thought they should, but from which purchasing is difficult and tracking down value for money becomes nearly impossible.

Below is a collection of semiotic signs that communicate 'the future' and can be deployed in physical and digital stores. If you consider that we previously discussed Nature and Tradition in terms of things and processes that are unspoiled by human or technological interference, the semiotic code of the Future is more or less the opposite of that. Here, we find celebrations of human achievement, not in the area of meticulous handcrafts, but in a realm of well-funded laboratories and space stations staffed by visionaries, science boffins and digital engineers. You may notice that the Future, like Nature and Tradition, is to some extent imaginary, fed by wishful thinking and science fiction. This is all good news for brands and retailers, as it offers a lot of flexibility and creative opportunity.

## Materials

Materials appear at the top of the list because they even outrank colour for their ability to suggest the future. Consider highly engineered textiles such as Kevlar and the Mylar foil that is used to make the shiny silver blankets used in extreme sports and emergency rescue situations.

Although not usually considered 'materials', sound and light rank highly in our collective fantasies of the future because the general public is intrigued by things like the seemingly infinite applications of sonic waves and lasers, including in eye surgery and dentistry.

## Colours

White and silver are fully expected here: it's interesting that the future is rarely imagined as particularly colourful. Blue may feature as a highlight – it is capable of suggesting the brilliant bluish-white light of scientific investigation.

## Typefaces

Follow tech brands by choosing skinny, sans-serif typefaces. It's not fashionable now to use futuristic typefaces that are too extreme, because they date quickly, like the 1980s 'computer' fonts that are rendered in chunky pixels. Follow the example of Apple and choose something sleek and restrained. Less is more.

## Store furniture, category management and merchandising

Because the future is a large-scale fantasy, expressing it in store also works best on a large scale. I've seen it done very well in shopping centres, airports and metro stations, where there is money and space to play around with novel design and architecture. Where achievable, futurism can be found in:

- architectural exoskeletons, such as putting glass elevators on the outside of a building rather than hiding them inside opaque shafts;
- responsive pathways and fixtures – environments that change their lighting or sound when a human is passing;
- large, swooping, curvy shapes that contradict the grid aesthetic of a conventional supermarket or warehouse;
- a return to nature with plants and even water features integrated into the organic, flowing design of buildings and their interiors;
- attention to positive sensory experiences while shopping – a space designed so that shopping is not accompanied by smells such as raw meat or other people's sweat; an elaborately designed space can be positively therapeutic – clean, hygienic bubbles of artificially stimulated sensation, where delicate aromas combine with soothing music;
- upsetting the conventions and traditions of retail – for example, if the typical supermarket has set an expectation that there should be a lot of product and not a lot of staff, you can display futurism by swapping that ratio, so that you offer only a limited range of items but have lots of staff to explain and sell them; Apple stores are usually well staffed, while most customers are there to purchase only a handful of core items.

## Sensational and exciting

There are many times when a brand or retailer wants to communicate 'sensational' and 'exciting' to the shopper. Categories that particularly feature this type of meaning include alcohol and soft drinks; food, especially confectionery and snacks; cosmetics; entertainment; some fragrance, especially brands targeting men; automotive; technology. Retailers are very interested in 'sensational and exciting' when they have seasonal festivals to celebrate, when they are running a promotion and when they operate in sectors where shoppers have heightened expectations of some kind of an 'experience', such as ice cream parlours, toy stores and fashion boutiques.

If we pause for a moment to consider the words 'sensational' and 'exciting', we may notice that there's something visceral about them. They describe physical experiences within the body. In psychology, the term for this type of sensation is 'arousal'. Arousal refers to a state of alertness that exists at one end of a dimension, where the other end is sleep. Arousal is a wakeful but emotionally neutral physiological state that then has to be interpreted by the human mind. It may be perceived as either pleasurable or unpleasant, largely depending on the context. In marketing, we are of course mainly trying to produce positive arousing experiences such as 'feeling excited', although even negative experiences have their place, as with roller coasters and horror movies. If this sounds a bit technical, there's a reason why I'm telling you. Reducing potentially vague and subjective marketing concepts, such as 'sensational' and 'exciting', to this simpler, more objective state of 'arousal' helps us to appreciate the full range of techniques available to retail marketers to stimulate shoppers. Anything that makes the shopper feel more awake is capable of being interpreted as pleasure.

The simplest way to achieve this is to identify the conventional appearance of things (for example, a supermarket trolley) or normal practice (for the soft drinks aisle, let's say) and then take the more arousing aspects of the scenario to extremes. Below are a few specific examples.

### *Store furniture, category management and merchandising*

I visited a French supermarket, possibly a branch of Carrefour, which was large enough to have an electronics department. The department borrowed semiotic signs from nightclubs, with striking results. The black ceiling (unusual in itself) was the location for dramatic, multicoloured spotlights pointing in different directions, making the area unusually stimulating for a grocery store and suggesting adult pleasures.

## Pack formats

Exciting packs do more than simply act as containers. For example, they may deliver an experience in their own right, by making a sound or delivering haptic feedback when opened (think of Pringles: 'once you pop, you can't stop').

## Colours

Avoid the fluorescent colours of highlighter pens. The clever way to use colour to create sensation and excitement is to take consumers by surprise. Wash large areas with your brand colour, repackage items in limited-edition seasonal colours, or introduce colour into spaces that are usually sombre or overlooked.

## Materials

Novel materials generate excitement. Throughout the 2000s, there was a shop in London called Playlounge, which sold toys for adults. I don't mean this in the sense of the adult entertainment industry but rather that they were selling desk toys, accessories, collectibles, novelties, books and T-shirts. Playlounge won awards for retail design, including some highly innovative shelving. The standard grey steel shelving units were replaced with a honeycomb structure of orange and yellow Perspex. Fixed to the wall, it offered the shopper an array of cells or containers in which the contents were only partly visible. The shopper would have to dip their hand into each cell and pull out an item in order to fully discover what was in there. The simple act of removing an item from a shelf for closer inspection becomes a surprising event.

## Digital

This is an obvious place to exploit the attention-getting qualities of movement and sound. This is about more than video: the distinct opportunity offered by digital platforms is interaction. For example, Nike has a feature on its website that enables people to design a pair of trainers. After more than ten minutes of designing a high-top sneaker in acid yellow and royal blue, I now feel somewhat of a sense of ownership of my imaginary shoes, which are priced at just over £100 ($140) and require registration as a Nike

Member as a condition of purchase. While this is, arguably, a design selected from a pre-set menu, I was involved in making decisions about the product, interacted with some fun design tools and slightly deepened my relationship with the brand.

## Power

Power is an interesting type of meaning that is closely related to perceptions of efficacy (for example in medicines or cleaning products). It may, but need not, overlap with futurism, or position itself as something bigger and better than mere nature. Both medicine and cleaning are about the triumph of human innovations such as vaccines and bleach over the more threatening and hard-to-control aspects of nature such as viruses and microbes. As well as the above categories, power is found in areas such as sport and e-sport, automotive, pharmacy, and training and coaching in fields such as weight loss, fitness, business coaching, sales and personal branding. Power is also found in the comms and design of service brands such as Amazon, FedEx and UPS.

Claims of power usually rest on the ability to do something specific. They may rest on the expertise of a company, or on effective product ingredients, or both. Sociologists often talk about power in terms of the ability of individuals and organizations to make change. This change may be regarded by participants as a zero-sum game where, in order for one entity to control power, another entity must be deprived of and subject to it. This isn't a trivial observation because, at the moment, younger consumers in many countries are very suspicious of power. They don't necessarily respect experts and are alert to possible exploitation.

From a retail point of view, the way to handle this suspicion on the part of consumers is to assure them that your store or brand makes them more powerful so that they can achieve their goals, whether that is getting a package delivered or changing the world. People know what they are trying to achieve, whether it is social justice or just scrubbing the draining board, so focus on telling them about the efficacious results of their actions, rather than having your brand take all the credit itself. Here are a few examples.

### *Store furniture, category management and merchandising*

Stores that mainly target men often make committed use of symbols of power. As I write this, I'm looking at a photo of a new branch of Foot

Locker, which opened a 'Community Power Store' in Vancouver and another in Toronto, in late 2020. Dramatic spotlighting and lots of black signage make the store environment seem both exciting and adult – even in the children's department. But there's more going on here, it's not a nightclub aesthetic as seen in the Carrefour electronics department. The aesthetic is more industrial than that. Stores like these are where the warehouse-like aspects of retail find a useful role. Grey steel shelves are matched by grey steel benches (for trying on shoes). The grey flooring is made to look like glistening, wet concrete (and is probably vinyl). The ceiling, from which large, plain, white lights hang, has exposed pipes and vents. Where there is industry, there is action. Where there's heavy machinery, there's power. This store doesn't just sell shoes and T-shirts, it sells a dream about the power to make change.

*Pack formats*

Packaging that leads the way in the semiotics of power is especially found in categories such as whey protein supplements for bodybuilders and products such as engine oil for automotive care. The giveaway signs include large tubs and containers that look heavy, and canisters with a handle moulded into the packaging for safety and ease of lifting. Look also at household cleaning products that feel like guns: packs with triggers, nozzles and spray features (women enjoy using these just as much as men). You might also use formats that close securely with a screw thread, clasp or bolt.

*Materials*

Thick, strong plastic, metals, girders, iron bars. There's less emphasis on natural materials such as wood unless they have been fashioned into industrial objects such as pallets and crates.

*Typefaces*

Typically, these are thick, blocky and upper case. They may be slanted to indicate progress and forward movement. Typefaces that imitate stencils are popular in this Power code because they enhance the industrial, made-for-work aesthetic.

## Colours

Conventionally, black and silver are used because they are 'macho' and futuristic colours. Perhaps surprisingly, there's quite a bit of bright orange, because it communicates bright, breezy practicality; it's not the colour of vague dreams and fantasies. Laundry products can be a bit like this, such as Tide, which is all about power and efficacy. Also consider Home Depot, the US home improvements store, which uses every semiotic sign listed in this section.

If it occurs to you that semiotic signs for power seem to be clustered around ideas of masculinity, I agree with your assessment. Within and outside retail, the marketing industry is quite comfortable addressing men with signs and symbols of power and, indeed, regularly struggles to address them in any other way. In contrast, our industry has not devised a consistent and effective way of addressing women concerning their power. We are quite happy to sell them extra-powerful toilet cleaner or stain-removing toothpaste, but we do not consistently or effectively invite women to explore their own strength or ability to change the world. Attempts by marketers to talk about women's empowerment frequently backfire, as you will see in Chapter 6. In this section I cite masculine examples of semiotic signs for power because I want to show you the most graphic examples, and because that is how power is nearly always expressed by marketers: in masculine semiotic signs. Perhaps this will change in the future. As marketing and retail usually reflect the values of the wider society in which they happen, I propose that the timid and frequently ineffective attempts of marketers to talk about power and women are a reflection of a society which is, in fact, deeply uncomfortable with women possessing real power and, increasingly, is uncomfortable with the concept of 'women'. That is, I am not entirely blaming marketers and retailers for this poor state of affairs. It's difficult and risky for marketers to invent and successfully communicate ideas that don't already have traction.

## Global and local

'Global' and 'Local' are not literal descriptions but are meanings that businesses often want to convey in stores and shopper experiences. They are interpretations on the part of the customer that can be actively encouraged and produced, using the right semiotic signs.

The important thing is to be clear about why you are trying to evoke these ideas in the mind of the customer. Global can be a great message when you are operating in categories such as beauty, where we are selling a fantasy involving the out-of-reach lifestyles of celebrities. Some brands that have a global presence, such as Coca-Cola, Nescafé and perhaps Starbucks and McDonalds, are selling the idea of an experience that is consistent around the world, so a global appearance works well for them.

Despite this, there are also many times when there are good reasons to appeal to a sense of place and locality. I don't mean in the sense of selling fantasies of the exotic in places and products to consumers who are located elsewhere. In this case, I mean appealing to people on their own terms, using familiar signs, like the bull mascot of the city of Birmingham, UK. Sometimes global and local can be brought together and combined in the same offering. Here are a few suggestions.

### How to be global

As global consumer culture expands and advances, a semiotic code emerges in brands and retail that is recognizable around the world. In fact, this code is recognizably North American, because the US led the world in developing global consumer culture during the second half of the 20th century. People all over the world are capable of recognizing American semiotics, which have become the conventional semiotics of the global brand, although this may change during the 21st century as China exerts a stronger influence on the brand landscape. Pending this development, you can achieve the international 'Western' look with the following semiotic signs:

- Large premises with correspondingly large fixtures, signage and furniture. Think of US 'big box' stores such as Walmart, Target and Barnes & Noble.
- Rest areas where shoppers can pause and sit down – if your store is large, they might be doing a lot of walking.
- Shopping carts with built-in cup holders. Thirst-quenching beverages, in the form of a soft drink or a coffee, fuel time on the shop floor and give a more leisurely aspect to the experience of shopping. Make drinks available at the store entrance to help people switch into 'browsing mode'.
- Pack formats need to be large. People might have driven some distance to reach you and they didn't make that journey to leave with tiny packages. They don't need to be unconventional shapes.

- Colours are frequently loud (because brands are competing with each other and because they are individually confident). On packaging, the brand name occupies nearly all of the valuable real estate on the front of the pack.
- Marketing includes a rational reason to believe in the store or product.

## How to be local

If you want to give your global brand some local flavour, my advice is to work with local artists and designers to help you incorporate semiotic signs into your marketing that are going to resonate with local audiences. Consumers like the glamour of big international brands, the giants of global consumer culture, but they like it even more when brands acknowledge and recognize local habits and tastes. Each region of the world has its own design traditions in which skills and techniques may have been honed over many years.

Even though we are almost out of space in this chapter, I want to draw your attention to two compelling examples of art that is intimately connected to place, and which all marketers can learn from.

> **LOCAL AUTHENTICITY IN ART**
> *Haitian painter Tomm El-Saieh*
>
> Artist Tomm El-Saieh was raised in Haiti and retains strong links to the country, even though he currently lives in Miami. Tomm's paintings are rich in Haitian aesthetics and culture but are very different from the modern reproductions of folk art that are sold to tourists, which you can find all over the internet if you care to look for them. This for-tourists folk art leans in the direction of simplicity, even cuteness. Scenes such as markets and villages in rural landscapes are sentimentally rendered: here is a tree, here is a stream, a house with a thatched roof, people fetching water, wandering chickens. As Tomm says (Goyanes, 2018), 'They always need to put the chicken in there, or it always leads to the face.'
>
> Tomm is doing something different, and it is his work that I recommend to you. While tourists look at Haitian culture from the outside, seeing nothing but streams and chickens, Tomm El-Saieh understands it from the inside. His abstract paintings pulse with life and are visual transliterations of Haitian music.

They capture the colours and shapes of abundant Haitian flora without being obvious and they are capable of resonating with people within Haitian culture quite as much as those who are outside it. They have a lot of authenticity, which we marketers spend a great deal of time searching for.

*German, Philippine and Mexican street art*

One great way to get to know a culture is to look at street art. Lately, I make a habit of including street art on my list of data that I want to include in any semiotic project, especially if there are multiple countries involved. I did this quite recently on a food project which spanned Germany, the Philippines and Mexico. Street art around the world has some features in common: it is far more unofficial than official; it skews young; it is often political, expressing both local history and current affairs. There are also differences at the level of region and culture, which you will be able to spot if you spend a bit of time looking at it.

In my food project, I found the German street art was the darkest in hue, and the most 'edgy', confronting the viewer with provocative subjects while at the same time displaying a taut sense of humour. Speaking of which, the street art of the Philippines has a big sense of humour and was the most culturally diverse art in my data set, reflecting the wider culture in that region, which combines influences from Asia, Europe and the Americas. As for Mexico, the street art perhaps had the biggest heart. It very often centres on larger-than-life human faces whose expressions range from big, punchy, emotions such as love, to more abstracted states such as wisdom and spiritual reverie. Interesting examples can be seen here (there are many more): www.theartnewspaper.com/news/mexico-city-street-artists-celebrate-the-lives-of-women.

If you plan to be global-but-local, you'll also want to think about enhancing your shopper's experience in the context of specific local markets, which may have physical and economic constraints and opportunities. Flexibility in this matter can help you achieve a balance where your brand's visual identity looks the same all over the world, but you alter aspects such as packaging formats and signs that showcase hero products so as to meet the shopper where they are, in the version of reality that they normally inhabit. For more about the semiotics of global and local marketing, there's some discussion in Chapter 2, plus a short list of techniques that work globally at the end of Chapter 11.

This chapter has ranged across a number of topics that are capable of being quite emotional for consumers. I hope that it is clear that there is much that a brand owner or retailer can do to stimulate powerful thoughts and feelings connected to ideas such as 'nature', 'the past' and 'the future'.

> Because we've packed in rather a lot of detail, this could be a good time to pause and think about your own brand or retail outlet.
>
> - Which of the various meanings in this chapter would you like to see flower in the mind of your customer?
> - Which semiotic signs could you apply within the constraints and opportunities of your own business?
>
> Make a short list, and then we'll move on to Chapter 5.

## References

Goyanes, R (2018) Tomm El-Saieh brings his rhythmic paintings to the New Museum Triennial, *Cultured*, https://www.culturedmag.com/tomm-el-saieh/ (archived at https://perma.cc/HT5C-7UUX)

McKinsey & Company (2019) The innovations behind China's Singles Day shopping phenomenon, https://www.mckinsey.com/featured-insights/china/the-innovations-behind-chinas-singles-day-shopping-phenomenon (archived at https://perma.cc/CJ3G-K2H3)

# 05

# Shopper needs and behaviour

*Or, 'How I bought 21 items of clothing in one day after buying next to nothing for a year'*

> WHAT'S COMING UP
>
> This chapter discusses topics that are familiar to retail marketers, such as needs and shopper missions. It offers a new view of these topics in light of changed or accelerated shopper behaviour during and immediately following the pandemic.
> By the end of this chapter, you will be able to:
>
> - respond to new, accelerated or enhanced consumer needs, in line with social trends;
> - co-operate with consumers as they imaginatively promote desires to needs and search for ideal experiences;
> - benefit from the ability of shopper missions to trigger further missions, this being a better strategy than trying to disrupt them;
> - recognize and support the wide variety of stories that consumers tell themselves and which guide every step of their shopper behaviour.

## A shopper's story

It was a Monday morning in May. I was at my desk in London. A more normal state of affairs is hard to imagine. Since the pandemic began more than a year ago, I seemed to be at my desk 100 per cent of the time. Having stayed indoors for 14 months, my spending habits had changed. Food deliveries increased, while new cosmetics plummeted to zero. Clothing purchases also hit a floor – the only items purchased in over a year were underwear, socks and T-shirts.

Twelve hours later, I had purchased the following items, all from my desktop PC:

- five sweaters from Joules (we could say that two of these were a 'planned purchase');
- five pairs of linen trousers from H&M;
- a five-pack of Fruit of the Loom T-shirts from Amazon;
- three pairs of light cotton dungarees from eBay;
- a pair of New Balance trainers from ASOS;
- two men's shirts from Ben Sherman.

I spent roughly £450 across six online retailers, with the bulk of the spending going to Joules, H&M and ASOS. This figure represents around 85 per cent of the amount that the average person in the UK spends on clothing in a year, or had been in the habit of spending, pre-pandemic (ONS, 2018).

I admit to being rather bashful about telling you this story, of which there is more to come. I don't usually reveal my own shopping behaviour in this much detail. But that day was different from a normal day, and not just because I was buying clothing where previously I hadn't bothered. It was a bit different because I was taking screenshots and careful notes.

Although the experience felt personal and individual, it was in line with larger trends that unfolded in the local economy and the retail sector. A report by the BBC (2021), 'Shoppers stuck at home shun new clothes in 2020', detailed the following trends:

- Overall, clothing sales slumped 25 per cent in 2020.
- But sales of comfortable indoor clothing, such as loungewear, increased.
- Online spending continued a sharp upward trajectory from previous years, now accounting for one-third of retail sales.
- Online-only fashion retailers such as ASOS reported strong sales.
- Clothes shoppers generally don't like the risks attached to not being able to try things on before buying but were obliged to absorb it when high-street stores closed.

In addition, throughout the pandemic year of 2020, anecdotal reports proliferated in consumer culture, in which new, slightly shameful forms of behaviour were revealed, such as 'drunk shopping on Amazon' late on a Friday night (a Freudian substitution by younger adults who would once have used the sacred occasion of Friday night for socializing or romance). Some consumers reported that their personal spending dramatically increased or became inexplicably erratic, with purchases being an ambiguous mix of the frivolous and the necessary, such as novelty homewares and items that might or might not be gifts.

As I watched this change in shopper behaviour all around me, at the same time as detailing my own shopping on this particular day, I was reminded that I've regularly felt unsatisfied by the language we marketers use when we talk about 'shopper'. 'Shopper missions' seemed to describe only a small part of what was going on. 'Need' appeared to be highly subjective and changeable. 'Purchase decision trees' started to look increasingly abstract and distant from reality. On top of that, a lot of things seemed to be missing from the conventional, retail-marketing way of talking about shopping. I noticed that shopper behaviour was fluid and messy rather than linear. The most surprising observation was that dozens of stories permeated shopping behaviour and guided its direction. They were stories of the past, the present and the future; stories of the self and stories that were woven into the fabric of relationships.

That's what this chapter is about. Shopper needs are evolving and the way we think about them as retail marketers needs to evolve too, so that we can keep up.

## Control, comfort and rewards

When I prepared myself to shop, that Monday morning in May, I knew I would purchase multiple items. I didn't know exactly how many (which worked to the benefit of several retailers by the end of the day) but I did know that when I found the item I wanted, I would purchase a few versions of it. I've done this often. I especially do it with grocery shopping. I don't particularly enjoy shopping, but I do enjoy the idea that future eventualities are taken care of, so if there's something that I like enough to buy one of, whether it's a pair of shoes or a packet of biscuits, I will normally buy two or three. It's the same with books and most other categories, with the idea that I am saving myself from future shopping down the line. As you can probably guess, these are little acts of self-deception in which I shop quite as much as people who say they enjoy shopping, if not more so, and it leads to more biscuit-eating than is good for a person.

What's going on? One the one hand, this type of shopping behaviour can be rationalized as a highly responsible thing to do, as when Mark Zuckerberg frames his multiple grey T-shirts as tangible evidence of commitment to his business. Look at this often-quoted remark from a public Q&A session in 2014 (Workopolis, for example):

> I really want to clear my life to make it so that I have to make as few decisions as possible about anything except how to best serve this community. [...] That's what I care about. Even though it sounds silly that that's my reason for wearing a grey t-shirt every day, it is true.

Using Mark Zuckerberg's example, I had a rationale all worked out. As part of the work-from-home demographic, I'm on Zoom meetings constantly, I need to look smart, I feel that my clients are starting to notice that I'm wearing the same two sweaters on repeat, one red, one lime (not at all the same thing as wearing 18 grey T-shirts on rotation) and I want to rationally solve the problem by buying multiple items of workwear now. In my imagination, this will save me a lot of getting-dressed time in the mornings. On the other hand, there's an underlying need for control, which is evidenced by a closet full of repetitive, even identical, clothing. In fact, such a closet is itself a semiotic sign, as you may know if you've ever read or seen *Fifty Shades of Grey* and its precursor *Nine and a Half Weeks*, in which a wardrobe full of identical suits is presented as the rather alarming sign of a controlling personality.

Consumers who found during the pandemic that their personal spending increased, or became erratic, are, I propose, not controlling personalities but are managing uncontrollable circumstances. They are using shopping to reduce their anxiety as well as benefiting from the comfort of self-gifting. In fact, there's a lot of anxiety around. In 2017, the World Health Organization estimated that 264 million adults around the globe have anxiety. That, if anything, seems a low estimate, but was notable for a 15 per cent increase within ten years. In the UK, the Office for National Statistics published a report on 15 June 2020 which described spiking levels of anxiety due to the pandemic and estimated that 19 million UK adults were experiencing 'high levels of anxiety'. In 2021, the Harvard School of Public Health published an article in which Professor Michael Barnett said it looked likely that '2020 will be the worst year for opioid overdoses that we've ever had.' The opioid epidemic in the United States, to which Barnett, refers, has a lot of economic and sociological causes, but, at the level of individual behaviour, a great deal of opioid abuse is self-medication for psychological distress.

My point is this: controlling and comforting behaviours are often a response to anxiety and other kinds of discomfort. The pandemic may have accelerated behaviours like drug abuse and erratic shopping on Amazon, but it did not cause them. Even the simple act of staying indoors predates the pandemic. If the development of the department store in the late 18th and early 19th centuries brought people, notably women, out of the house (which it did by transforming shopping into both a leisure activity and a public spectacle), then the invention of the internet returned everyone home again (Lury, 2011). The pandemic simply gave people more reasons to shop for comfort, control and rewards while stuck indoors. On 3 May 2021, British newspaper *The Telegraph* ran an article, 'Vaccinated but won't go out?', on 'Covid anxiety syndrome', the hallmark of which is an overuse of coping strategies, according to Marcantonio Spada, professor of addictive behaviours and mental health at London South Bank University, and Ana Nikčević, a psychology professor at Kingston University. Coping strategies that are highly sensible during a pandemic, such as staying indoors and observing hygiene, become impossible to leave behind. It feels easier and safer to stay inside.

Staying indoors, we of course find ourselves online. The work-from-home demographic soon found that it was spending 24 hours a day indoors. For millions of people, working hours revolved around meetings on Zoom and Teams, which gave people plenty of chances to scrutinize and feel anxious about their appearance. Then, in the evenings, adults who were trapped indoors spent their time on Netflix or the PlayStation Network, or on their phones, using social media. I like social media as much as the next person, but there are well-publicized statistics about the correlation between social media use and anxiety (Karim *et al*, 2020), and we don't have to look very far to find some of the reasons why this relationship should exist. Social media platforms expose us to millions of other people, to a degree that is historically unprecedented. Each person is exposed to millions of other people's tweets and Facebook, Instagram, YouTube and TikTok posts. Each exposure amounts to a microscopic social interaction: one person speaks, the other is spoken to. The internet being what it is, with its lowered inhibitions, taste for controversy and high incidence of 'keyboard warriors', some of those interactions are going to be negative. That this would have an effect on mood and then mental health is unsurprising. The tech devices that deliver the salve of 24-hour, indoor shopping opportunities are the same devices that deliver anxiety for which the salve is required.

This is how some shoppers got themselves into a negative feedback loop of anxiety–shopping–anxiety. I admit that, for a while, I became one of those people.

## Actions for marketers

Society is changing rapidly. Retail is in a period of transition. Digital culture and global mass culture gather strength. Anxious individuals argue with strangers on Twitter and then make themselves feel better with new pyjamas, video games and hats that were selected to be worn on camera rather than outdoors. Some shopping is neurotic (maladaptive, driven by negative thoughts), and, as business owners and marketers, we may want to take an ethical stance on that. At the same time, we need consumers, and most economies need retail, so we have to find ways to survive and thrive. Here's my advice.

### CONTROL

Control is important to many people, and Mark Zuckerberg's decision to sacrifice sartorial variety in exchange for better control of his life is both plausible and has a moral basis – in his improved commitment to work – that resists criticism. Among consumers who can afford to shop for non-essentials, there are marketing opportunities in selling control and simplicity.

- This can manifest in 'basics' and 'essentials' ranges for people who follow Zuckerberg in not wanting to make decisions.
- It can mean home control systems, which could be anything from an app that schedules home management routines to stacking containers or a robot vacuum cleaner.
- It can mean financial products and services that help people find satisfaction and relief in controlling their finances.

### ANXIETY

This is a worldwide problem. While we do not want to encourage it, it is difficult to blame consumers for taking opportunities to make themselves feel better. There are marketing opportunities in selling comfort, and I don't just mean in obvious ways, like anxiety-reducing yoga classes and apps that remind you to breathe, useful though these things are.

- Creative activities provide comfort to consumers that is more long-lasting than passive activities such as consuming internet news and gossip. When people are engaged in making things, their mood improves and there's usually a sense of achievement at the end. Help your customers to discover their creative potential.
- Unhappy people benefit from positive and uplifting experiences, which can include doing things to benefit their community, helping and encouraging others and having positive interactions with animals. Some Londoners find relief from the pressures of city life in Verve, a café that encourages people to visit with their dogs and incorporates a grooming service and 'doggie hotel' as a well as a licensed bar for the humans.
- The process of shopping (searching, selecting, buying) often triggers anxiety in its own right. The process needs to be as smooth as possible. I'll show how some of the bumps could be ironed out in the next section.

## Shopper needs and missions

There's a lot of talk in retail marketing about shopper missions, and even more about needs. I've been sceptical of these concepts for a long time, but it's usually not a good idea to start demolishing foundational ideas in marketing when you're in the middle of a project for a client whose organization has invested a lot of money in them. The world is changing, though, and there's a fixed, static quality to needs and missions that is causing them to get left behind.

### Mission

This was an idea that mapped fairly well onto a time when everybody went out to the shops with a shopping list of things they needed. The idea that caught marketers' imagination was the big, weekly grocery shop. In this version of events, shopping was planned. People didn't leave their homes, travel to the supermarket and walk around the store for the fun of it. They were there to buy food, in fact a whole week of meals. And food is essential to survival: it really is a need.

Mission was a very useful concept for describing these kinds of shopping trips, and still is, to the extent that they still happen. It encouraged retailers to realize that shoppers could use a little help finding the things they came in for. But it also encouraged marketers to expand the twin ideas of needs and missions to situations that became less and less applicable. Leisure shopping, the kind people do in old-fashioned malls to be sociable and for recreation, is more or less the opposite of a mission. The whole point is that there is no mission to be completed, unless 'being sociable' is a mission. As for more contemporary shopping occasions, consider a person who loads up Instagram, scrolls through a few posts and notices a video about luxurious-looking hand cream that is offering discounts on bundles. There's a 'shop now' button, and the person clicks through to see if the bundles are an attractive deal, which they aren't, because they include other items such as soap. Is this a mission? Only in the very loosest sense of the word, and only for a few seconds. Is there a need for hand cream? Apparently not. A need for value for money? It seems rather a stretch when the bundle is rejected because it includes unwanted items and not because it lacked wanted items or was overpriced.

### Need

*Need* is a word that grows in value when it describes things that people cannot do without, such as food and shelter. Needs are so important that it is easy to see how their fulfilment results in missions: they are a matter of survival. But need reduces in value (that is, in descriptive and explanatory power) when it is conflated with wants, for which we already have a word. Wants do not necessarily result in missions, nor in direct action. They can hang around vaguely in the back of people's minds for weeks or years. They can result in unplanned impulse purchases, and they are capable of never reaching fruition, with no loss to the individual.

Now, I don't want to be reductionist about needs and their indissoluble connection to physical survival. The situation is more interesting than that. Recall that semiotics concerns representations of reality; the stories we tell ourselves about reality and the way that reality is actively constructed and shaped by our self-talk. Precisely because of its connection to the essentials of physical survival, Need is a powerful ingredient in the way we characterize our own shopping behaviour to ourselves and others. With a little bit of linguistic engineering, we can upgrade all sorts of trivial wants to the status of need, to give ourselves permission to purchase. For marketers, the key thing is not to get sucked in to taking these accounts at face value. Need is a much more interesting and useful concept when we make a point of observing what consumers are *doing* with it, which includes a lot of creativity and post-hoc rationalizing.

## *How 'a couple of sweaters' turned into 21 items of clothing*

Here's a summary of my Monday shopping expedition, which I documented in real time, because I wanted this chapter to be anchored in reality, including the version of reality that I constructed on a moment-to-moment basis to justify and fuel my own shopping behaviour.

The episode began with a constructed need: 'I need a couple of new sweaters for work.' Like most other so-called needs, this one was fragile. I have clothes. I do not lack clothes. But of all my sweaters, only two were immediately at hand, the right size and therefore in regular use. I spend a lot of time in Zoom meetings and was becoming self-conscious about my plumper, greyer, pandemic appearance. Thus, 'I need it for work' immediately became available as an appropriate reason for buying new clothes.

It took me a few visits to the websites of familiar brands to find the type of jumper I was looking for (wool content, plain design, bright colour). By the time I found the item I had in mind, or something close enough, I was bored and frustrated. I did not wish to shop for clothes again for a long time. I placed three versions of this jumper in my basket, because that was how many colours it came in.

Far from being a completed mission, anxiety immediately reared its head. What if the sweaters don't fit? I was guessing my size. What if there's something about them that I don't like? I had a look around the store's website (it happened to be Joules) and placed two more sweaters in my basket as 'insurance options'. These were linen rather than wool and one even had stripes, so it turns out that my initially strict criteria meant little when making insurance purchases. I made the purchase. Item count: 5.

Imagining myself in the happy situation of being able to find an appropriate outfit each morning, I reflected on the fact that I was down to two pairs of linen trousers, both of which needed a wash. Already tired of shopping, I searched 'linen trousers women uk', landed on the H&M website and purchased five pairs of trousers in record time, a fraction of the time I had been willing to invest in buying jumpers. Item count: 10.

What goes under jumpers? If you are me, it is T-shirts. As with sweaters, I like plain styles but bright colours. I went to Amazon and purchased a five-pack of unisex Fruit of the Loom Ts. It's the third time I've purchased that particular multipack. I wear these T-shirts every day and it's the closest thing in my real-world shopping trip to my self-congratulatory fantasy of being a bit like Mark Zuckerberg. Item count: 15.

The H&M purchase was making me twitchy. I had bought three different styles of trouser but I was vaguely concerned about size. What if none of the trousers fit? At this stage, I was starting to feel a bit guilty about spending so much money, so I went to eBay and snapped up three pairs of light cotton dungarees (same style, different colours) for a knockdown price. Item count: 18.

That evening I had a phone call with my son. We chatted about shopping and looked at websites while we were talking. We discussed trainers and I sneakily purchased a pair of New Balance trainers at £75, even though I was not going out, had no place to wear them, and was now feeling very guilty about splurging money on clothes. I remember a distinct thought of 'in for a penny, in for a pound' passing through my mind as I paid for the shoes. Item count: 19.

On the same phone call, I listened to my son's experiences with buying men's shirts – in his last job he would pass a branch of department store Debenhams en route to work and would call in to look at the menswear. He'd managed to buy a Ben Sherman shirt at a great price. But I was unconvinced that he'd chosen the right size and I felt bad about spending money on myself, so I went to the Ben Sherman website, picked out two shirts in what I considered to be the right size, and ordered them to be delivered to his house. Item count: 21.

As you can see, only two of 21 items could be categorized as 'need' and then only rather tenuously. All the rest of it was driven either by emotional states such as doubt, anxiety and guilt, or by fantasies about future occasions of getting dressed, which are the subject of the next section.

## *Actions for marketers*

- Acknowledge that shopper missions are a relatively small part of shopping. If you own a grocery store where most people still attend the premises to do a weekly 'big shop', it remains a useful concept. But many other types of shopping are unplanned, spontaneous and depend on there not being a mission, because missions are work, and what's more they seem to require conscious attention and acknowledgement. It's hard to let your shopping excesses slip unnoticed under your own radar when there's some mission involved.

- The recovery of malls and physical stores might depend on the above change in our thinking. If all shopping is about completing missions, there's no reason for anyone to move away from Amazon. As wonderful as this is for Amazon, it makes life difficult for traditional stores. However, if a big part of shopping revolves around leisure and social relationships, as well as fantasies, then this is an area where traditional stores can compete. If we are going to hold on to these physical premises, then they need to be destinations that provide experiences for individuals and groups – experiences that cannot be achieved online.

- If shoppers aren't on missions, then we marketers can stop trying to 'disrupt missions', a very common ambition among my clients when they want people to switch to a different brand or simply realize that something new is available at the fixture. There are far better opportunities available to us than disrupting missions that might not exist in the first place. What I offer instead is the insight that buying one thing tends to lead to buying another thing to support it (this is called the Diderot Effect and is well documented – see jamesclear.com/diderot-effect, for example). If a purchase solves a problem, then likely as not, it will also generate a new problem. This is your chance to get involved. Try replacing the traditional idea of a shopper mission with a branching tree of shopping activities. Where there is a willingness to make one purchase, it is often possible to stimulate further purchases of 'insurance options', 'add-ons' and services that alleviate anxiety, such as 'true' sizing and tracked delivery.

- We marketers and retailers are not compelled to believe our own hype about every wish or whim being a need. It is more sensible and ultimately more profitable to recognize that while some things may be needs from the outset (let's say things like staple foods and soap), other things are not needs and never become needs, like buying an ice cream at the beach. Still other things are not needs but are positively and constructively upgraded to the status of need *in cases where the consumer intends to give themselves permission to buy* – that is, 'I just wanted' (a professional ice-cream making machine, a holiday or a new car) will not do, for whatever reason. Observe *how* wishes are upgraded to needs (for example, 'I need it for work') and convert these mechanisms into retail marketing actions, such as an area of the store or product range labelled 'for work'.

## Stories: why they matter and what you should do about them

The stories we tell ourselves – and other people – are important in shopping, but they are hardly mentioned in marketing literature that is overwhelmingly concerned with rational and economic matters such as missions and decisions. The distinct perspective of semiotics invites us to pay very close attention to stories about shopping, because none is original or unique (they are all iterations of stories that have been told before and will be told again), and as such the stories of one consumer are the stories of many consumers. Semiotics also asks us to notice that reality, for example the reality of a 'need' for new clothes, is shaped by the stories we tell ourselves. It's not sitting around awaiting scientific discovery and measurement. It's an organic and changeable thing that flowers in the fertile soil of words.

As I documented my own shopping spree even as it progressed (almost completely in private and alone until the phone call at the end), I counted an astonishing six kinds of stories that worked together to put £450 in the hands of retailers and caused 21 items of clothing to be delivered to addresses in London and Birmingham, where clothes already existed. In this section, I'll show you the stories and suggest marketing actions at the end of each one.

### Stories about the self

Consumers regularly tell themselves stories about 'what sort of person I am' and use this to explain and facilitate all kinds of behaviour, including shopping. From the moment that I first fabricated a 'need' for new clothing, I knew that there would be multiple purchases and I anticipated and facilitated it by telling myself a story that I notice I've re-told in this chapter. I was a bit like Mark Zuckerberg, I flattered myself. I am a single-minded professional. 'Zuck', as I might refer to him if he were my friend, does not hesitate to buy multiple iterations of the same item if it fits in with his business plan.

The Zuckerberg interview in which he explains his grey T-shirt habit also takes the form of a story. I am not suggesting that it is untrue; it is entirely plausible. At the same time, it is a *representation* of Mark Zuckerberg's daily life. Zuck is presenting himself in a certain way and asking the interviewer to accept it. I've done the same thing in this chapter, claiming that I don't love shopping, even though I did plenty of it, and highlighting the moments when I was bored and frustrated.

What we can learn from this is that a refusal to participate in the enjoyable aspects of choosing clothes is a form of identity work in its own right, just as much as shopping for fun. People who don't want to 'do' fashion still need to wear clothes and they still choose according to the stories they tell themselves about who they are.

> **MARKETING ACTION**
>
> Stories about the self are not unique, people borrow them from a limited set. Use this insight to create stories and marketing campaigns which match the stories that people tell themselves, rather than the stories that brands want to tell, which are rarely the same thing.

## Stories about relationships

My shopping spree started by telling myself a story about need. As I mentioned earlier, I do not need clothes, because I have clothes. If I wanted to be deliberately sceptical, I would say that the illusory experience of having 'only' two jumpers was a product of my lack of interest in my own domestic affairs, because I like being at my desk, where I concern myself with other people's domestic affairs. I had only two jumpers which were within arm's reach, which is not the same as having only two jumpers in total. But although I am sharing this more sceptical story with you now, it is not the story I told myself at the time.

The story which initially triggered the shopping spree began with a sense that people might start to notice that I was perpetually wearing the same two outfits on Zoom. I spend a lot of time in meetings, there could be up to six each day. I see some people multiple times each week. I became slightly paranoid as I thought of my two jumpers being shown on camera over and over again. In the story I told myself, people noticed my outfits (likely untrue) and thought of unflattering explanations. In particular, I started to worry that people would think I was wearing and re-wearing them without doing any laundry. This story, supported by no empirical evidence, was so compelling that the thought of continuing to wear the same two jumpers on Zoom calls became painful. It was at this moment that the 'need' for a couple of replacement jumpers became manifest.

> **MARKETING ACTIONS**
>
> Most people are very keen for others to think well of them. They want to fit in and appear normal. Use this insight to sell products and brands that help people feel that they have met the standards of 'their' community.

## Stories that are shared and circulated

To some degree, all the stories in this section are culturally available stories. They are made from publicly available semiotic signs, such as 'work' and 'laundry', and they express culturally relevant themes, such as 'time management'. Despite this commonality, some stories are more publicly expressed than others. While I didn't hear any of the people I met each week worry out loud that their colleagues might think they weren't doing the laundry often enough, I did hear many colleagues and business associates telling a related story.

The pandemic had not been kind to most people's appearance. Business associates who I knew well, particularly women, fretted openly about the grey hair, wrinkles and weight gain that had resulted from 14 months indoors. One person told me a story about an associate of hers who broke down in tears on a Zoom call because of the terrifying prospect of having to return to business meetings that take place in real life. That is, as much as Zoom has everyone inspecting their own faces in larger-than-life detail, it also has a filter that improves the appearance of one's skin, and only the top half of people's bodies are visible, hiding thickened waistlines around which the clothes of 2019 will no longer quite fit. These stories, in which people grieve the loss of formerly attractive selves and fear the public exposure of the new self, circulated everywhere; in business meetings, in middle-class newspapers, on the internet. They circulated in the same stream as stories about vaccinations and the economy.

> **MARKETING ACTIONS**
>
> Monitor the mass media and social media for widely circulated stories that express needs, problems and heightened emotions. This is your chance to make people feel better. People don't necessarily want weight-loss programmes: we aren't trying to capitalize on their anxiety. But they do want chances to feel better, so spread around some happiness.

## Stories about future events

Having first convinced myself of the need for new jumpers, I built and maintained desire with an attractive fantasy about a perfect morning. It was another story that I told myself. In this fantasy, I am getting ready for work and an immaculate, well-fitting outfit presents itself, immediately at hand. Everything is ready, pressed and folded. I put it on, knowing that I am going to look good all day. I'm even having a good hair day.

As I was shopping, I repeated this story to myself, long after the first Joules jumpers were discovered. It was this story that created further need and drove further purchases such as the linen trousers, even though there was no hint of a need for new trousers at the beginning of the process. As a matter of fact, some days later, after all the shopping had arrived (mostly in sizes that fitted) I even made an attempt at cutting my own hair, not too badly, as it turned out. It was another example of one shopping action leading to another. If the new clothes had not been good, I might not have bothered, but they were good, and the improved appearance of my clothing led to dissatisfaction with my hair, which I attempted to improve myself. This involved yet more purchases, this time on Amazon, consisting of hairdressing scissors, dye, new brushes and other not-strictly-essentials.

> **MARKETING ACTIONS**
>
> We marketers have always known that fantasy is important in selling products, but we have not always acknowledged how fantasy causes one purchase to trigger another. But in societies that emphasize continual self-improvement and fear of ageing, fantasies of a better version of the self are especially potent. If you didn't know that a sweater can sell a pair of scissors, now you know.

### *Stories about past events*

As I searched online for clothing, recollections of past events were just as important as fantasies of the future. I make no claim that these recollections were perfectly factual, because that is not where they got their power. All memories are to some extent reconstructive (Loftus, 2017, for example) and it is the reconstructed stories that we tell and retell ourselves that make a difference.

I issue these disclaimers because the negative stories had a practical effect on my shopping behaviour. I avoided Amazon because I'd previously bought jumpers that turned out to be synthetic material and unravelled at the neckline as soon as I got them out of the packaging. I also avoided a well-known British department store that should have been an obvious choice for the type of sweater I was looking for because I was once treated rather humiliatingly by a customer service representative to whom I tried to return some shoes. Experiences like these make a long-lasting impression on consumers and can leave them with a lifelong aversion to certain retailers. In fact, both of these experiences, the unravelling jumpers and the unkind customer services person, were more or less deliberately encoded at the time, in the way that one makes a mental note of things.

Positive stories of past events also guide behaviour, to the extent that I ended up on the Joules website looking for sweaters for no better reason than because I'd purchased wellington boots that pleased me two years earlier.

> **MARKETING ACTIONS**
>
> This is a good time for direct-to-consumer brands to give assurances of quality. Consumers who once trusted Amazon for everything are slowly forming the view that Amazon doesn't actually make anything and guarantees very little. As online shopping continues to expand, the results become less certain, and this is a way in which smaller DTC brands and retailers can get ahead.

### *Stories that recount shopping trips, after the fact*

At long last, at the end of my day of shopping, there were stories that involved other people in a direct way. This was the moment when the shopping started to be fun. I spent time on the phone with my son, who lives in another city. In families that are not geographically close, phone calls are important and the topic of conversation doesn't matter too much. It's all about bonding, showing concern and sharing experiences. We shared opinions about various brands and styles of trainers. He told me about his Debenhams experiences and I told him about a branch of Gap that I used to pass on my way to work, and would have bought from many times, except that they were never open early enough. This conversation led to the purchase of two shirts, with which he was pleased.

I'm sharing these rather intimate family details because the literature on retail marketing leads me to think that we've forgotten how intimate shopping can be. One of the best shopping experiences I've ever had was in Gantt in New York, again with my son. Correctly perceiving me as the one who would be paying for the goods, staff gave me a comfortable chair and a glass of wine as a matter of priority, as soon as I arrived, and only then was my son escorted around the store to try on clothes. This type of experience supports social relationships and is one way in which physical stores and traditional retailers have a chance to shine.

> **MARKETING ACTIONS**
>
> The pandemic separated families and friendship groups and of course some families suffered tragic losses. Shopping has always been somewhat of a social activity, but it holds the promise of taking on a new status when people are finally reunited.

This has been a very personal chapter, and perhaps it needed to be, because the books I read on retail marketing in preparation for writing it were distinctly lacking in human truths and emotions. I share my stories of excess, anxiety, doubt, love and other emotions because they are central to shopping, as it was and as it will be in the future. Shopping has a role to play in comforting people and preserving their relationships and this is a reason for all retailers to feel hopeful.

In the next chapter, we'll take a look at people having enormous fun with shopping, in another way that is largely overlooked by marketing literature.

## References

BBC News (2021) Shoppers stuck at home shun new clothes in 2020, 22 Jan, https://www.bbc.co.uk/news/business-55762644 (archived at https://perma.cc/8WJW-XZWQ)

Harvard School of Public Health (2021) A crisis on top of a crisis: Covid-19 and the opioid epidemic, https://www.hsph.harvard.edu/news/features/a-crisis-on-top-of-a-crisis-covid-19-and-the-opioid-epidemic/ (archived at https://perma.cc/YY24-Y7TX)

Karim, F, Oyewande, A A, Abdalla, L F, Chaudhry Ehsanullah, R and Khan, S (2020) Social media use and its connection to mental health: a systematic review, *Cureus*, **12** (6), https://www.cureus.com/articles/31508-social-media-use-and-its-connection-to-mental-health-a-systematic-review (archived at https://perma.cc/UP2L-T279)

Loftus, E (2017) How can our memories be manipulated? *TED Radio Hour* podcast, 13 October, https://www.npr.org/transcripts/557424726?t=1621208218033 (archived at https://perma.cc/86GJ-T3N4)

Lury (2011) *Consumer Culture*, Rutgers University Press, New Brunswick

Office for National Statistics (ONS) (2018) Family spending in the UK, https://www.ons.gov.uk/peoplepopulationandcommunity/personalandhouseholdfinances/expenditure/bulletins/familyspendingintheuk/financialyearending2018 (archived at https://perma.cc/4AGP-PE6G)

ONS (2020). Coronavirus and anxiety, Great Britain, available at: https://www.ons.gov.uk/peoplepopulationandcommunity/wellbeing/articles/coronavirusandanxietygreatbritain/3april2020to10may2020 (archived at https://perma.cc/VLP4-WY7T)

Workopolis (2014), The reason Mark Zuckerberg wears the same shirt every day, https://careers.workopolis.com/advice/the-reason-mark-zuckerberg-wears-the-same-shirt-every-day/ (archived at https://perma.cc/L8VH-JZ3R)

World Health Organization (2017) Depression and other common mental disorders global health estimates, https://apps.who.int/iris/bitstream/handle/10665/254610/WHO-MSD-MER-2017.2-eng.pdf (archived at https://perma.cc/LD53-4TF2)

# 06

# Shopping and identity

> **WHAT'S COMING UP**
>
> Welcome to Chapter 6, the last of four chapters concerning big topics of social change and consumer culture. This chapter is about identity.
>
> Consumers use brands and shopping as tools to express their individual identities, their political affiliations and their tribal allegiances. In some cases, they will buy and invest even when a rational approach would suggest they are acting against their own interests. Brands and businesses need to understand this behaviour, and semiotics offers a new point of view.
>
> This chapter also includes discussion of diversity and inclusivity, which organizations know to be important to consumers but do not necessarily know how to enact, especially at the level of retail marketing. The third big topic in this chapter is conspicuous consumption – displaying one's wealth, possessions and brand choices.
>
> By the end of this chapter, you will be able to:
>
> - identify the emotional pay-offs for shoppers who at first glance seem irrational or biased;
> - be more inclusive and anticipate what is coming next as thinking about diversity and inclusivity evolves;
> - provide shopping experiences that are rewarding for vigorous shoppers and consumers.

## The Legend of GameStop and Wall Street Bets

2020 was a tough year for most consumers, with the many fatalities and casualties of the pandemic, job loss or insecurity, economic contraction, political upheaval and social isolation. As a constant observer of people, it was a time in which I became very interested in happiness, because it seemed to be in such short supply.

As 2021 opened, extraordinary events started to occur in the stock market, centring on GameStop, a formerly successful but ailing chain of stores with a headquarters in Texas. GameStop sells physical copies of video games (products that these days are mostly digital downloads) and also gaming hardware (which consumers increasingly purchase online). Business was declining, in line with the overall decline of high street and shopping mall retail. People said that GameStop would be the next Blockbuster – once a thriving chain of stores that rented out movies on VHS video tapes and DVDs, which has now been replaced by on-demand streaming services such as Netflix, Hulu and Amazon. Hedge funds were shorting GameStop's stock, which is a fancy way of saying that they were placing bets that the business would fail. Its fate was sealed, or so it seemed.[1]

The extraordinary events were sudden, gigantic and totally unpredictable gains in GameStop share prices. Figure 6.1 shows a page from Google Finance

FIGURE 6.1  Spikes in GameStop shares, Google Finance, March 2021

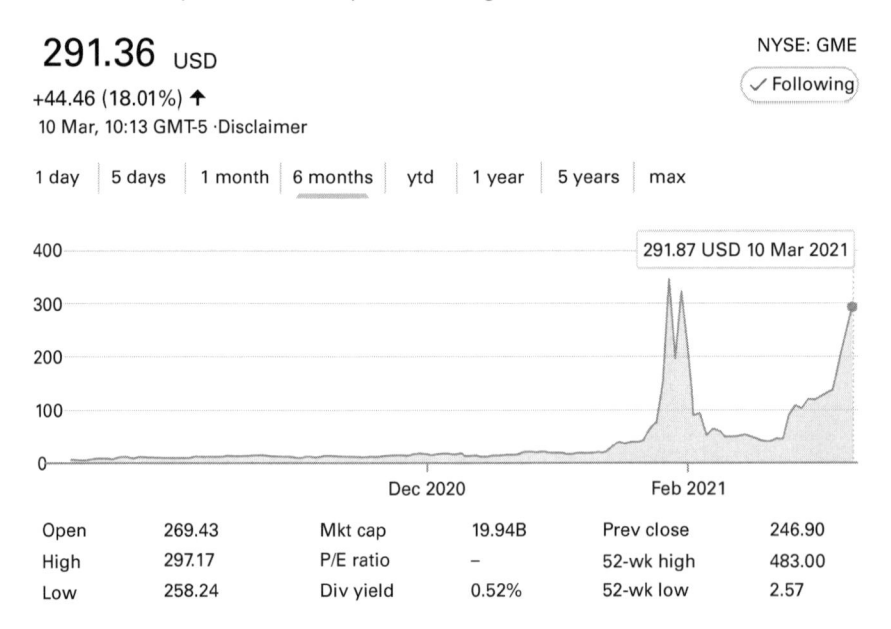

**291.36** USD

+44.46 (18.01%) ↑
10 Mar, 10:13 GMT-5 ·Disclaimer

NYSE: GME
✓ Following

| 1 day | 5 days | 1 month | 6 months | ytd | 1 year | 5 years | max |

291.87 USD 10 Mar 2021

| | | | | | | | |
|---|---|---|---|---|---|---|---|
| Open | 269.43 | Mkt cap | 19.94B | Prev close | 246.90 |
| High | 297.17 | P/E ratio | – | 52-wk high | 483.00 |
| Low | 258.24 | Div yield | 0.52% | 52-wk low | 2.57 |

plotting the behaviour of the shares over a six-month period, captured on 10 March 2021. You don't need to be a financial analyst to see that something very unusual and special is happening at the end of January, where prices peaked at a whopping $483 per share. As you can see from the right-hand side of the graph, after seeming to return to a floor, prices then jumped again at the beginning of March. I don't claim to know where the line on that graph is heading, but we can see that something remarkable happened.

Most people agree that at least the first two spikes at the end of January were caused by retail investors – mainly casual day traders – acting en masse to purchase GameStop shares, which drove up the price. These day traders congregated in a group called Wall Street Bets (WSB), which is part of Reddit, a thriving social media platform and a compelling brand. The hub of consumer action was therefore easy to find, and I went to investigate what was going on.

I joined Wall Street Bets, first as an observer and later as an owner of an impressive two shares in GameStop, because sometimes things are easier to understand when you have skin in the game. I arrived just in time to see group membership expand from 2 million to 9.5 million in around six days. What I discovered there was a geyser of happiness, in full force, billowing clouds of joy and tangible, visceral excitement. People talked about feeling as though they might burst. Here are a few quotes from the days of the initial spikes in January.

> I can feel the serotonin kicking in. (leelooodallas, 2021)
>
> I HAVE NEVER HAD THIS MUCH ADRENALINE. (IceFabulous7202, 2021)
>
> This is the most fun I've had since the pandemic started. (TheRealSamBell, 2021)
>
> This is the most exciting thing I've ever witnessed. (brennychef, 2021)

And finally, there is this response from Reddit user Twl1 (Wall Street Bets, January 2021). It is worth quoting in full because it captures the special nature of the euphoria that engulfed the group as the shares kept climbing and climbing (emphasis in the original):

> It's the energy. There's more than electricity on this board right now, there's real, actual **energy**.
>
> Old internet was alive with possibility and pure, unhindered creativity. We didn't have stringent mods, repressive ToS, or platform identities limiting us. We weren't split up by politics and misinformation, so we just did whatever

made us happy in the moment. It was always just 'us', the internet nerds, banded together in our own little sphere of influence that other people didn't even want to bother to penetrate. We could make whatever we wanted a reality, and logging on to your favourite websites was always a dive into a pool of infinite possibility.

I'm new here, but the way WSB has banded together over these past two weeks has completely captured that spirit: The idea that random idiots on the internet working together can make something truly special, and that's not just at the core of the internet; it's at the very core of the human spirit. THAT's the energy you're feeling right now.

Raw, unmitigated possibility, and it's beautiful to behold.

God speed everyone. May we never forget these days.

Tw1l, although a new member, eloquently describes a powerful cocktail of joy, love, fellowship, creativity, nostalgia, revolution, pride, victory and belief in the future. For at least a two-week period in January 2021, almost the entire active membership of Wall Street Bets was drunk on this cocktail.

From the perspective of 'the real world', a place awarded considerable status in Tw1's post, the behaviour of this rabble of retail day-traders was not only irrational but uninformed. Each day, WSB thronged with new posts in which people who had been investing for a week haphazardly explained it to people who had started that day. As a group, they (and after a certain point, we) collectively made a colossal investment in a bubble that seemed guaranteed to burst, and braced ourselves to lose the money. I have never seen people happier about the prospect of losing money and I don't think I've seen a better example of people appearing to act against their own interests in their sheer determination to make and hold on to a purchase. Who among us, as brand owners, retailers and marketers, wouldn't love to inspire anything close to that degree of passion in our customers?

## *What does semiotics have to say about GameStop?*

As GameStop share prices exploded in January 2021, the financial press and then the mainstream press tried to explain what was going on, with some difficulty. The overwhelming tone of these stories was that of a cautionary tale. Certain doom was predicted. Readers were warned that this is not how investing is supposed to go. You are supposed to undertake due diligence and research your investments. You are supposed to have a strategy and an exit plan. You are at least supposed to know what an exit plan is. You should take all reasonable measures to avoid going bust. 'A lot of people are going to lose all their money and it is very concerning', they said, and so it went. They were not wrong, but this is how far a strictly economic or rational analysis will get you when you are faced with exuberantly irrational behaviour.

In fact, when I came to look at it, Wall Street Bets both craved material gains (with very much talk of taking share prices 'to the moon') *and* showed little fear of loss. Losing one's investment did not constitute losing the game, a principle that business and finance journalists found hard to get along with. What's more, on top of this casual, chaotic-neutral approach to investing, in which any outcome was a good outcome, WSB celebrated and revelled in its irrationality and lack of real understanding of finance. In fact, at that time, it was very much part of the USP. People who misguidedly attempted to post sensible financial advice on WSB were often reminded, 'Sir, this is a casino', and individual posters frequently referred to their ape-like smooth brains and their habit of eating crayons. This is the culture that WSB built for itself.

This is the **reality** that Twl1 intuitively describes, in which the creative human spirit finds innocent and irrepressible expression in a universe of unlimited potential. Although hastily assembled, the dynamic and seemingly bizarre reality that WSB built was so real that it protruded into versions of the world that affect everyone, where there are banks and hedge funds and chains of retail stores with uncertain futures and unexpected strokes of fortune.

Semiotics is a style of thinking and a type of research practice that examines the **versions of reality** that consumers inhabit, and which they craft and build using culturally available resources. Let me highlight a couple of semiotic conclusions concerning this story, then I'll supply a bit of marketing advice for brand owners and retailers.

### FEELINGS OUTRANK FACTS

This is a commonly noted aspect of contemporary Western culture, which in turn makes a contribution to global consumer culture and eventually impacts on international relations. I am not going to get into the geopolitics of it here; this is just to note the real-world impact of popular movements in ideology and philosophy. To put it in simple language, the events of January 2021 made WSB investors feel amazing, and that is something that people will pay for. The new version of reality that WSB built finds itself, or found itself at that time, in conflict with a powerful but uncomprehending reality used by banks and hedge funds. The moral of the story is that reality is flexible and comes in many versions. Energetic struggles over reality are playing out all around us and this will continue into the future. Life is tough and conflict can be stressful, but the good news for marketers is that people will take *and make* happiness where they can find it.

### THE VERSION OF REALITY USED AT YOUR COMPANY MIGHT NOT HAVE MUCH IN COMMON WITH THE VERSION USED BY YOUR CUSTOMERS

I don't just mean, 'Consumers sometimes have funny ideas and exhibit strange behaviour, so you should do some market research.' It's not just that consumers misunderstand your category and business model, get things wrong and apply different labels to your everyday business concepts. The more valuable insight is that the version of reality that lives in large organizations, as well as the highly specific version of reality that persists in the marketing industry, is just as 'made-up' as the version your customers are using. Getting close to customers might mean abandoning a lot of what we thought we knew about what we are selling. Being willing to think flexibly is key, and semiotics certainly encourages and cultivates that ability.

---

#### RETAIL MARKETING TIPS

- **When your customers' energy is up, invest your energy in keeping it there.** If you knock them off their perch just when they are happiest, customers experience that as a worse betrayal than chronic and low-level failures of customer service. This is why WSB investors easily forgave small, unsatisfying experiences they'd previously had as customers of GameStop, while they were enraged by the *other* retailer in this story, Robinhood. Robinhood provides the mobile app on which many US retail investors buy and trade their shares. A high-profile court case (Cnet, 2021, for example) was launched to investigate whether Robinhood behaved unlawfully when it shut down retail trading at the exact moment when prices were going sky-high. The app was flooded with one-star reviews because it let customers down at the precise moment when they were at the height of their glory.

- **People like finding new friends and banding together to make new stuff.** Reddit, the social media platform of which Wall Street Bets is a small part, claims to have over 430 million active monthly users and counting. It has

> done brilliantly out of the GameStop saga, if it needed more brand awareness. This is not to say that if you are the owner of a grocery store, you need to change direction and start a tech company instead. It is a recommendation, however, that you look for the things your customers are *trying* to create and help them build it. What's going on in your community? Maybe your customers are banding together to feed their children, make art or celebrate occasions that are important to them. Identify ways of getting involved. Help people out. Loan them a bit of space, start a club, help them find each other.

## Diversity and inclusivity

Among the companies that I work with – retailers, brand owners, ad agencies and consumer insight agencies – most are anxious to be diverse and inclusive. They realize that these are the hot issues of the day. They know they will be scrutinized by consumers and 'called out' if they do the wrong thing. For many organizations, this can be a rather hit-or-miss affair. They are not quite sure of the difference between diversity and inclusivity, and occasionally their efforts to do the right thing backfire. It is not my plan in this book to burden you with more theory than we need, but allow me to introduce you to the idea of **commodity racism,** if you haven't met it already. It is useful and helps brands avoid mistakes, and the underlying mechanism applies to more than just race, extending into other kinds of appropriation.

To put it simply, businesses often assume that what minority groups want is 'representation'. The thinking goes that marketing and advertising routinely ignore people who aren't tall, blond, white, heterosexual and conforming to the beauty standards of global consumer culture. Therefore, it is thought, the problem can be relieved by introducing more brown people into ads. Sometimes the company will go even further and have a recruitment drive that results in more diverse employees. This is the essence of 'diversity'. Simply add people who look different, and shake, then serve.

The problem with this is captured in the concept of commodity racism. It has had lots of good explanations in academic literature; one is Susan Willis's essay (1990), 'I want the Black one: Is there a place for Afro-American culture in commodity culture?'. Anne McClintock (1995) is also an important figure in this style of thought, but we'll stick with Willis for the moment because she talks more about shopping.

The problem for the Black shopper, says Willis, is not that she fails to encounter any representations of herself in stores, it is that she encounters what she calls Black replicants. If you imagine a range of dolls which is Caucasian in appearance, and then, in the interests of diversity, you add one or two dolls to the range that are the same model, but the skin tone is a bit darker and they have dark hair, then you haven't created a diverse range of dolls. At best, you've created a white doll that has a tan and at worst you've created a replicant, a science-fiction type of creature that is a black *version* of a white person. This doesn't help people of colour to feel included. In fact, it causes them to realize that white culture and white capitalism don't see Black people as fully human (Willis, 1990).

Here's an example. Pop musician Katy Perry has her own fashion brand, Katy Perry Collections. In 2019, Sky News, for example, reported that two similarly styled pairs of shoes in the range had to be pulled after consumer complaints. One version was beige and the other black. Both have human features. Both have blue eyes and red lips. According to reports at the time, consumers complained because they considered the shoes to be racist. Katy Perry Collections is a US brand. The US is a place where people of colour have their own material, economic and political struggles. These go largely unnoticed by the white majority, who choose the black shoe, the black baby doll and the Black entertainer, because Black people are novel and are there to be consumed.[2]

I know this is a scary story, so let's talk about how inclusivity is different. If the problem with diversity is that it often makes people feel alienated and pushed out, then inclusivity makes them **feel that they belong**. Diversity means making sure that your culturally white grocery store stocks big bags of rice as well as tiny ones, because you know or assume that minority ethnic customers have bigger households to cook for. **Inclusivity** means placing those big bags of rice with the other rice products and not making your customers walk to the 'ethnic aisle' to purchase ordinary, staple foods.[3]

Inclusivity would have seen Katy Perry Collections encouraging collaborations with minority designers and giving a platform to young people in less-advantaged positions. It was a missed opportunity to 'lift as you climb'. One brand that does this well is fashion retailer ASOS, with its Collusion range that targets Gen Z consumers. Collusion clothes are developed with teams of six young consumers who work alongside creatives. The result is clothing that the target demographic has had a hand in making. Clothing is unisex, fits all sizes and is sustainable, reflecting Gen Z values and not merely superficial aspects of their appearance.

*How does semiotics give us new insight into diversity and inclusivity?*

Semiotics, at least in the world of brands and marketing, is characterized by two key activities:

- noticing semiotic signs and figuring out what they mean;
- finding out what changes in society or culture are connected to these meanings.

The reason why we want semiotics as part of our repertoire for thinking about brands is that it helps brands to avoid a Katy Perry situation before it happens. Both pairs of shoes, beige and black, are semiotic signs. They were semiotic signs before they had human faces applied to them (think of the different connotations of a high-heeled satin shoe versus a steel-tipped boot). But the addition of human faces was the real turning point. Now the colour of the shoes is attached to the idea of the colour of skin, and that means people are going to have strong opinions about it. The brand has strayed into territory where it needs to be careful. Applying a little bit of semiotic analysis at the design stage helps to anticipate and head off these problems before they become triggers for public distress.

The other reason why we need semiotics in the mix is because culture changes quickly. Semiotics watches that change unfold, so it can usefully flag up whether some piece of brand communication is well timed. Like many British people, I've shopped countless times at Paperchase, a stationery company that was founded in the UK in 1968 and now operates internationally. Paperchase sells decorative notebooks, gel pens and many other items that sit just at the border of 'home and office ware' and 'giftware', making it a popular destination for self-treating. It is one of so many retailers that has been hit hard by the COVID-19 pandemic. There have been store closures. It has goodwill among consumers – most people want it to survive.

I was therefore sad to see Paperchase get into hot water on Twitter in March 2021, when a well-intentioned product failed to hit the right note. The product in question is an A5 notebook, retailing at £7. The cover of the book is decorated with simple line drawings of 24 bottoms, mostly plump and rounded, clad in decorative and revealing knickers of the type usually marketed to women. The viewer (the shopper, the Twitter user) could reasonably infer that they are women's bottoms. The product was listed on the company website as 'A5 magazine pants notebook'. The product details included the following text (the notebook was part of Paperchase's 'Equilibrium' range):

> Equilibrium is a vibrant collection of powerful pieces designed to celebrate and promote unity, diversity and inclusivity.
>
> Sending positive vibes to our female community and anyone else who celebrates inclusivity with our A5 notebook featuring an ensemble of pants!

Further web copy concerning the Equilibrium range included:

> Feel empowered everyday by our Equilibrium pieces that aim to uplift and motivate with inspiring slogans, funky prints and diverse representation.[4]

Twitter (which by no means represents all consumers, but certainly a loud and influential segment) was displeased. Users demonstrated a very incisive analysis of that empowerment, as well as being able to spot failures of diversity. Here are some of the comments from Twitter.

> **Diversity**
>
> I know what happened. Some bloke said 'I know, let's tell them that even the ones with fat, lumpy bums, matter. They'll love that.' (Walton, 2021)
>
> Why are they all white bottoms? (Truth and Beauty, 2021)
>
> **Empowerment**
>
> Thank you for this inspiring symbolism. Every time I wish to feel more empowered I pull my pants down and look at my own arse in the mirror. You've really nailed it. (Purple Sneakers, 2021)
>
> If it was empowering, people with power would be doing it. Men, however, are not using notebooks with pictures of male bums on them. Ergo, it will not give women any power whatsoever. (OverCaffeinated, 2021)

On that latter point, if it's not clear, the argument is that 'empowerment', a concept that appeals to women in numerous ways, once meant 'gaining actual power' – for example by becoming financially independent, getting an education and gaining positions of influence at work and in public office. This is a type of empowerment that feminism was almost solely concerned with until sometime in the late 1990s. Note that these are material concerns: they concern the economic and political struggles of a group that has been denied liberties (which is why it was once called 'women's lib'). Later, the meaning of 'empowerment' changed, as you will see.

This was harsh criticism for Paperchase to endure. It replied to its Twitter complainants as follows (Paperchase, 2021):

> This image has become a symbol of female empowerment and recognized as such in this form, we are proud to be supportive of this. We have also seen similar themes elsewhere. We have received great feedback from customers at the positive message it drives.

Paperchase had the reasonable expectation that the Equilibrium range would land as they wanted it to. I know where Paperchase 'saw similar themes elsewhere'. The 'pants' motif in popular discourse concerning women's empowerment has been noticeable for ten years or more. There are items such as greetings cards, postcards and enamel badges on sale on Etsy that also feature line drawings of disembodied female bottoms in underwear and slogans such as 'put on your big girl pants', meaning 'be brave today'. Some of this type of merchandise is purchased as giftware and is part of a category of cute and pink 'Stuff' that is bestowed on female cancer patients (Ehrenreich, 2010). Talk of 'putting on your big girl pants' as a way of coping with the everyday fears and challenges of womanhood was also visible on social media platforms that attracted a female audience. I'm absolutely willing to believe that Paperchase did some market research and had positive feedback.

The type of empowerment that Paperchase had latched on to is a late-flowering version, where material and economic concerns are replaced with an emotion: something along the lines of 'feeling good' or 'feeling capable'. This is an ideological shift and the 'pants' motif was part of that more recent wave of thought. Recall the importance of feelings and their ability to outrank facts, discussed earlier with regard to GameStop. Feeling empowered is as good as *being* empowered, or nearly, or perhaps even better.

It was the right message but the wrong timing.

The Twitter-using public discovered the new Pants notebook at the exact moment when there was a swelling of protest concerning violence against women. There had been a documented upsurge of violence against women during the COVID-19 pandemic when so many people were ordered to stay at home (United Nations, 2020, for example). What's more, Paperchase is a British company, yet within the UK the pandemic had coincided with criminal attacks on women that made national and international news. It wasn't the right time to sell images of body parts or promises of feeling empowered, when feeling empowered would not have saved any of the women whose lives had been violently and prematurely ended.

Paperchase has been a much-loved brand and even its critics do not want to see it fail. Semiotics pays attention to the *version of reality* that consumers are experiencing and helps businesses to avoid the problems of introducing new products with semiotic signs and marketing strategies that test well in market research but are becoming dated and are thus vulnerable to sudden changes in public mood.

We've covered some difficult topics in this section. Below are some concise retail tips.

---

RETAIL MARKETING TIPS

- **Avoid commodity racism by not depicting people of colour as novel, alternative 'versions' of white people.** They are not dress-up costumes for white people to play with and for white companies to profit from.

- **Achieve inclusivity by designing and marketing with people rather than for them.** If you wish to target some specific consumer group, such as a particular ethnic group, a gendered group, an age cohort, a political group or any other group, don't stop at market research. Get them involved in helping to create better products and customer experiences.

- **Remember to follow through in your commitment to inclusivity by hiring a diverse range of employees and making sure they feel welcome.** The last part is key. It's vital to include them at all levels and make sure they feel engaged and listened to.

- **Arrange items in store to show that you recognize that there's no 'wrong' way for a customer to be themselves.** Whatever minority group they happen to be a part of, you want them to feel welcome in your store. Don't hide the plus-size clothing in the basement. Don't hide the big bags of rice in a special aisle. People are just trying to go about their lives, buying leggings and groceries.

- **Look at your store, fixture and products, and list their semiotic signs.** A semiotic sign is a human face on a shoe; a pair of knickers decorating a notebook; signage that depicts white, able-bodied and clearly gendered people as the 'right' sort of people; a supermarket aisle labelled 'ethnic', 'Asian' or 'international'; words such as 'empowering'.
    - Check whether these words and images mean what you think they mean.
    - Think: Is there anything going on in the news that suggests you shouldn't use this semiotic sign even if it worked previously?

## Conspicuous consumption: when more is more

One of my favourite photos ever on Instagram was posted by someone I know: a former student and occasional freelancer. The young man is still in his 20s, has a talent for personal branding, is photogenic and recognizes a photo opportunity when he sees it. His IG account is a meticulously curated collection of photos in which he models designer fashions in various attractive locations, such as upmarket bars and restaurants and historic buildings. But my favourite photo shows him sitting on the floor in a supermarket, in clothes by Gucci.

Let me be clear: when I say 'supermarket', I do not mean Fortnum & Mason or Harrods – those historic and luxurious department stores that also sell edibles. I mean Waitrose. Waitrose is at the top end of the British supermarket chains, but the fact remains that it is a supermarket. It has the grid-like aisles, steel shelving and rows of dustbin liners, laundry detergent and canned pet food that are found in supermarkets everywhere. It is a nice supermarket, but it is not exceptional. Why would my friend want to get on the floor in a supermarket, in his expensive clothing, to have his photograph taken?

As it happened, Waitrose had recently refreshed its wines and spirits department. This part of the store, which is rivalled only by kitchenware (ceramics, gadgets) in its ability to increase the basket value of shoppers, was demarcated by change. Steel fixtures changed to wood and soft lighting and spotlighting was introduced in place of the uniform glare that can be found in the main body of all supermarkets that are thinly disguised warehouses. The bottles of wine instantly looked cared for and the overall effect was one of a wine cellar. In fact, it was even more inviting than some 'real' wine cellars, which frequently use steel racks. The combined effect of these semiotic signs (the wine bottles, the wooden shelving, the careful lighting) was enough to create a photo opportunity and a good enough reason for my friend to get on the floor in his designer clothes and pose artfully for the camera, as though the wine cellar were his own. The photo then appeared on Instagram as part of the ongoing collection. As any regular Instagram user will tell you, keeping up an account like this is a lot of work and one has to be constantly on the alert for opportunities to create content.

Not every consumer is a content creator and only a few can afford head-to-toe designer clothing, but most people are users of one or another social media platform and the implicit command to keep feeding it with attractive photos is hard to resist. There are plenty of rewards to be had, ranging from social approval in the form of 'likes' and comments and even job opportunities and free gifts from friendly brands. Indeed, if you are young and in need of a job, it might be very important to stay visible. Looking your best is more than mere vanity, it is a part of the work of personal branding which younger cohorts of consumers accept as the price of admission to desirable career paths.

Women are also well represented among consumers who buy things with one eye on their photogenic qualities. In their book *Brandsplaining* (2021), Jane Cunningham and Philippa Roberts patiently advise brands on how to be less patronizing in their marketing communications, while at the same time recognizing that women do, in fact, enjoy the categories that marketers always knew they were excited about.

> Most women do love thinking about homeware, beauty and fashion (beauty and fashion are described as key interests for 80 per cent of women) [...] They are not 'trivial' or unimportant subjects but the source of huge amounts of interest and satisfaction. [...] They are enjoyable, hobbyist, fun and highly, highly creative.

Again, this isn't simply about vanity, even though it might look like vanity at first glance. Just like the young career-seekers, these women are doing a kind of work. They are caring for themselves and their loved ones by making the world a slightly more beautiful place, and they are displaying success; that is, a mix of economic success (as demonstrated in discretionary spending) and success in understanding and playing the game of being an individual in circumstances of late capitalism.

### Semiotic analysis: reality and representations of reality

It is a truism that people's real lives are not quite as their Facebook and Instagram photos would have you believe. We have accepted that these are **representations of reality** and not simple, unmediated reality itself. Indeed, this acceptance is so widespread that it has become a trope used successfully by amateur and professional content creators to strengthen their relationship with their audience. Thus, a beauty or fashion influencer may draw attention to the fact of their being in a supermarket (and not, after all, a wine cellar) and encourage viewers to laugh with them at the absurdity of the situation. The middle-class office worker who has been displaced to a home office because of the pandemic puts on make-up for Zoom meetings while at the same time using Twitter to jovially reveal the cluster of dogs, toys and small children that had to be hastily swept out of shot. Despite the fact that 'everyone knows' that the highly aesthetic version of everyday life depicted in social media photos isn't real, it persists, and we keep eating it up.

Ever conscious of social class and the demands of capitalism, sociologists have tended towards the view that this type of willing, co-operative display (such as taking photos of yourself, making videos, putting yourself and your home on Tik Tok, Instagram, YouTube or Facebook) is about conforming. If we wanted evidence in support of this theory,[5] we need look no further than TV 'makeover' shows in which individuals who are 'failing' in some aspect of self-management or self-presentation are redeemed (or not), on camera, in the hands of experts. For example:

- *Supersize vs Superskinny* and *The Biggest Loser*, in which obese or underweight participants try to adjust their diets and praise is rationed accordingly;
- *Hot Mess House* and *Get Organized with the Home Edit*, concerning the redemptive effect of tidying up one's house and organizing possessions;
- *My 600lb Life* and *Hoarders*, which are not so much makeover shows as cautionary tales of what happens when non-conformity is not reined in.

While the academic sociologist has good reason to be attentive to the political aspects of these modern-day morality plays and the ways in which they enforce homogeneity and consumer spending, marketers may look at things differently. As Cunningham and Roberts point out in *Brandsplaining*, people positively enjoy crafting semi-truthful representations of reality, and consuming the representations of others. Many people are fortunate enough to discover that their tastes and choices fit in with the choices that their culture allows, and crafting these stories can be affordable if you have a decent mobile phone, some spare time and a little disposable income. You can get a satisfying, and satisfactory, tweet or Instagram post out of an arrangement of novelty candles and flower planters, a plate of cupcakes, an attractively decorated to-do list, an artist's easel or a row of repurposed Mason jars. You don't absolutely *need* exaggerated gym muscles, cheek and buttock fillers, hair extensions or holiday photos from Dubai or Marrakech – it merely helps.

Whether our politics align more with left-leaning academic sociologists or with the idea that free-market capitalism creates wealth and opportunity, the fact remains that consumers enjoy crafting representations of reality that do not need to be firmly anchored to any objective truth in order to succeed. Indeed, Baudrillard (1995), one of the great thinkers who contributed so much to semiotics, offers as a semiotic prompt, the question, 'Is any aspect of the thing I am looking at a simulation?' The question is not a complaint or an appeal to nature; it is more an observation that a lot of things are simulations, and people often like the simulation more than the original object, if there is one. They like manicured parks and golf courses more than they like untamed wilderness; they like the Cinderella castle at Disney more than they like historical castles and they like faux wine cellars more than they like either actual wine cellars or supermarkets that look like supermarkets.

*Retail marketing ideas*

SHOW CUSTOMERS HOW TO ENVISAGE THEMSELVES
When people look at your products, they envisage how the product or service, once purchased, will fit into their life. They can see themselves baking the cake, wearing the sportswear, playing games on the new laptop, laughing at their cat in its new bed and astonishing their children with the exact princess or superhero costume of their dreams. When people have these visions, they are imagining what their life could be like if it were not so full of work, laundry and tax returns. And the visions they are entertaining are highly photogenic. There's a saying in digital culture: 'Pics or it didn't happen.' That's how important these visions, small acts of creative consumerism and the resulting photos are. They let you know that you are here. You are alive now. Your life has moments of beauty and each one is a success, even and especially if the rest of your life isn't quite like that.

Use your digital or physical retail space to show people how to imagine themselves and their future photos. Yes, we've always had some 'lifestyle' photography in stores but photo-library stock dates quickly and tends to lack human warmth. In contrast, photos taken by contemporary humans are generally much more on-trend and permitting of tiny imperfections that help other humans to better imagine how the products on sale will manifest in their own life. Unsplash is a good resource, at the time of writing, and it's also a great idea to work with local artists when you are targeting specific markets.

PEOPLE LOVE COLLECTIONS, MODULAR RANGES AND AN ARRAY OF COLOURS
There are easy wins here for retail marketers. Stationery retailers are often great with Instagram and know how to present collections of disparate products in photos that are saturated with blue, pink or sunset orange. We could do much more of this in merchandising in physical stores, with homewares,

for example. The point is not that the shopper necessarily wants an entirely blue kitchen, but the deep blueness of the display is a sensory kick all by itself and cries out to be photographed, and a purchase means that the shopper can take a little piece of it home with them, like owning a fragment of a rainbow. It's not your entire display that they envisage in their kitchen, it's that one milk jug, but the jug needs to justify itself with its obvious aesthetic qualities to gain admittance to their dreams.

### YOUNGER CONSUMERS ARE ESPECIALLY INTERESTED IN THINGS THAT MAKE THEM FEEL UNIQUE, ARE TRANSFORMATIVE OR REVEAL UNEXPECTED TRUTHS BENEATH THE SURFACE OF CONVENTION

The seemingly different points in this heading are connected to an underlying aspect of how the younger Millennials and Zoomers of our time experience themselves, at this moment in history. They know they are different from previous generations (and indeed it is the privilege of all cohorts of young adults to perceive this). In Western and Westernized countries, they are highly individualized. Older adults sometimes mistake this for 'special snowflakes wanting to be special', but in fact individualism is now such a powerful force that working out how exactly you are different from everyone else is mandatory and requires considerable effort. Letting people know that they are special and precious exactly the way they are relieves some of that pressure.

Transformation and the revelation of unexpected truths are outcomes of a society that makes individuals responsible for working on and crafting themselves. Where are the rewards of expending all this effort on personal branding and self-construction if there are hard limits on what is allowed to be achieved? If there are limits on how individual a person can be or how much crafting they are permitted to do, then what is the point of trying to co-operate, beyond the minimum required to have friends and get a job? Younger cohorts are ready to meet the challenge of being works-in-progress, constant self-creators, and because of this they are interested in products and services that transform, and which reveal truth and reality as malleable, able to be negotiated.

Attract their attention as shoppers by doing the following things:

- **Invite them to create their own customized bundles.** I speak of customization and personalization in later chapters of this book (for example, Chapters 7 and 8), this is just a reminder that people like having something that is unique to them. The Build-A-Bear Workshop is a little like this.

Writer and actor Felicia Day (2016) described the pleasure of creating a Santa doll in a ballet costume; an item which is clearly possible to achieve in store but is outside the range of outcomes that perhaps any other customer would have chosen.

- **Provide transformative experiences,** in store or out of store. A lot of people of many ages and genders would like to be a monarch for a day, travel back or forward in time or try out a different profession. As long as we are very careful to avoid the type of exploitation seen in commodity racism, we can attract consumers by confirming that they are right to believe that they can be whatever they want to be.
- **Reveal hidden truths.** This can be simple, like the eraser on my desk that starts out as a rectangular cuboid and gradually turns into a snow-capped mountain as the outer edges rub away. It could be a tall, juicy burger that turns out to be vegan. It could be something counter-intuitive such as cold-brew tea in countries that usually drink it hot or it could be conceptual, at the level of the famous Dove Campaign for Real Beauty, in which diverse bodies are revealed as more beautiful than the professional-model kind.

In the next four chapters we'll take a thrilling ride into the future, which should help you to find more ways to activate the ideas discussed here.

## Endnotes

1. A detailed and instructive account of the story appears on the Wikipedia page 'GameStop short squeeze'. You may also be interested in a story in the *Financial Times* of 22 June 2021, 'Hedge fund that bet against GameStop shuts down'.
2. See also Arthur Jafa's short film, *Love is the Message: The Message is Death*, 2016.
3. Thanks to Shazia Ali for this insight.
4. This chapter was written, and the Paperchase site accessed, in March 2021. By September 2021, the product was no longer visible on the website and the description of the 'Equilibrium' range has changed to include: 'Make a statement with punchy prints, positive slogans and fiery colours across innovative stationery and gorgeous gifting options. Paperchase will also be donating part of the proceeds from the collection to the charity CAMFED – Campaign for Female Education.'
5. See, for example, work by sociologists Tania Lewis, Bev Skeggs and Helen Wood.

# References

Baudrillard, J (1995) *Simulacra and Simulation*, University of Michigan Press, Ann Arbor

brennychef. This is the most exciting thing I've ever witnessed. [Reddit] 29 January 2021. www.reddit.com/r/wallstreetbets/comments/l7ly4a/people_are_risking_their_lives_to_wage_war/gl81wfy/ (archived at https://perma.cc/QFE2-693X)

CNet (2021) 'Robinhood backlash: What you should know about the GameStop stock controversy', www.cnet.com/personal-finance/investing/robinhood-backlash-what-you-should-know-about-the-gamestop-stock-controversy/ (archived at https://perma.cc/AV9E-Y582)

Cunningham, J and Roberts, P (2021) *Brandsplaining: Why marketing is still sexist and how to fix it*, Penguin Business, London

Day, F (2016) *You're Never Weird on the Internet (almost): a memoir*, Sphere, London

Ehrenreich, B (2010) *Smile or Die*, Granta, London

IceFabulous7202. I HAVE SPENT ALL WEEK STARING AT MY PHONE. I HAVE NEVER HAD THIS MUCH ADRENALINE. [Reddit] 10 March 2021. www.reddit.com/r/wallstreetbets/comments/m1xhlc/gme_megathread_for_march_10_2021/gqgsqod/ (archived at https://perma.cc/WFZ7-FLWT)

leelooodallas. I can feel the serotonin kicking in [...] [Reddit] 05 February 2021. www.reddit.com/r/wallstreetbets/comments/ld4v2q/daily_discussion_thread_for_february_05_2021/gm4ett1/ (archived at https://perma.cc/GJJ9-SVM9)

McClintock, A (1995) *Imperial Leather: Race, gender, and sexuality in the colonial conquest*, Routledge, New York

OverCaffeinated. @excess_caffeine. If it was empowering, people with power would be doing it. Men, however [...]. [Twitter] 19 March 2021. twitter.com/excess_caffeine/status/1372938883042844674?s=20 (archived at https://perma.cc/V7WT-GL2M)

Paperchase (2021) Collections: Equilibrium, www.paperchase.com/en_gb/collections/equilibrium (archived at https://perma.cc/PU5S-2N68)

Paperchase. @FromPaperchase. This image has become a symbol of female empowerment & recognised as such in this form, [...]. [Twitter] 19 March 2021. twitter.com/frompaperchase/status/1372865822398554113 (archived at https://perma.cc/SH85-GQW9)

Purple Sneakers. @PurpleSneakers3. Thank you for this inspiring symbolism. Every time I wish to feel more empowered I pull my pants down [...]. [Twitter] 19 March 2021. twitter.com/PurpleSneakers3/status/1372990843284430849?s=20 (archived at https://perma.cc/TA3U-VGYX)

Truth and Beauty. @trashalou. Also @FromPaperchase why are they all white bottoms?. [Twitter] 19 March 2021. twitter.com/trashalou/status/1372978972858925061?s=20 (archived at https://perma.cc/U824-SYR2)

Sky News (2019) Katy Perry 'saddened' as her shoe line is taken off shelves for being racist, https://news.sky.com/story/katy-perry-saddened-as-her-shoe-line-is-taken-off-shelves-for-being-racist-11635345 (archived at https://perma.cc/G5SG-D2LS)

TheRealSamBell. This is the most fun I've had since the pandemic started. [Reddit] 02 February 2021. www.reddit.com/r/wallstreetbets/comments/lal105/gme_discussion_thread_for_february_1_2021_part_4/gloll0j/ (archived at https://perma.cc/7ZAR-DRDS)

Twl1. It's the energy. There's more than electricity on this board right now, there's real, actual energy [...]. [Reddit] 29 January 2021. www.reddit.com/r/wallstreetbets/comments/l7iorh/gme_overnight_pajama_party_megathread/gl79uo6/ (archived at https://perma.cc/BAR5-K4KK)

United Nations (2020) The shadow pandemic: Violence against women during Covid-19, www.unwomen.org/en/news/in-focus/in-focus-gender-equality-in-covid-19-response/violence-against-women-during-covid-19 (archived at https://perma.cc/V3MM-MPNM)

Walton, A. @coolAngieWalton. I know what happened. Some bloke said "I know, let's tell them that even the ones with fat, lumpy bums, matter [...]. [Twitter] 20 March 2021. twitter.com/coolAngieWalton/status/1373257339302723590?s=20 (archived at https://perma.cc/5P7L-HKCA)

Willis, S (1990) I want the Black one: Is there a place for Afro-American culture in commodity culture?, *New Formations*, 10, Spring

**PART THREE**

# The future

# 07

# The future of business

> **WHAT'S COMING UP**
>
> The world is changing very rapidly, driven by technological innovation. In Chapters 3 to 6 I argued that some things, like desire, begin and end with consumers and can be only *influenced* by business and marketing. But in this and the next three chapters, I concentrate on aspects of retail and shopping, technology and the future, which are largely caused and controlled by business, because businesses have money and technical capabilities that are beyond the reach of most private individuals. In this chapter, we dive straight into the deep end to consider some of the largest aspects of business and the evolution of capitalism.
>
> By the end of this chapter, you will be able to:
>
> - design opportunities to promote your business and its products that are firmly focused on providing benefits to your customers, not just to the business;
> - find an alternative to the popular approach of continually reassuring consumers that they are special even though big data is making them feel like a rat in a maze;
> - list a number of different ways of helping your customers feel that they have some control and a hand in shaping reality;
> - use a case study of China's Double 11 shopping festival to identify some of the factors that make it successful, and apply them to your own business;
> - design better, more satisfying and engaging loyalty programmes;
> - recognize and support both creative work and play – these are the most appealing aspects of a tech-enabled future, the part that your customers most look forward to.

## The behavioural futures market

*A short introduction*

'Behavioural futures market' (Zuboff, 2019) is a useful phrase that describes a newly emerged, technology-driven economy where money is made not from selling things to people but from selling reliable predictions about their behaviour or selling their behavioural data itself to other organizations.

Consumers have not always been aware that the behavioural futures market exists, but they are certainly beginning to realize. They may not all read books like Shoshanna Zuboff's but many have seen other depictions of that market, such as Netflix's docudrama *The Social Dilemma* (2020), which chillingly spelled out how people have their behaviour and their emotions manipulated by algorithms.

For better or worse, the behavioural futures market is unambiguously controlled by businesses, not by consumers. It is leaving a lot of people feeling anxious and disempowered. At the same time, there's an appetite for technology among consumers when they feel that they are allowed to 'drive'.

*A little more depth*

Even before the rise of behavioural futures, retail experts such as Herb Sorensen (2016) were remarking that margin on retail sales is only about fourth on the list of profit sources for large retailers. The major sources of profits listed by Sorensen are: rebates, promotional allowances and slotting fees; cash float that accrues interest; real estate that can be bought cheaply and sold later; and, in fourth place, margin on sales, which largely exists in service departments such as deli counters and in-store pharmacies.

In the time since Sorensen wrote the first edition of his book, the retail landscape has changed dramatically. Today, the world's largest retailers are not purely retailers but tech companies such as Amazon and Alibaba, which happen to have a retail arm. Before the digital age, retailers used sales figures and their knowledge of their local communities to stock items deemed most likely to sell. It involved elements of guesswork, hope and intuition, as well as the sales figures themselves. But because of the almost breathtaking ability of organizations such as Amazon to reach into people's lives and gather their data, particularly through voice-recognition assistants such as Alexa, which can be built into homes and cars as well as cell phones, the tech companies now have quantities of data on human behaviour that are historically unmatched.

All of this is worrying for consumers, even though they love the convenience of being able to shop from any location and control their smart homes using only their voices. Data analytics 'works' in the sense that it correctly predicts behaviour, and the behavioural futures market makes money, but it leaves consumers feeling unsettled, mistrustful and concerned for their privacy. (See the report at truata.com/2021/05/19/personal-data-consumer-report/, for example.) People like the benefits that technology brings, but they become fearful when the benefits seem one-sided and they are not sure exactly who is benefiting on the other side of the transaction.

## The unique perspective of semiotics

If you have any familiarity with academic psychology, or if you read about behavioural futures markets, you may have noticed that what we see being implemented is a form of behaviourism. Popular in the 1940s, behaviourism is a school of thought in psychology that revolves around the idea of stimulus and response. You've heard of it if you've ever come across the experiments of B F Skinner, who found that rats, pigeons and dogs could be trained to exhibit certain behaviour (such as pressing a lever) when the action was systematically rewarded. They could even be trained to respond with involuntary behaviour such as salivation to a cue such as a bell ringing, where the bell was usually followed by a reward.

The key thing about behaviourism is that what we call the mind isn't strictly necessary for the system to work. It isn't necessary for the organism (the rat, pigeon, dog or online shopper) to think or possess any free will. The organism, the 'something' that resides in between the stimulus (a bell; a sponsored ad on Amazon) and the response (salivation; a lever-press; a click-through) is a black box. We don't know what's going on in there, and it doesn't matter as long as the stimulus and the response are reliably connected. Consumers usually place a high value on the idea of their own free will and are capable of becoming upset when they perceive that a powerful external system is over-riding it.

When some users of these systems, such as some brands and retailers, would prefer to avoid upsetting customers, they usually respond by borrowing ideas from liberal humanism (see Barry, 2017, for example). That is, they reassure consumers using ideas that they are likely to endorse, telling them that they are special and unique. Data-driven targeting is repackaged (very successfully) as 'personalization' – because what could be nicer than a tailor-made service? Consumers are further invited to generate even more data by writing reviews, creating wish lists, filling out their profiles and doing other economically useful activities in exchange for rewards or the chance of a reward. All of this creates at least the illusion of the consumer's individuality and free will being respected. It works – so successfully, that I am not going to tell you not to use it. I even think it's a good idea in cases where it has been designed so that consumers genuinely and demonstrably benefit from it. However, it's not a new approach. Your competitors are probably already doing it.

Semiotics uses a different approach altogether. Deferring neither to the reality of the consumer as a machine nor a mysterious and unique organic being, it instead asks how reality itself is manufactured, collectively and at the level of culture. When humans get together in groups, they actively create *versions* of reality, principally through shared communications. The results can be found in all the places where cultures exist: in organizations, in local communities and in special-interest communities, such as those organized around religious beliefs, political identities and beliefs about wellness and illness. Where does this get us? It means that businesses are not limited to reassuring consumers that they are unique, different and special, and instead yields this insight: **people want to shape reality, not have it shaped for them.**

## Actions for retail marketers

The chance to have a hand in shaping reality is something that any size of store or brand can build into its offering, even though the four specific actions below try to be future-facing and therefore lend themselves to the use of technology where it is available. Here are some things that you can offer, through clever marketing communications or through branded experiences, which connect with the most sought-after aspects of living in the digital age. Offer your customers opportunities to:

1 **Mould and shape reality.** Give people a chance to vote on how the store is managed, how its space is used, which charities it supports. UK supermarket Waitrose hands out green plastic tokens at the point of sale that represent a small amount of money that Waitrose will donate. Customers choose where the money goes by dropping their tokens into one of three boxes representing different charitable causes (and these change over time).

2  **Own something.** Waitrose is part of the John Lewis Partnership, which is employee-owned, so that each staff member is a colleague in reality and not in name only. It's great for the reputation of John Lewis, and not just among employees. You probably have a subset of super-customers who could be offered the chance to buy shares early or at a preferential rate.

3  **Make a mark; make something of lasting value.** In 2015, furniture store IKEA held a competition. Children around the world were invited to send their drawings of real and mythical creatures: bats, dinosaurs and some creatures that don't have names. IKEA selected ten of these drawings and transformed them (with great fidelity and accuracy) into soft toys, then put them on sale at child-size prices, as part of a charitable collaboration with UNICEF and Save the Children.

4  **Perform magic.** Anthropologists and writers on technology both like to point out that 'magic' is a word we use when we can't explain how something works, but the same sensation results when something works better or differently than expected. If you can afford technology, use it to offer a surprising and delightful experience. I'm reminded of the delight people show when staircases unexpectedly light up or make a sound. The same people could be thrilled by motion-sensing devices at fixtures that make flowers bloom when people walk by, or when they stop to inspect the display.

> EXERCISE
>
> For consumers, the number-one issue regarding the behavioural futures market is control. People instinctively dislike feeling that they are being controlled by external, largely invisible forces such as algorithms. At the same time, they are very attracted to the idea that they can control things themselves.
>
> Whether you have a large or small budget, whether you are a retailer or a brand owner, ask what you can do to restore a sense of control to your consumer. This could include things like:
>
> - **Trust and honour systems**
>   Danish negotiation adviser Keld Jensen, writing for Forbes (2016), describes the perhaps surprising findings of Honest Tea and WHSmith who both implemented honour systems in asking for voluntary, non-enforced payment for tea and newspapers respectively. US company Honest Tea found that 94 per cent of customers paid in full. UK stationery retailer WHSmith found that

> even though some people took newspapers from a box without paying, it recovered more than 100 per cent of the cost of the newspapers, because the difference was made up by customers who deposited coins worth more than the value of the newspaper (perhaps because they couldn't be bothered to find the right change). Consider also the amount that stores spend on policing customers to make sure they don't escape without paying and you may see an advantage in using honour systems that have the added bonus of making people feel good about themselves.
> 
> - **Asking people what kinds of things they want to see in your store**
>   This may seem redundant if you already have solid quantitative data based on sales, but taking data from people is not the same as asking their opinion. Digital and even physical stores could introduce vote-up and vote-down buttons concerning not just products but every aspect of the retail offering, such as promotions, customer service desks and customer facilities such as rest rooms. Reflect the changes. Give people a sense of control and ownership of 'their' store.

## Double 11

### A short introduction

The Chinese shopping festival Double 11 barely needs an introduction. Originating with Alibaba's Singles Day in 2009, it increases each year in size, reach, engagement, volume of sales and revenue. The biggest day of the festival is 11 November, but it has expanded over time so that festivities now begin as early as 21 October.

It was closely watched by the business community in its November 2020 iteration, because the date was about eight months into global experience of the COVID-19 pandemic. The event's performance was regarded as a prediction of how China's retail sector would withstand and recover from the pandemic. In fact, it once again exceeded expectations. Reports appeared on 12 November that Alibaba and JD.com 'racked up around $115 billion in sales during the Singles Day shopping event, both setting new records' (Kharpal, 2020).

## A little more depth

The expansion and seemingly unstoppable success of Double 11 naturally has multiple components and variables, but it is nonetheless easy to pick out a few prominent features.

### HUGE BUILD-UP TO THE EVENT

As noted above, Double 11 expands in time as well along other dimensions. A longer shopping festival that is spread over three weeks rather than one day offers more retail opportunities in an obvious way. Brands keep consumers interested using various techniques such as creating scarcity, through limited-edition variants and limited, early-access availability. Shopping is more social in China than in Western culture, and consumers recruit each other into the event across social media platforms, collecting rewards for sharing content and participating in group activities such as games.

### GAMIFICATION

This includes, but is bigger than, sending consumers on a quest or journey around a shopping platform such as Alibaba's Taobao, in search of red envelopes that eventually become vouchers, discounts and other prizes. Taobao guides the consumer to experience these activities through well-developed, branded games with attractive graphical user interfaces. These games change each year (Daxue Consulting, 2020): in 2019, Taobao had consumers compete to build virtual skyscrapers; in 2020, the emphasis changed to co-operation and consumers nurtured and raised virtual kittens.

### MULTI-CHANNEL EXPERIENCE

For years, Singles Day and then Double 11 has been a televised event similar to the US Superbowl. It makes full use of celebrities. US singer Taylor Swift was a special guest in 2019, as were the UK's David and Victoria Beckham in 2016. More recently, live streaming has become important; it grows over time, discovers new applications and generates sales all by itself. As reported by *Forbes* (Forrester, 2020), 17,000 brands participated in live streaming in Double 11 2019, generating RMB 20 billion ($2.9 billion) in gross merchandise value (GMV). Beauty brand WHOO generated $14 million in GMV in six minutes. As for 2020, celebrity live streamers such as Weiya and Li Jiaqi were reported by *Forbes* to have generated RMB 7.8 billion in GMV as early as 2 November, nine days before the main event. Superficially similar to US television's Home Shopping Network, live streaming is a relatively exciting and personal experience in which consumers follow people and brands whose content they already enjoy, so as to discover new products, witness demonstrations, hear reviews, participate in a conversation and collect token rewards in exchange for their attention.

## The unique perspective of semiotics

As always, semiotics has something new to say about developments like Double 11. A new point of view arises when we reconsider behavioural events (measured in the amount of GMV generated within a set time frame) from the point of view of humans acting en masse to create meaningful experiences, tell stories, build their own culture and have a hand in shaping history.

The key point that I want you to take away concerning Double 11 is as follows. Its multiple, distinctive features, such as the tense build-up, the team games and the active involvement of key opinion leaders (KOLs – independently successful influencers), add up to a highly energetic, mass experience. Like the Super Bowl and the FIFA World Cup, it is a chance for humans, who some people say are herd animals, to come together in a large mass and experience heightened emotions. When we add to this the year-on-year advancements in technology seen in Double 11, which make the event incrementally more personal, more ambitious and more novel, the mass of humans enjoys a sense of *rushing headlong into the future*. The event also represents a *wealth creation opportunity* for individuals – not because of the small amount of income a person can generate in coupons and tokens, but because, in our emerging, global, digital culture, every individual is their own brand. Double 11 is a chance to make content, not merely to consume it, and to grow one's own audience by latching one's own brand onto the most dynamic event of the retail year. This is a version of the future that a lot of people want; especially younger people and especially markets such as China where shopping is already more social and more fully integrated with technology. It is a utopian vision of a technology-dominated future, in which everything is sociable and sensational; not the dystopian, fearful vision, in which people worry about being spied on.

There's one more important point to make here. Above, I remarked that live streaming is only superficially similar to selling via channels such as the Home Shopping Network. Streaming does not only happen in support of traditional consumer brands; it is also found on consumers' own social media, on e-sports platforms and in the ever-expanding adult entertainment industry. Fans' loyalty to their preferred KOLs and performers can be intense, and they will offer 'tips' and other kinds of payments in return for the performer's attention, such as acknowledging them verbally, saying their name, thanking them for their donation and responding to their comments. Streaming brings with it different expectations from watching TV, including the expected chance of drawing closer to attractive individuals and aspirational social circles. These emotionally rich yet distant and rather one-sided relationships are an example of parasocial relationships, which we will discuss in more detail later.

## Actions for retail marketers

Double 11 succeeds on many different levels. Semiotics adds a set of questions about reality and how it is constructed. Double 11 is a highly constructed event. Deliberately fabricated, it is fairly recent, and its conspicuous and constructed-ness is part of its appeal. Here are just a few ideas inspired by Double 11 that you can apply to make the most of your retail store or consumer-facing brand.

- **Co-operate with business partners** to create participatory events across multiple locations. It would be overstating the case to claim that business rivals Alibaba and JD.com co-operate over Double 11, but the event has grown to a size that more than accommodates them both. A promotional event that is confined to a single store or even a chain of stores is less exciting for shoppers than an event that seems to temporarily override day-to-day rivalries. Large, multi-agency events deliver a feeling of momentum: progress and movement into the future. If Double 11 itself is out of reach, great results can still be achieved by working with local business groups, chambers of commerce and city councils to organize local festivals – of food, entertainment, the culture and local pride of a specific city, and so on.
- **Show people something they haven't seen before**. Double 11 is nothing if not dynamic. It changes on a moment-to-moment and day-to-day basis because of time-limited promotions. It changes year on year. It offers new visual spectacles. You may not be able to afford Taylor Swift, but there are far cheaper ways to reveal something novel. If you would usually decorate your store with balloons and children's beach toys to celebrate a summer sale, try an underwater theme with mermaids instead. If your customers like to take selfies, give them a photo opportunity using novel seating or an inflatable tree to stand under, or some similar item drawn from human imagination that isn't part of the everyday world.

- **Reality is an experience that consumers can access through doing things in real time, with real people.** It's especially enjoyable when those people perceive that they found and chose each other because of a common interest. Consider organizing shopping events and promotions that exclude no one but are organized around specific themes, whether it is locally popular sports, fandoms such as science fiction or 'good cause' campaigns such as veganism. Make choices based on what your local and core customers seem to care about. Give them a chance to feel that something special is happening for 'their' people because your store or organization has noticed and believes they matter.

> **EXERCISE**
>
> An exercise that I regularly benefit from in my work as a semiologist is 'having the experience'. When I see retailers and brands inviting consumers to participate in something interesting, I will quite often sign up for or get involved in whatever it is. Reading about retail innovations in the business press is one thing, but experiencing it for yourself is another thing altogether. Here are some things you could do.
>
> - If you're interested in a category or sector that has trade shows and expos that admit consumers, go along as a consumer. You may or may not have an exhibition stand of your own, but, even if you do, get someone from your company to attend only as a consumer, visit all the stands, consume the entertainment, eat at the restaurant, get a drink at the bar, collect samples and gifts and use the rest rooms. Acting as a consumer, try to extract as much value from the event as possible.
> - Install and use some shopping apps. If you've never used AliExpress (Alibaba's retail arm for international customers), install the app, try it out, see how it feels. I'm looking at the AliExpress app as I write this paragraph, and it couldn't be more different from Amazon. Right on the front page and before making an account or logging in, I'm being offered 'coins', 'freebies', 'coupons' and 'new user gifts'. There's a ticker counting down the number of days left in a sale (19), and there is a separate, week-long event called Super Brands Week, offering customers chances to score discounts of 'up to 60%'.
>
> Use your research findings to make a list of ideas. What went well? What could be improved on? Which aspects could you implement for your own retail store or brand?

## Play-to-earn

*A short introduction*

Games, gamification and the games industry are recurring topics in this book, particularly these four chapters, which are focused on technology and the future. The reason these topics are not confined to their own short section are because:

- The games industry is enormously wealthy and profitable, and substantially pandemic-resistant. Retail is struggling and could use some new ideas and help.
- Tech companies invest in both games and retail. For example, at the time of writing, Tencent Holdings Ltd owns 20 per cent of JD.com, Alibaba's nearest competitor in retail, and 40 per cent of Epic Games. Cutting-edge retailers benefit from transferrable insights and cross-industry expertise.
- The games industry evolves over time and grows innovative business models that retailers and other businesses can learn from.
- Marketers who are still trying to 'gamify' out-of-date business models are missing the point that the games industry is showing retailers new ways to conceive of retail and marketing.

'Play-to-earn' describes an emergent business model in the games industry. The industry is alert to customer experience and is willing to design opportunities for people to hand over their money that customers themselves enjoy and experience as a benefit.

*A little more depth*

Let's get right to the point: consumers have realized that there is an attention economy in which they are participating. At this point, many consumers around the world could not pay any more attention to their screens if they tried. They are already giving technology all the attentional capacity they have. They are increasingly aware of their attention as a resource that is being competed for by various shopping apps, entertainment providers and social media platforms. They are starting to expect something in return, which is where play-to-earn comes in.

If you're not very familiar with the games industry, here's a short breakdown of what happened. When video games first emerged, people bought disks with games on them. Today, it is still the case that individual games (or, in fact, their licence keys) are on sale in exchange for a one-off, up-front payment and the premium brands can set prices at around $60. This is a considerable investment for many consumers, especially on top of paying for gaming hardware. After a while, the industry realized that a mix of other models would better serve both it and its customers.

First, there was a move to a subscription model, where games are no longer products but a service. This helps to reduce the initial outlay by the customer and sets up a long-term revenue stream for the publisher or retailer, as long as it regularly issues new content.

Then came 'freemium' games such as *Fortnite* and *Candy Crush*. Free at the point of access, users of the software pay to acquire exclusive content or digital assets. This model is not universally popular with gamers and is sometimes called pay-to-win.

After that came the new model: play-to-earn. The consumer whose expectations rose when they realized that brands were competing for their attention can be satisfied when they are compensated for the valuable resource of attention that they are being asked to hand over. The hallmarks of play-to-earn are:

- The game allows users to own certain assets.
- These assets increase in value when the game is played.

When these two conditions are fulfilled, the game need not even be free to access. *Axie Infinity* is an online game that bears some resemblance to Nintendo's *Pokémon*: users create, battle and trade small, digital creatures called Axies. Joining the game requires the initial purchase of a team of three Axies. Because Axies are individually identified with non-fungible tokens (NFTs), they are unique assets that are capable of retaining and growing value over time. That is, if you imagine starting out with a small and weak Axie, which you train so that it wins battles and gradually becomes superior to the others, you now have the option of selling your unique Axie for more money than you used to purchase it. The currency underlying *Axie Infinity* is Ethereum-based cryptocurrency. It has an exchange rate with traditional currencies such as US dollars. Today's Axie Marketplace informs me that prices for Axies start at $350 (and remember, I'll need to buy a team of three to play the game). This is a steep entry point, yet buying in confers the chance to sell at a profit later. The Marketplace shows plenty of Axies on sale at prices over $1,000 each and in theory there is no upper limit. The key points are:

- Axies are unique assets, owned by the customer. The customer may dispose of the Axie as they please, including selling it for real money.
- The monetary value of Axies rises when the game is played.

## The unique perspective of semiotics

*Axie Infinity* is an example of the agile thinking of the games industry and its ability to capitalize on both new *technology* and the new consumer *needs* that technology provokes. For me, *Axie Infinity* is good to know about because it helps me to see what is missing from the customer loyalty programmes that are commonly used by retailers and which may not prevail in a fight for attention with tech giants such as Alibaba. It offers a new angle on retail, and semiotics is all about looking for a new perspective on familiar mechanisms.

To take a concrete example, *Axie Infinity* causes me to notice the difference between eBay Bucks and Alibaba's Coins. eBay Bucks used to reward customers by giving them Bucks worth 1 per cent of the value of their purchases. Bucks could be turned into gift cards, redeemable by the user, on a quarterly basis. In 2021, the scheme has been replaced by one where rewards are earned by using an eBay Mastercard, which seems like rather a return to traditional banking. Aspects of this scheme to note:

- It is difficult to see where a real sense of ownership exists in points that are in no way different from anyone else's points.
- Points accrue from purchases (in a very consistent and remote way over which the user has minimal control). Points do not accrue from any other activity.
- Points don't increase in value when more people use eBay.

Alibaba's Coins are different. They can be used in part payment for purchases, so they turn into real-world goods and services in a fairly immediate way. Alibaba is good at thinking up new ways for app users to win coins, for example through mini-games and supporting Double 11 by sharing content. Simply opening an app can be enough to net a few coins; a gesture that acknowledges the preferential treatment that the user is giving to this app and not to a competitor. Coins accumulate in exchange for attention and not solely in exchange for purchases. Shoppers know that their attention is valuable and they are compensated for it. Mechanisms like mini-games help them to feel that they have genuinely won something: it was not a fait accompli but involved chance, risk, competition or collaboration.

The key take-away is this: retailers who are competing for attention (and I think that's all retailers) will need to find ways to succeed in an emerging play-to-earn economy. Consumers seem to like arrangements that give them a sense of ownership and control, where their achievements have lasting value and where they are rewarded for thinking about you and not someone else.

## Actions for retail marketers

As you can see, play-to-earn is more than just a system for attaching loyalty points to purchases. It's also more than applying a game-like skin to an old business model. As well as user ownership and assets that retain or grow in value over time, play-to-earn products provide these features in a context of solid insight concerning the question of why play is enjoyable. Here are the key elements, according to expert academics in the field such as Vahlo and Hamari (2019).

Play is fun. People describe the experience as pleasant and relaxing. Play is immersive: you can lose yourself in it and forget your everyday worries. Play is sociable: play-to-earn models are good at building-in sociability, as is Double 11. Play gives a feeling of competence. It's possible to make measurable progress. Play offers chances for autonomy. The game-player, software user or shopper is empowered to make independent decisions and is given a degree of control.

Fun, immersion, relatedness (being sociable, being connected to others), competence and autonomy are building blocks that you can use to design satisfying and engaging experiences. Add play-to-earn mechanisms and you have a chance of competing successfully for attention, as well as getting ahead of competitors who still don't know why play matters.

> Further exciting insights are coming up, but in the meantime, take a look at your retail store or consumer facing brand. Ask these questions:
> - *If you have a loyalty programme already in place, what is it rewarding?* Rewarding people for giving you their attention, even in a small way, acknowledges their point of view, in which their time is important.

- *What can you give consumers to control?*
  If you have an app, could it be more customizable by the user? Do you have something that they can work on, grow or own?
- *How many ways can you see to recognize their skill?*
  Could the discerning purchases of those customers who are foodies, wine buffs or who have an eye for quality be acknowledged for their expertise?
- *Is it fun to shop in your store?*
  Is it relaxing? Does it help to relieve people of the burden of everyday cares?
- *What could you do in store to help people feel that their repeated investment of time and energy retained some value over time?*
  Play-to-earn products get 'better' the more you play them, and when larger numbers of people play. them. Can you introduce a promotion or loyalty reward that gets better as participation increases?

### EXERCISE

As in the previous section, my best advice to you is to 'have the experience'. Find one free-to-play game and one play-to-earn game and feel the difference for yourself. You will be able to experience the lows as well as the highs and see more clearly which elements could work for you in getting consumers to spend their attention on your brand. As you explore the free games on platforms such as Facebook, you will learn more than just which themes you prefer between sports games, racing games, puzzles, mystery adventures and so on. More importantly, you'll experience the mechanisms that underpin these games, such as collecting items, races against time, games in which interaction with others is more of a selling point than the game itself.

Then have a go with some play-to-earn games. You'll see how different they are and how much they vary. You'll also be able to see for yourself which aspects consumers are less happy with and how they could be resolved. Not every game is perfect; not every retailer has it all worked out. Alibaba's coins and red envelopes are easy to get, but some customers complain that you have to do a large amount of gaming to amass a tiny reward. At the other end of the scale, play-to-earn games like *Axie* and *Zed Run* can be financially rewarding to play, yet put up barriers to entry in the form of buy-in prices or other complexities. Frank Partnoy, writing 'My wild ride into the crypto world' for the *Financial Times* (16 July 2021), gave a thorough description of his attempts to make money using a horse racing game. He succeeded, but getting started was more difficult than he expected. See how your experience compares.

## Creator economies and decentralized economies

### A short introduction

#### CREATOR ECONOMY

This is an economy in which people – your customers – are not merely consumers but rather, or also, creators of content that others then consume. The type of content being created varies by platform. On Patreon and Medium, it is longform writing. On Twitch, it is mostly live streams of video gaming (for all levels of ability). On YouTube and TikTok, people broadcast and attempt to monetize video content that ranges across comedy, gossip, political commentary and adult entertainment. The customers or users of these applications reward and support their favourite content creators in various ways. Increasingly this means 'tips' (offered on a goodwill basis at a moment to suit the customer, a lot like tipping a bartender) as well as payments to access exclusive content, buying merchandise, taking out subscriptions, purchasing ad-free experiences, and various other models. Some people think that the creator economy is what comes next, when the attention economy has gone as far as it can go.

#### DECENTRALIZED ECONOMY

This is the name for an economy that diverges from centralized operations. The emerging creator economy is an example of decentralization, but it is not the whole story. Decentralization is bigger than the entertainment industry. It also lives in the tech industries, where it includes the invention of new kinds of money. The premise is that not all money has to be controlled by the IMF, the US Federal Reserve, the European Central Bank, the People's Bank of China or other central organizations. Decentralized currencies are privately owned currencies that have an exchange rate with USD and RMB but exist outside the systems that control them. The decentralized currencies you might have heard of are Bitcoin, Ether and perhaps Dogecoin, a sometime favourite of Elon Musk.

*A little more depth*

If you are new to these topics, as many retailers and brand owners are, it's a lot of information to take in. To simplify, I have a couple of real-life stories for you. They are well-documented elsewhere – I offer a short summary here.

Alexandra Cooper is a young woman who founded a podcast called *Call Her Daddy* in 2018. It concerns sex, relationships and the experience of being a younger adult in the present day. Cooper has a seemingly inexhaustible supply of topics, an exuberant personality and is camera-friendly. The show is wildly successful. This success led to a tussle between Cooper, her former business partner, and Barstool, the platform that originally hosted the *Call Her Daddy* show. After a struggle, Cooper broke free and accepted $60 million from Spotify as part of a three-year contract. Her podcast is now ranked number five of all Spotify's podcasts. In 2020, 10 per cent of Spotify was owned by Tencent Holdings (which also has shares in JD.com and Epic Games, as mentioned above).

Addison Rae Easterling will be 21 by the time you read this. Based in California, she dances in short videos on social media platform TikTok. Her career began in 2019. Since then, she has amassed 81 million followers. The bulk of her income comes from the traditional sources of the successful influencer: brand endorsement deals and her own merchandise. Predictably for someone of her evident mass appeal, she is branching out into acting and music. She has become friends with the Kardashians and is thought to be one of TikTok's highest earners (Brown, 2020). TikTok is owned by Chinese company ByteDance, which claims to entertain 800 million daily active users across all its platforms (Lahiri, *nd*).

You could reasonably argue that a creator-driven economy is not fully decentralized when it ultimately serves the same few tech giants that are responsible for the attention economy. You would have a point. But the creator economy is a series of steps towards decentralization, in which people want to own the means of production and break free from being treated as machines or passive organisms that do nothing but make purchases and view advertising. These appetites for control and creative activity are recurring themes in parallel areas of decentralization, such as cryptocurrencies NFT collectibles and meme stocks. It all contributes to one big picture that links the teenagers stacking shelves in a rural village supermarket and dancing in their bedrooms at the weekend to people like Elon Musk and Jack Ma, aspirational figures around whom cults of personality have grown.

## The unique perspective of semiotics

The task of semiotics is to think critically about the version(s) of reality currently inhabited by both businesses and consumers. With the emergence of the creator economy, what new realities are being ushered in?

Some writers on business and technology are just as enthusiastic as content-creating consumers. Indeed, there's plenty to be enthusiastic about. Consumers appear to be getting what they want, which is full personhood, recognition, chances to express themselves. It's easy to see the utopian aspects of blossoming creator economies. Writing in *Forbes,* marketer Kian Bhaktiari (2021) exemplified this point of view.

> We are now seeing the distribution of individual creativity at unprecedented scale. Creativity is integral to the human experience ... for the first time, we can harness the collective creativity of the masses to benefit the many, not the few.

But if semiotics teaches you anything, it is that there is always another version of reality sitting behind the one that you are being directed to look at. In this case, we don't have to look very far to find it. The creator economy is not simply about everyone having a great time. There is economic insecurity. It especially affects young people who are trying to get started in life. The COVID-19 pandemic cost a lot of people their jobs. Retail used to employ more sales staff and shop-floor workers than it does now. It's more and more difficult to even entertain the idea of buying property. In the US, kids dance on TikTok and hope for their big break. In the Philippines, their peers scrape a living that's just above subsistence level by charging commission for training other people's virtual animals: the Axies and digital racehorses that are priced beyond the reach of their own purchasing power and are owned by people who enjoy technology and are cash rich but time poor.

Have you ever run into those memes that set up a contrast between 'Me at 23' versus 'My parents at 23'? They are simply assembled collages in which two identical men, father and son, contemplate their life goals and opportunities. The point of the meme is for Millennials and Zoomers to display their dramatically reduced life chances. 'My parents at 23' are shown starting a family with no considerations or constraints beyond desire, and buying a large house in which to raise the family. There are no financial or other obstacles. 'Me at 23' is an identical man with no wife, family or house. All are beyond his reach. What he has instead is a small number of 'likes' on his latest tweet or Facebook post. This is what society has offered him.

Not every aspect of the creator economy is fun and fluffy. Some of it involves economic struggle and feelings of being denied reasonable human ambitions. I'm telling you this because when consumers – your customers – create, share and circulate these memes and other messages on digital platforms, they're trying to tell you something important. They're trying to let everyone know about the exact nature of deeply felt injustices, and economic and generational tensions. Marketers and product designers are usually very interested in pain points: when we know what's causing people difficulties, then we can offer solutions that they are going to respond to.

*Actions for retail marketers*

In all probability, your customers are already creating content in one way or another, whether it's just posting 'good morning' messages on local WhatsApp groups or counterbalancing unemployment and lack of traditional jobs by building themselves up as one-person, multi-platform entertainment brands. Marketers are forever looking for new consumer needs that they could potentially address, and the emergence of the creator economy seems to be accompanied by a lot of needs. Here are some suggested ways for retailers and consumer-facing brands to get involved.

- **Creators need an audience and a platform.** Take opportunities to provide those things, especially to creators who are aspirational figures to your customers, or in whom they feel a sense of investment or ownership. If you have a traditional bricks-and-mortar store, who are the most loved people in your community? Can you give them a platform to speak or a spot in your store communications? Tmall and Taobao are great at designing events where people are encouraged and helped to put their content in front of a wider audience.
- **Making content is an endless task.** Those of your customers who are creators are caught up in a commitment to making new content and that means they need a steady stream of new ideas as well as props and locations. That's where your promotions come in, organized around whatever you are celebrating in store, whether it's families, baby care, local

schools, local key workers such as medical personnel, the local arts and music scene, local sports, or whatever categories you especially want to promote, such as fresh produce for cooking from scratch, or personal care products that create the feeling of a spa at home.

- **Facilitate and reward play.** The key insight here is that being a content creator in even a small way is a form of work. Work is recognized as different from play, in that it is externally motivated (people need to earn money) and compelled (most people have to work even when they don't feel like it). In a sense, work has colonized play, which leaves 'real', uncoerced play as something comparatively scarce. Lush Retail Ltd has traditionally done a good job of giving shoppers chances to play in store, dropping fizzing bath bombs into tubs of water. Nike invites play when it gives consumers the chance to design their own shoe as well as taking part in branded, online, multi-player fitness events.

---

### EXERCISE

Consider your retail business or consumer-facing brand and ask the following questions.

- What can you do with your marketing or business model to show that you are on the side of 'the people'? Decentralization is exciting to consumers because it represents an opportunity to resist and to attempt to take control of their own lives.
- What are you doing, or what can you do, to position yourself on the right side of the divide between 'big business' and honest 'folks'?

If you've recently shed staff, some of those people are included in a population of different kinds of content creators who have in common the objective of supporting themselves. You may not be able to create hundreds of new jobs if you are in a situation where you have stores that are closing, but you can go out of your way to be a business that is friendly to creators and supports their efforts. List some things that you could do.

Using customer feedback, identify the playful (non-compulsory, spontaneous) aspects of your customer's journey and build on them. Give people chances to interact with displays, make things, try things out.

In the next chapter, we'll look more deeply into what's going on with consumers: why they aren't very happy, how they're trying to fix it, and what businesses can do to help in a situation that business itself created.

## References

Bakhtiari, K (2021) The creator economy, NFTs and marketing, *Forbes*, https://www.forbes.com/sites/kianbakhtiari/2021/04/18/the-creator-economy-nfts-and-marketing/?sh=565768ac1204 (archived at https://perma.cc/B24B-YXVV)

Barry, P (2017) Beginning Theory: *An introduction to literary and cultural theory*, 4th ed, Manchester University Press, Manchester

Brown, A (2020) TikTok's 7 highest-earning stars: new Forbes list led by teen queens Addison Rae and Charli d'Amelio, *Forbes*, https://www.forbes.com/sites/abrambrown/2020/08/06/tiktoks-highest-earning-stars-teen-queens-addison-rae-and-charli-damelio-rule/?sh=503ef9f50874 (archived at https://perma.cc/4YD8-42BJ)

Daxue Consulting (2020) The craze for e-commerce gamification in China, from charity to Double 11, https://daxueconsulting.com/gamification-in-china/ (archived at https://perma.cc/5LT7-NU7A)

Forrester (2020) What to expect on singles' day 2020, *Forbes*, https://www.forbes.com/sites/forrester/2020/11/02/what-to-expect-on-singles-day-2020/?sh=8865036723fe (archived at https://perma.cc/2H5H-BKKZ)

Jensen, K (2016). Allow people to steal from you – it's good for business: why the honor system is creating profit, *Forbes*, https://www.forbes.com/sites/keldjensen/2016/06/30/allow-people-to-steal-from-you-its-good-for-business-why-the-honor-system-is-creating-profit/?sh=443fc3e357e2 (archived at https://perma.cc/6KAP-VNMW)

Kharpal, A (2020) Alibaba, JD set new records to rack up record $115 billion of sales on Singles Day as regulations loom, *CNBC*, https://www.cnbc.com/2020/11/12/singles-day-2020-alibaba-and-jd-rack-up-record-115-billion-of-sales.html (archived at https://perma.cc/HTY2-VUMR)

Lahiri, T (*nd*) Facebook finally has a serious Chinese rival, *Quartz*, https://qz.com/1564270/bytedance-video-app-tiktok-rival-to-facebook-reached-1-billion-downloads/ (archived at https://perma.cc/8RJ8-YP33)

Sorensen, H (2016) *Inside the Mind of the Shopper*, Pearson FT Press, Upper Saddle River

Vahlo, J and Hamari, J (2019) Five-factor inventory of intrinsic motivations to gameplay (IMG), https://trepo.tuni.fi/bitstream/handle/10024/117607/Five_factor_inventory_2019.pdf (archived at https://perma.cc/VHG6-FP2Q)

Zuboff, S (2019) *The Age of Surveillance Capitalism*, Profile Books, London

# 08

# The future of consumers

> **WHAT'S COMING UP**
>
> This is the second of four chapters about the future – a matter in which businesses exercise greater control and incur greater responsibility than do individual consumers. The previous chapter was about the future of the whole business community and ranged across topics such as big data, the behavioural futures market, cryptocurrency and the changing nature of work. This chapter continues the story by looking more deeply at the future of consumers: your customers. The rapid pace of social and technological change means there's a lot going on that affects them personally and is beyond their control.
> By the end of this chapter, you will be able to:
>
> - respond to human unhappiness in ways that genuinely benefit people and communities, not just businesses;
> - create opportunities for people to experience meaningful social and emotional connections; understand parasocial relationships and their implications for marketing;
> - identify the aspects of the technology-driven future that make people feel happy and excited, and offer people a variety of ways to experience freedom.

## Sicknesses of consumer culture

*A short introduction*

Reality is in crisis and so is mental health. Like climate change, we've known this was coming for a long time but lately its symptoms are more and more visible. As consumers, we eagerly enjoy and benefit from reality-enhancing experiences and products, and we are certainly busy users of social media. We like having Siri and Alexa do things for us. We like taking delivery of our purchases on the same day we placed the order. Yet a lot of people are really unhappy and some of the skills and abilities that distinguish us as humans seem to be in decline.

As with climate change, all of us in the business community share some responsibility for what is happening. Most businesses have learned to do at least something in the area of reducing their carbon footprint. Now could be a good time to pay the same attention to the happiness and mental health of the consumers on whose purchases we rely.

## A little more depth

Every scientific study has its limitations. Sample sizes have their limits. Most studies can only hope to address one or two hypotheses. Even making scientific news available has its constraints. Despite this, evidence that there is something *wrong* with us is starting to pile up. In fact, there's so much evidence that, in the space available here, we will have to run through the headlines very quickly. If you have time for more reading, all these topics are worth exploring individually and suggestions are provided.

First, let's note the **global context**. Along with climate change, people are contending with widening economic division, the worldwide opioid epidemic (UN, 2021) and the global obesity crisis (WHO, 2021): all at least as consequential and long-lasting as COVID-19. Social change that is driven by rapid technological innovation happens within this context. Facebook launched in 2004 and the iPhone in 2007.

Technology gives birth to the attention economy and its offshoots, including one we haven't mentioned yet: the **outrage economy** (Harvey, 2019). The content that people see on social media, from news to memes and everything in between, is algorithmically directed so that people are shown more of whatever makes them engage, comment and share. Politically polarizing content, along with various kinds of hate speech and gruesome crime news, are all extremely effective in the intense contest for attention. People might *like* cat memes but what gets them *reacting* is any and all kinds of content that make them think that other humans are bad and wrong, and that the world is full of things to be feared.

There is **spiking anxiety and depression**. Poor mental health correlates with social media use. Clicking 'like' on Facebook and even updating one's own status sends self-reported mental health into decline, discovered University of California academics in a three-year study published in 2017 (Shakya *et al*). More kids than ever are on anti-depressants, and at a younger age. The UK-based National Institute for Health Research (NIHR) reported in 2020 that 'the number of 12-to-17-year-olds prescribed anti-depressants in England more than doubled between 2005 and 2017'. In 2021, the World Health Organization reported that one in 100 deaths are suicides.

In 2010, a landmark study by social psychologists at Michigan University (Konrath *et al*) registered a **catastrophic loss of empathy** among students compared with previous cohorts. Empathy had declined by a shocking 40 per cent since the 1970s, with most of the loss occurring during 2000 to 2010. In 2021, a report by Onward, a British think-tank, said that the number of Brits aged under 34 who have one or no close friends has tripled in ten years (Blagden *et al*).

**Attention spans have shrunk.** In 2015, Microsoft published a hotly discussed report (McSpadden) which appeared to show that average attention spans had shrunk dramatically, from 12 to 8 seconds, in the period from 2000. Methodologically disputed (Maybin, 2017, for example) the story persists because it seems to line up with our subjective experience that it is hard to concentrate. People check their phones a lot. They report increased difficulty with reading (Griffey, 2018).

**Creativity might be becoming more limited and conservative.** In 2013, psychologists Howard Gardner and Katie Davis published some extraordinary research. In a carefully designed study, a team analysed the creative output of teenagers – their visual art and creative writing – and compared cohorts of the early 1990s and the 2000s. The creative products of the later cohort were far more complex and more professional. What they gained in professionalism, however, they appeared to lose in imagination.

**Depersonalization is becoming a problem.** This is another huge topic that recurs later in this chapter. For now, let's just note that in 2019, a YouTuber called Jak Wilmot rather bravely wore a VR headset for a week, awake and asleep, and experienced depersonalization. The point to notice is that it was not a depersonalization or loss of reality with regard to his own self. He did not question his own existence. Rather, it was other people who became depersonalized. When he was taken outside for a walk after finally removing his headset, he remarked that passers-by appeared to be avatars.

## The unique perspective of semiotics

We just covered an expansive range of topics. I know it is a lot to take in. A substantial part of the preparation for this book entailed getting a grip on each of these subjects individually so that I could see how all the pieces fit together (and indeed this is a hallmark of semiotic research, even when one is not writing a book). Having pieced the jigsaw together, at least momentarily, as the pieces keep multiplying, here's the big picture that I can see.

> **Technology is evolving faster than our human ability to cope with it.**
> This is not the sole cause of human unhappiness, but is a major contributor. As humans, we have not yet learned to mitigate the harms or ensure the benefits of the tools that we have invented. Largely driven by business, digitally manufactured realities are exerting costs and pressures on consumers, but not yet delivering their expected rewards.

Right at the start of this chapter, I commented that reality is in crisis. It's common to say this kind of thing in conversations about fake news and its implications for democracy: subjects that are too large for this book. But not knowing whether to believe the news is just the tip of the melting iceberg. The far-reaching erosion of reality is best illustrated, as is often the case, with a story about the details of real life, so that's why I want to share with you a vivid story of Sherry Turkle's, in case you have yet to read her groundbreaking book *Alone Together* (2017).

In 2005, anthropologist Turkle took her daughter to the American Museum of Natural History in New York. Waiting in a queue, which positioned her in front of a display of living, ancient Galapagos tortoises, she entered a conversation with her daughter and then other families about whether the reality and authenticity of the living creatures had any value. The value was not very great, it turned out. Children, in particular, were unimpressed, thinking the display dull and unhygienic as well as being a shame for the tortoises. They said they would have preferred robots.

As remarkable as this is, the real punchline of this story is when Turkle later relates it to an executive at Disney. Turkle reports:

> He said he was not surprised. When Animal Kingdom opened in Orlando, populated by 'real' – that is, biological – animals, its first visitors complained

that they were not as 'realistic' as the animatronic creatures in other parts of Disneyworld. The robotic crocodiles slapped their tails and rolled their eyes – in sum, they displayed archetypal 'crocodile' behaviour. The biological crocodiles, like the Galapagos tortoises, pretty much kept to themselves.

This crisis or loss of value in reality was predicted a long time ago, by the leading thinkers in postmodernism, in the 60s and 70s (for example, Baudrillard's (1981) observation that people often like simulations more than they like 'the real thing' becomes truer with each year that passes, and there are more examples of that in this and my previous book). This is a good thing to the extent that businesses can best satisfy customer needs with simulations that are relatively low-maintenance and involve less of a burden on tortoises.

However, individuals are already experiencing a lot of the negative fall-out associated with a mass shift to life online, as when they become casualties of culture wars, or they lose their jobs in retail. Moreover, they are not yet having the mind-blowing experiences they see in Steven Spielberg's 2018 sci-fi adventure *Ready Player One* and which they eagerly await. I think there's a reward gap for consumers, and it's keenly felt when people are starting from low baseline levels of happiness.

In a moment, I'll recommend some actions for retail marketers. In the meantime, if you haven't seen *Ready Player One,* which is simultaneously dystopian and a complete shopping list of everything that consumers have ever hoped for from VR, you should see it. I'll wait.

## *Actions for retail marketers*

The story so far, at least the way I am telling it to you now, is that people are very unhappy. One of the reasons is that we have got ahead of ourselves with technology. We have invented powerful new tools around which it is possible to build wildly successful business models. But we have yet to work out how to mitigate harm and prevent system malfunction and abuse. What's more, there's a reward gap for most people. Peering into a small screen isn't, in itself, much fun, and the VR headsets available to consumers now are reminiscent of the brick-like objects that people carried around in the early days of mobile phones. We still don't have flying cars. Amazon delivery drones are something, but they are not quite what science fiction led us to expect and hope for.

I think that we in the business community, including retailers and marketers specifically, need to step up to the challenge. **It's a win-win for everyone if we make it our goal to respond to human unhappiness in ways that genuinely benefit people and communities, not just businesses.** Putting this into practice can be guided by the insight that specific kinds of unhappiness imply specific opportunities to make people feel better. I will list a few in the exercise below, but first let's consider one place that many consumers agree is 'the happiest place on Earth': Disneyland. Viewed through the lens of contemporary unhappiness, what Disney has to offer seems more relevant than ever.

'The happiest place on Earth' is such a simple proposition. It's bold and to the point. How does it deliver, and how does it meet the needs discussed here?

- **Nostalgia**
  For adults who grew up in the US, a trip to Disney is a step back into childhood: something that nearly always feels comforting and reassuring for adults. One could see how that increases in value when adults are experiencing spiking mental distress.

- **Emphasis on families**
  By 'families', Disney means real-world relationships which exist offline. There are opportunities to make family memories. A generally wholesome and innocent atmosphere.

- **A seamless experience**
  Disney parks are a protected bubble and the company has very clear prescriptions for how park staff should behave and interact with guests, so as to avoid puncturing anyone's fantasy. It's a very carefully managed environment where security is a priority. It's safe for kids. Guests aren't carrying weapons.

This is on top of all the other things that Disney does well, such as exclusive merchandise and a talent for bringing things – objects, fantasy characters – to life. I wanted to mention this specific example so we can see strategies working together as a whole package. Let me conclude this short section with a quote from the website of a community called Wholesome Games. The point of WG is to collect, curate and showcase video games that the WG community has decided are compassionate, hopeful and comforting. In an industry where the highest-profile games have traditionally revolved around macho, dark and violent themes, WG unapologetically embraces games that are peaceful and uplifting. Here's the quote: *'Sometimes it's a radical act to make dark or upsetting art, and sometimes it's radical to make hopeful art in times of adversity.'*

This is my overall advice. Let's use our skills in marketing and retailing to make shopper experiences that are compassionate and hopeful. In dark times, it's the courageous thing to do. Examples coming right up.

---

EXERCISE

If you're a small or medium-sized retailer, or even a larger company, you may feel that a worldwide decline in mental health and happiness is beyond your power to change. But there is nothing stopping us trying to improve matters. Here are some of the resources we may have as retailers:

- **Space**: premises or a digital platform.
- **Budget**. I know many retail businesses aren't wealthy, but we still have more money than the average customer, and better spending power.
- **People**. If your retail business employs more than one person, then you can benefit from teamwork.
- **Knowledge of what sells locally**: what kinds of things make people happy locally.
- **General knowledge of business and marketing:** what kinds of things make people happy everywhere.

Look at whatever resources you have available as I suggest some ways of meeting specific types of distress. Make a note in the margin of this book when you see a fit.

- **Anxiety**
  There are many ways to combat anxiety. People like 'safe spaces', which may be expressed as 'Here is a quiet spot for differently-abled shoppers to sit down' or 'This area is safe for kids to play and explore' or 'Everyone here has been verified and is a genuine account.'

- **Not being able to tell what is real**
  Give people some real-world experiences – all the better if they can become involved in creative activity. Offer some physical experiences and live performances. Music performed and heard in person is different from listening to a digital stream. Most paintings are much more impressive in

> person than they are on a screen. Give people chances to play creatively using their hands and their imaginations. Be sincere in offering this opportunity. It needs to be play first, not surveillance disguised as play. We want to rebuild trust, not undermine it.
>
> - **Loss of empathy, intimacy and human connections**
>   Give people opportunities to be kind and trustworthy to each other. If you're looking for inspiration, there's a digital product (I'm reluctant to call it a game) by Popcannibal called *Kind Words* that recently won a BAFTA in the UK, in the category 'Games Beyond Entertainment'. The default state of the software is that it plays quiet and soothing music while the user studies or does other productive work. At the click of a button, the user can choose to receive and read short messages, written by real people, in which they express anxieties and ask for emotional support. The user may reply to none or to any of these messages with their own words of sympathy or advice. People want to reach out to each other. There's more about relationships in the following section, coming next.

## Relationships

*A short introduction*

The discussion in the first section of this chapter ranges across many different kinds of human distress. Here I want to explore just one aspect in more detail. Being on social media and conducting relationships in public or semi-public virtual spaces is a source of anxiety and, at least some of the time, places stress on those relationships. One can recite examples without difficulty, because we all know people this has happened to. Users of Instagram and Facebook report constantly comparing the imperfect state of their real lives with the curated exhibitions of their friends' lifestyles. Teenage cliques and bullying behaviour used to be largely confined to school hours and are now conducted with even more fervour out of hours, over everyone's phones.

Because online communication presents many difficulties, heated and irreconcilable disputes arise between people and their families, their employers, and the friends they made on the internet yesterday. Relationships are fragile and under threat. But there are some things that marketers and customer experience designers can do to help people feel happier and promote societal benefits.

*A little more depth*

THE PROBLEM

I only have a few words available to say this, so I will get right to the point. In her book *The Age of Surveillance Capitalism* (2019), Shoshanna Zuboff diagnoses the problem as follows. It is not merely that tech makes us envious, insecure and prone to falling out with each other. Historically unprecedented use of technology to understand ourselves and each other has led to depersonalization of an even deeper kind than experienced by Jak Wilmot in his experiments with virtual reality. Zuboff pulls no punches in saying that we have evolved populations of tech users who: are unable to put down their devices and cannot tolerate being disconnected; have an unstable sense of self and feel merged with the hive mind of the internet; need to control others and are arrested in the development of their ability to handle relationships, something that normally arrives with maturity. These are strong words, but are as good an attempt as any I've seen at getting to the core of our newly developed, proliferating problems with ourselves and each other.

WHAT'S GOING WELL

Sometimes, tech platforms allow the best of humanity to shine through. In 2014, a Norwegian couple who were coping with the death of their son were suddenly overwhelmed by the realization of how much he was loved and by how many (Schaubert, 2019). 25-year-old Mats had been living with muscular dystrophy, a progressive disease. Like so many people who spend a lot of time at home, he took up video gaming from a young age. By the time he reached adulthood, he was a respected player in an established guild – a common name for a collective of players who stick together. Mats' parents knew that he was a gamer but had failed to grasp its meaning, until his father successfully contacted one guildmate to let them know of Mats' demise. Emails started to pour in. Community fundraising allowed Mats' closest friends – people he had never met in person – to fly to Norway for the funeral. In locations across Europe, there were candle-lit vigils. As Mats' father expressed it: before his eyes, an entire society, a tiny nation of people took shape. Each of these people testified that Mats had 'transcended his physical boundaries' and 'enriched people's lives'. Pouring out love is something that humans do well, and it distinguishes us from machines. Hopeful and optimistic stories that restore faith in human nature arise when technology supplies people like Mats and his friends with chances to care for each other.

## PARASOCIAL RELATIONSHIPS

We can't close this section without mentioning parasocial relationships. Perhaps you've come across news stories about lonely people forming relationships with Siri and Alexa (Vlahos, 2019) for example, or about the latest generation of robot dogs (Vincent, 2021). These are parasocial relationships, which involve non-sentient objects and sometimes artificial intelligence. People like them, they deliver emotional benefits, and they can be easily deployed on behalf of brands.

Since its launch in 2020, 33 million people paid around $60 for Nintendo's *Animal Crossing: New Horizons*: a digital product, more a toy than a game, that is full of parasocial relationships with a cast of around 400 anthropomorphic animals. At any given time, about ten of these animals are present in your local and personalized version of the game. These villagers, as you will learn to call them, remember your name and make up nicknames for you. They ask about and remember your tastes. They have their own tastes and appreciate thoughtfully chosen gifts. They seem pleased to see you and know when you last met. They throw a party for you on your birthday. Much of the game's fan community revolves around the appreciation of favourite animals, called 'dreamies'. The world of *Animal Crossing* is a cosy and safe world, where you will never have to interact with a human when you don't want to, and your little animal friends are reliably soothing and comforting, as well as responsive to the nurturing effort that you invest in them.

## *The unique perspective of semiotics*

In digital culture, **people have weakened relationships with each other, but strengthened relationships with non-human entities**. It's not our job as marketers or retailers to fix this, but we can be sensitive to changed and new consumer needs when designing shopper experiences.

Semiotics challenges us with two key questions:

1 What versions of reality have we brought into existence, and what versions are we capable of imagining?
2 What kind of a society needs this thing (technologically mediated relationships, parasocial relationships) to exist?

People are avid users of technology, which like so many things is a solution and a problem rolled into one. The relationship between **social anxiety** and social media is a chicken-and-egg situation. On the one hand, people with social anxiety blossom on social media. They are finally able to talk to strangers. They come out of their shell, because everything is anonymous and safe behind a screen, or at least some of the time. At the same time, the revelation or exposure of our real selves online is risky and generates new sources of anxiety. Our selves and relationships are not only more technologically mediated but more public. Socially anxious people often fear being judged, but if that was once an irrational fear, it is no longer. Twitter is only too ready to judge you, and so are your local law enforcement operatives and the algorithms used by your bank. This is what we have brought into existence.

Because the human spirit can withstand a lot of pressure, and because we are creative and resourceful, our best efforts to help ourselves using the tools we have now also show the versions of reality that we are capable of imagining. **People want to invest in each other emotionally.** They want to see feelings come to life. The funeral of Norwegian gamer Mats Steen showed exactly that. The tech product – a video game that some people use as a communications tool – was not the main allure. What mattered was what the tech product permitted: a pan-European event, in real time, in which real people experienced and expressed love and compassion in a way that offered comfort to each other and especially to Mats' parents.

Mass culture shows that the public is very interested in, and slightly worried about, parasocial relationships. There's an ongoing, sci-fi fuelled fantasy about robot housekeepers and what that will mean for family life; it's a theme that people find intriguing and a little troubling. But at the safer and cosier end of the spectrum, parasocial relationships with **warm, friendly voices and cute mascots are meeting real needs.** Marketers have long known how to make good mascots: the Charmin bears in the US, the Cushelle koala in the UK, the Andrex puppy, to name just a few from the household tissue industry. It's just that businesses in some wealthy nations started to treat the mascot as dated, fearing that, in the constant rush of innovation, it might seem twee or unsophisticated. But in the newer, digitally driven versions of reality that we have now, twee and unsophisticated can be good things. It's a good time for mascots to make a comeback.

### *Actions for retail marketers*

Here's my overall advice. Cater for those with social anxiety. Design shopping experiences that build in reciprocal nurturing. Don't shy away from parasocial characters and relationships: the time is right.

**Socially anxious** people can be catered for in both physical and digital stores. Some people are overcome by crowds and noise; others fear awkward interactions with others. Use tech to tell customers when your physical store is not busy. Beauty and fashion stores are sometimes good at creating calming environments. Supermarkets are usually noisy, but if you have the space, quieter zones can be created around products like books, magazines, stationery and giftware. Provide a spot for an overwhelmed person to catch their breath, and place information about in-store promotions and facilities within reach. On digital platforms, a lot of people are triggered by flashing images, animations, loud colours and busy design, especially all together. Consider accessibility at the start of your design or give people the chance to mute or adjust aspects that they find difficult.

Give people opportunities to **nurture** each other. Some supermarkets have barrels or crates near the exit where people can donate an item of their shopping to a needy family – the one in my local supermarket is usually full. There's somewhat of a trend for people 'paying it forward' in Starbucks, where the customer at the till has their order paid for by the stranger behind them. Anonymity is part of the sweetness of the deal: the kindness of strangers, with minimal anxiety triggers. Not all shoppers love this trend, as it can cause lines to move slowly in physical stores, but this is a logistical problem, not a failure of the concept. Remember that most people like to see some visible change in return for their efforts. Design something into the system that yields visible results.

**Parasocial relationships** are achievable. You don't need to be as wealthy as Apple or Nintendo and you absolutely can link parasocial appeal to a brand mascot, especially if you can place a digital version into an app or you can make it into a stuffed toy. In recent decades, US and Western European cultures seemed to think that they had grown out of cute mascots; the Pillsbury Dough Boy and the Energizer bunny started to seem like relics of former times. In Mexico, however, people have never stopped loving brand mascots, and in Japan there's no incompatibility between being an adult and loving the innocent face of Pikachu. As I wrote this chapter, I became the owner of a pink bunny rabbit called Emily, whom I 'adopted' through London-based company Loved Before. (You can see her in Figure 8.1.) The company solicits donations of pre-owned stuffed animals, which are spruced up and sanitized before being 'put up for adoption' at about half the price of a new equivalent. Proceeds support the Make a Wish Foundation that fulfils the dreams of children with terminal illnesses. The amount of good-

FIGURE 8.1  Loved Before

Emily was named after her previous owner because she always wanted whoever had her next to remember the adventures they once had. Loves honey and board games.

Reproduced with kind permission from Loved Before

will and loving expression built into this business model is hard to over-state. Emily is named after her previous owner, who wants to be remembered. Second-hand stuffed animals are not usually considered a premium product, but in the hands of Loved Before, their history adds to the value of both the toy and the organization.

> EXERCISE
>
> In this section, we've delved into some deep human emotions and needs. People are anxious and lonely and there's a lot at stake. That's why I want to end this part of the chapter by asking you to consider a similarly big topic, which is **virtue**. I am sure your business agrees that ethics are important. Perhaps you already have a corporate social responsibility (CSR) programme in place. Perhaps your company has a vision or a mission statement that

expresses ambitions such as 'helping everyone to be a little bit more healthy' or 'connecting people through technology'. Comparing these commonplace things to the gaping emotional and social needs of today's consumers, I want to suggest that we are not going far enough. It might be time to start talking about virtues: things like compassion, truth and beauty.

If your organization or brand had one key virtue from which everything else followed, what would it be? In an uncertain age, your business and your customers stand to benefit from your moral backbone.

## Future objects of desire

*A short introduction*

The final part of this chapter is about wants and the things we long for. Specifically, it is about the products, services and experiences we will want *in the future*, which are largely going to be conceived and designed by the business community rather than its customers. As noted earlier, there seems to be a noticeable gap between the things that consumers feel they were led to expect from a digital revolution and the things they actually have. I can get a coffee and a sandwich delivered in record time, but I don't have powers of mind control, and I can't cheat death, halt climate change or fly to the Moon. Despite the frustrations of the nascent version of the future that we've managed to develop so far, many people remain very happy and excited about technology-assisted futures that could come to exist. At the heart of this happiness and excitement is a longing for freedom.

*A little more depth*

Let's get straight down to business. Below are 12 ways in which affluent consumers will use their purchasing power to access the future of their dreams, if only business will keep inventing ways to make it available to them.

1 **Luxury.** Consumers who are attracted to luxury will continue to want the best of everything: the best watch, the best winter coat. In a world of over-processed products, there will be increased desire for material and moral **purity** of ingredients and processes.

2. **Exclusive access** to hard-to-get goods and services. Not everyone will be able to take a leisure flight into space with Richard Branson, Jeff Bezos or Elon Musk, but some people will.

3. **Objects that are precious** because they are unique will continue to be valued: jewels, some works of art. Non-fungible tokens (NFTs) create new kinds of authenticity of digital objects, creating more rare objects for people to collect and own.

4. Seeing **things that have never been seen before**. This is a really craveable experience. This is why Jeff Bezos talks about wanting to see Earth from the window of a spaceship, because seeing something with your own eyes is different from looking at a picture. It's also why gamers want to play the latest fantasy games before they are ruined with spoiler videos all over YouTube.

5. Being able to **live in desirable areas**. Cities aren't going to die. They will continue to act as magnets for people with money who want to be under an increasingly sophisticated digital umbrella. (There's a section in Chapter 10 on smart cities.)

6. Things that **improve one's digital self or one's life online**, such as prime virtual real estate and exclusive digital fashions. Valuable real estate exists in *Decentraland*, a VR platform and traversable virtual space that is decentralized but has high barriers to entry. In digital fashion, technology is still at an early stage, but the hope is that eventually digital couture will be fully wearable.

7. **Smart devices.** People want smart homes and futuristic cars. Some of the people who are now among the world's richest and most able to access cutting-edge technology grew up watching futuristic fantasies on TV. Since childhood, they have looked forward to being waited on hand and foot by homes and vehicles able to anticipate their every need.

8. Better ways to **meet people**. Networking will grow in importance. People will pay for dating and introductions technology that delivers more certain results than Tinder. New markets for buying information about other people will open up, such as paying to know more about sperm donors and surrogates.

9. **Privacy, anonymity.** As life becomes increasingly more public, unfolding in digital space in front of a mass audience, people will pay more for privacy. Some will pay significant premiums to become invisible to the gaze of the public and the state, appearing to drop off the radar.

10  Already, people cannot wait to spend on premium healthcare and biotech: **life-extending and life-preserving services**. That means not only the most cutting-edge medicine when one is ill, but also enhancement technologies, such as nootropics and smart drugs, assisted reproductive technology, and genetic engineering.

11  Opportunities for material **self-improvement**, for example through education and entrepreneurial development. There will be more uptake of services such as media training and private coaches and mentors.

12  All services that increase one's ability to **attract desirable things** to oneself, which is almost but not quite the same as being wealthy. Its simplest expression is found in things like increasingly fast delivery services, but could also manifest as membership of an exclusive community that gets access to cutting-edge content.

## *The unique perspective of semiotics*

The long list of desiderata above amounts to a set of observations, but they are not yet analysis. Semiotic thinking begins at the point where we ask what new version of reality these items add up to and what overall purpose they serve for the people who believe in, subscribe to and invest in them.

When I look at the big picture, I see people who are excited because they feel that we are on the brink of something huge in the evolution of civilization. It might have been Yuval Noah Harari (2016) who said that when future generations look back at today, they will see a crucial moment when for the first time, and around the globe, everyone became connected to everyone else. The future has only just begun, yet it is full of barely imaginable rewards and threats.

I want to briefly mention a study conducted by Ericsson in 2019. It surveyed around 12,000 people spread across 15 major cities and asked them how they envisioned life in 2030. This isn't in itself unique, although it is one of the larger studies of its kind, but for me it distinguished itself with its remarks on privacy. Ericsson described around half the sample as post-privacy consumers. These consumers recognize that right now, privacy and data protection can be hard to achieve. They are confident that, in the future, laws and technology will tighten up, the better to protect privacy. At the same time, they seem very willing to hand over privacy, for example in the form of their own biodata. They reasonably expect that there will be more requests for this in the future and that privacy as we know it now will cease to exist. It does not dampen their enthusiasm. These respondents were the most enthusiastic about longed-for developments such as being able to operate software with one's mind.

I mention the Ericsson story because I see it as capturing something in the imaginations of consumers who are tech- and future-enthusiasts. What I see is a reach for freedom. What's more, this freedom has two distinct strands. There is freedom-from and freedom-to: freedom from theft, data leaks, annoying inconveniences, unwanted interference in people's relationships with technology; freedom to have new experiences, pursue new thrills, enjoy new benefits, see newly created things and go to newly created places. The Ericsson respondents want the freedom-from and the freedom-to, and they do not see one as the necessary price of the other.

## Actions for retail marketers

The twin concepts of freedom-from and freedom-to help us to think in a strategic way about what we could be doing as marketers. Further thought led me to view freedom-from as attempts to escape, while freedom-to is more like flight: it is a positive movement towards something. I see the 12 ways to buy a better life, listed at the start of this section, as organized into two kinds of escape and two kinds of flight. These concepts are distinct, yet broad enough to accommodate retailers and marketing efforts of all sizes.

### ESCAPE (BACK) TO REALITY

If you are checking off the list, here we encounter item 1, luxury, and item 3, precious and authentic objects, which can include newly minted kinds of authentic objects, such as NFTs. This is a form of resistance against mass marketing and mass production. It has been around for a long time and survives because objects that are unique and painstakingly crafted by hand remain at a premium in digital culture, which is nothing if not 'mass'. Use your store, buying power or marketing resources to offer the customer a temporary retreat into real things, created and loved by real people. This could be anything from a unique piece of furniture made by a master craftsperson to a kit that lets shoppers make things themselves.

### ESCAPE FROM THE BODY

Here we find items 6, things that improve your digital self or your life online, 8, better ways to meet people, and 10, augmented health services. All paid-up members of digital culture know that bodies hold a person back. With a very few exceptions, our bodies are older, heavier, poorer and less attractive than our avatars. Bodies are high-maintenance, difficult to transport and only function in perfect health some of the time. If you have a digital platform, find some ways for friend groups and pairs to shop together while maintaining the most presentable, digitally enhanced, 'best' version of themselves. If you have physical premises, make a priority of designing accessibility into the shopper experience, so that people can feel confident that their bodies aren't standing in the way between them and something fun.

FLY TO THE FUTURE
Here we find several items from the original list. They are 2, exclusive access, such as climbing aboard a spaceship, 5, living in desirable areas, 7, smart devices, and 12, attracting desirable things. All these are forms of wish fulfilment, in which we continue to live the lives we have now, on the Earth we have now, but with access to its most pleasing and comfortable aspects. Because of rapid technological change, the future feels very close and there's a sense that exclusive and premium services and objects function as tickets to that future. The spaceship will be leaving soon, and people want to be the first to climb aboard. But even smaller stores can make wishes come true in a small way, whether it's through fast, local delivery, or through encouraging fantasy or providing immersion.

FLY TO A NEW EDEN
Lastly, here we have item 4, seeing things that have never been seen before, often with the expectation of personal change, item 9, privacy and anonymity and item 11, opportunities for material self-improvement – that is, actually making your life better rather than making your avatar look better. The key point I want to make here is that many people share a sense that we have irreversibly ruined the Earth, or ruined society, or ourselves. There's a longing to start again, to have a second chance, to refresh nature and beauty, to make better choices, to find personal and maybe spiritual fulfilment. There's appeal in the idea of making past errors disappear and starting over. If your business doesn't have the ambition of helping people disappear or terraforming Mars, there are still dozens of ways to sell the idea of a fresh start: plants and seedlings, flowering tea – anything that grows and blooms; breakfast time as a new start to each day; gyms' and self-help programmes' fresh starts.

> **EXERCISE**
>
> People fantasize about the future. They fantasize about their possible and future selves and about the lives they could be living. Some of them have the disposable income to buy a little bit of the future and make it their own. Throughout this chapter, I've tried to regularly make suggestions that can be implemented even by companies that are not tech giants. At this point, it's your turn to take a look at your business and ask these key questions:
>
> - What can you offer that is real, authentic and hand-crafted? Think of some ways to market the product, service or experience as an escape from modern uncertainties and a return 'back' to a time when things were made with care.
>
> - How are your customers being held back by their physical bodies? Is anyone excluding themselves from your store or services because they think they are too old, too anxious, too differently abled or too far away? What can you do to reach out and include them?
>
> - What can you do to help customers feel that they are enjoying some of the benefits of the modern age? What can you do for them that previously they would have had to do themselves? Look for opportunities to surprise and delight with services that go the extra mile, or novelties that work better than expected.
>
> - If your customers could make a fresh start, what would it be like? Would it be improving their health, post-pandemic? If they have an account with you, would they like to be able to erase or hide the history of that account? Would they like your digital store to stop showing them sugary snacks and instead promote the healthier items in their own dietary repertoire, even though and indeed because of the fact that they mostly order snacks?
>
> Make a list. See what you can do.

# References

Baudrillard, J (1995) *Simulacra and Simulation*, The University of Michigan Press, Ann Arbor

Blagden, J, Tanner, W and Krasniqi, F (2021) Social fabric: Age of alienation, *Onward*, https://www.ukonward.com/reports/age-of-alienation/ (archived at https://perma.cc/94K6-LCZ4)

Ericsson (2019) 10 hot consumer trends 2030 – the internet of senses, https://www.ericsson.com/en/reports-and-papers/consumerlab/reports/10-hot-consumer-trends-2030 (archived at https://perma.cc/AJD9-CWZ8)

Gardner, H and Davis, K (2013). *The App Generation: How today's youth navigate identity, intimacy, and imagination in a digital world*, Yale University Press, New Haven

Griffey, H (2018). The lost art of concentration: being distracted in a digital world, *Guardian*, https://www.theguardian.com/lifeandstyle/2018/oct/14/the-lost-art-of-concentration-being-distracted-in-a-digital-world (archived at https://perma.cc/8WQD-NPUN)

Harari, Y N (2016) *Homo Deus: A brief history of tomorrow*, Harvill Secker, London

Harvey, D (2019). The outrage economy, *20MinutesIntoTheFuture*, https://medium.com/20minutesintothefuture/the-outrage-economy-870a23f65d9c (archived at https://perma.cc/WE6D-8BEH)

Konrath S H, O'Brien E H, Hsing C (2011) Changes in dispositional empathy in American college students over time: a meta-analysis, *Personality and Social Psychology Review*, **15** (2), pp 180–98

Maybin, S (2017) Busting the attention span myth, *BBC News*, 10 Mar, https://www.bbc.co.uk/news/health-38896790 (archived at https://perma.cc/7UP3-C4N5)

McSpadden, K (2015). You now have a shorter attention span than a goldfish, *Time*, https://time.com/3858309/attention-spans-goldfish/ (archived at https://perma.cc/D9VK-ZKQL)

NIHR (2020) Teenagers' use of antidepressants is rising with variations across regions and ethnic groups, https://evidence.nihr.ac.uk/alert/teenagers-use-of-antidepressants-is-rising-with-variations-across-regions-and-ethnic-groups/ (archived at https://perma.cc/2GVC-L4GG)

Schaubert, V (2019) My disabled son's amazing gaming life in the World of Warcraft, *BBC News*, 7 Feb, https://www.bbc.co.uk/news/disability-47064773 (archived at https://perma.cc/LY3L-E7LH)

Shakya, H B, Christakis, N A (2017) Association of Facebook use with compromised well-being: a longitudinal study, *American Journal of Epidemiology*, **185** (3), pp 203–11

Turkle, S (2017) *Alone Together*, Basic Books, New York

United Nations (2021) UN responds to the global opioid crisis, https://www.un.org/en/delegate/un-responds-global-opioid-crisis (archived at https://perma.cc/2X9B-38HU)

Vincent, J (2021). This $2,700 robot dog will carry a single bottle of water for you, *The Verge*, https://www.theverge.com/2021/6/10/22527413/tiny-robot-dog-unitree-robotics-go1 (archived at https://perma.cc/W6PF-J5J9)

Vlahos, J (2019) Hey Alexa, I'm lonely – why it's good to talk to your voice assistant, *inews*, https://inews.co.uk/news/technology/alexa-amazon-voice-assistant-loneliness-281361 (archived at https://perma.cc/RSM4-PXTY)

World Health Organization (2021) (1) Obesity and overweight, https://www.who.int/news-room/fact-sheets/detail/obesity-and-overweight (archived at https://perma.cc/PU64-NCBC)

WHO (2021) (2) One in 100 deaths is by suicide, https://www.who.int/news/item/17-06-2021-one-in-100-deaths-is-by-suicide (archived at https://perma.cc/DD2E-TUKY)

Wilmot, J (2019) I spent a week in a VR headset, here's what happened, vlog, https://youtu.be/BGRY14znFxY (archived at https://perma.cc/VHB6-RYPY)

Zuboff, S (2019) *The Age of Surveillance Capitalism*, Profile Books, London

# 09

# The future of retail

> **WHAT'S COMING UP**
>
> In this chapter, we get to grips with the rapidly developing, exciting and occasionally scary future of the retail sector. By the end of this chapter, you will be able to:
>
> - describe an ecosystem and say how it is different from omnichannel marketing, and understand how to apply this distinction to your business;
> - appreciate the radically different approach to retailing that is demonstrated by the large tech companies in China, which are leading the way;
> - future-proof a traditional grocery store or small physical store by making it relevant to the expectations of today's and tomorrow's consumers;
> - branch out with a digital presence in a way that avoids common mistakes and offers the best return on investment;
> - design a fully integrated online/offline shopper experience.

## Digital ecosystems

### A short introduction

*Ecosystem* is not just a new, more fancy word for omnichannel marketing. It signifies a completely different perspective on retailing, in which the goal is to have your consumer logged in to your business empire at all times, eschewing competitors. A 'good' ecosystem gives people as few reasons as possible to go outside the system, accomplishing all their daily tasks within it. Survival and competition in this context require consumer-facing businesses to work extra hard at branding. If you have a smaller business, you can also leverage the human face of your business, which is the one thing that ecosystems struggle with.

### A little more depth

Big tech companies change everything they touch. They change health, education, banking and retail, among many others. They cause radical change because they have the money to make things happen, but more importantly because they are not limited by ideas of 'the way we have always done things' in the sectors they colonize, or rejuvenate, depending on how you look at it.

This situation leaves traditional retailers, for whom retail is their only business, in doubt and uncertainty. Some are trying to cope by embracing omnichannel marketing, which means ensuring that you have a coherent presence on lots of platforms and media. Other businesses are still at the point of branching out and 'going online', often by designing websites with architecture that mimics physical stores. These actions are useful and I will not decline to give you advice on how to make the best of them. But at the same time, being fully future-facing means swallowing some difficult truths, such as the fact that the big players of the digital age do not care very much about marketing funnels, channels and e-commerce (see Zakkour and Dudarenok, 2019, for example). In their view, these are already redundant concepts. What they care about is ecosystems.

An ecosystem is a group of entities, in this case, businesses, that are in an interdependent relationship. They make money by co-operating so as to benefit from each other's capabilities. They aim to offer the consumer a complete ecology in which all their shopping, banking, household, leisure and work-related problems can be solved without ever having to leave the system. The customer is always logged in and does not depart.

Chinese businesses are leading the way towards the ecosystem. The Western business community has historically respected independence, expertise and vertical integration. Transport is not like selling groceries. Banking is not like entertainment. But the core competence of the successful Chinese business is making money.[1] This single-minded focus and lack of 'preciousness', as well as other misunderstood aspects of Chinese business culture, such as the common sense of what Westerners call 'copying',[2] all allow ecosystems to evolve. This is how Jack Ma grew the large ecosystem of Alibaba Group, comprising several different kinds of retail (Tmall,

Taobao, AliExpress, grocery store chain Freshippo, Lazada), consumer finance (Ant Financial, Alipay), cloud computing (Alibaba Cloud), entertainment, logistics and many more. It is an empire that no longer has Jack Ma on the board and is being 'rectified' (broken apart and its control redistributed) in the midst of an anti-trust government crackdown, but it remains the best example the global business community has yet seen of ecosystem thinking and profits.

## The unique perspective of semiotics

Let's ask some semiotic questions about what kinds of reality are being ushered in, and who they benefit. You can already see how a cleverly designed ecosystem benefits its constituent businesses. But how does it benefit the consumer? What good is it to them if the services they use every day are all owned by the same company? Consumers like ecosystems because they hate having to log into things and find passwords. An often-quoted statistic[3] is that one-third of all abandoned baskets in e-commerce are dropped when the system requires the consumer to enter a password. Other disliked aspects of online shopping that can trigger abandonment are the requirement to make an account and discovering an unexpected charge, such as a delivery fee, that wasn't factored into the customer's idea of the price. Of course consumers like ecosystems. They are great at removing obstacles, however tiny, that stand in between them and their desiderata.

The emergence of ecosystems is changing the shape of retail and it is also changing shopping. A well-functioning ecosystem incentivizes consumers not to shop around. There are lots of mechanisms that encourage staying within the system, including but not limited to: accumulating loyalty points, being able to see a complete historical record of purchases and receiving rewards in exchange for profile-building activities such as leaving comments and reviews. But there's more to it than this. The retail ecosystems implicitly understand that not all shopping is particularly interesting to the consumer. If I'm buying a pair of shoes, I might be highly motivated to view several alternatives and carefully read customer reviews. Not all purchases are shoes, though. My household consumes a lot of tea and the go-to product is Twinings Assam. Partly due to writing this book, I signed up for an Amazon subscription service, which will automatically send me four large boxes of this exact tea on a three-monthly schedule. In theory, I'll never again run out of tea or face the inconvenience of going out to get more. This is fully automated replenishment shopping.

This situation represents a problem for brands. At first glance, it looks like a win for Twinings, and it is certainly a win for Amazon. But the combination of two factors – the compelling ease and comfort of the large ecosystem plus the 'subscribe now and never think about it again' nature of automated replenishment shopping – means that there's a risk of everything merging into everything else. The tea starts to lose distinctiveness as a brand at the moment when I decide as a shopper to cease making choices concerning tea. Replenishment shopping is indistinguishable from being asleep. All stores are Amazon (or Tmall or JD.com). In this situation, brands and retailers that are not already the consumer's default choice have to work hard to stay visible and exert any appeal. There may be only two points of leverage: becoming better at branding – that is, becoming a much more distinctive brand with a clearer USP – and engaging people's feelings.

## Actions for retail marketers

Over the decades, I've worked with dozens if not hundreds of brands. Surprisingly few companies have a very clear sense of why their brands exist and how they are different from competitors. If that's you, now is the time to sort it out. Here are three reasons why it's time to pay extra attention to **branding**.

1. Finding your USP has never been more important because your competition is more intense and more global. Whether you are going it alone or planning to become part of someone else's ecosystem, you are going to be up against a lot of other brands, and you need to be 100 per cent certain how your brand is different.
2. Everyone will tell you that succeeding in today's ecosystems and especially in big shopping festivals is going to mean making a lot of videos, creating opportunities for live streaming, and ensuring online-offline integration. This is all perfectly correct, but you are not going to know where to start unless you have a clear vision for your brand and know what it stands for.
3. Building your own digital retail platform is ambitious when you are going up against companies like Amazon, but it can be done. Etsy was started in 2005 by iospace, a company of three people who built the site in as many months. In 2021, Etsy announced its largest takeover yet; a fashion reselling business called Depop, for which Etsy has paid $1.63 billion.[4] As it has grown, Etsy has faced challenges, such as complaints

that the platform has opened itself to drop-shipping and counterfeit goods. The reason why shoppers love Etsy consists in the idea of handmade items sold by the original craftsperson. Etsy has always known this (Malik, 2013), even when it was first setting off down the road of selling factory-made goods. The value of the brand, to customers, is the human connection.

Shoppers like Etsy because of the **feelings** it evokes. I've used the UK version several times (giftware, food, COVID-19 masks, stationery, even toilet cleaner) and, in my experience, the vendors have mostly, if not exclusively, been the same people who made the product, and all of them have gone out of their way to emphasize that they are real, individual humans and not faceless corporations. They've achieved this through various methods such as handwritten notes enclosed with the parcel, using both my and their names in the message; unexpected gifts with purchases (an unexpected GWP comes off as thoughtful; a GWP as a marketing mechanism at point-of-purchase feels like marketing); on the product page, natural-looking photos of the vendor and a rough indication of where they live. All of this creates a feeling of buying from a real human being with real feelings and a real life. This is increasingly valuable in an age where algorithms and big data are making shopping automated and faceless.

### EXERCISE

Here's a short checklist of ecosystem questions for your business:

- What is your brand's USP? What is the one thing that makes it unlike competitors?
- If you plan to place your branded product or smaller retail business on someone else's ecosystem, have you found anything that it offers to help you create more of a branded presence? For example, in the games industry, Steam (owned by Valve) and Epic Games (40 per cent owned by Tencent) regularly hold 'publisher sales', which introduce shoppers to the full range of products offered by publishing companies who have at least one hit product that consumers recognize.
- Are you in a position to place your product or retail business in a smaller ecosystem? Despite the best efforts of large ecosystems, people can be triggered to look elsewhere, especially when their 'home' system is

> perceived to have done something wrong. Amazon, for example, has experienced negative press concerning a fine of $888 million by the EU over mishandling of data and privacy (Bodoni, 2021). A smaller system carries fewer brands, giving yours a better chance of visibility.
> 
> - What or who can you add to your brand to help it seem more real, personal and human?

## 'I have a traditional grocery store or a small physical store'

### A short introduction

Let's say that you have a traditional kind of store. It has physical premises, the size of which may be generous or modest. It has all the usual kinds of things found in traditional stores: physical products that are for sale, aisles, fixtures, in-store signage, tills and, of course, packaging. Bigger stores, such as the larger supermarkets, may also have trolleys, car parks and service counters. This section suggests some ways to help your store become more future-facing.

### A little more depth

It's time we talked about Freshippo, formerly known within China as Hema. It is one of the retail arms of Alibaba – specifically, the arm dealing with physical stores and fresh groceries. Freshippo owes some of its success to the large ecosystem of which it is a small part, and I will return to it in the next chapter when we discuss smart cities. For now, let's just observe that it embodies a lot of future-facing ideas that could be implemented by independent competitors. There are currently around 250 Freshippo stores in China (Statista, 2021). If you are outside China, you can watch videos about Freshippo on Alibaba's YouTube channel.

What's exciting about Freshippo from the shopper's point of view? It has two stand-out features: novelty and choice. Novelty is found in Freshippo's deployment of the latest in-store technology. Of course, novelty soon wears off, but right now there's still a feeling of newness to Freshippo's constellation of technologies, such as payment mechanisms that use face recognition and using QR codes to select and place products in a virtual basket.

Novelty is also found in the activity at ceiling height: the shopper who looks up will see bags of groceries travelling around the store, suspended from a kind of monorail. The reason they are there is because each store doubles as a fulfilment centre. This is where choice comes in. There's a huge effort to offer shoppers as many choices as possible, not just in the products themselves but in the way that they shop. You can go into a Freshippo store and shop in a traditional way, carrying a physical basket, paying at a self-service checkout and leaving with your groceries in your hand. Alternatively, you can order in store or remotely using the app and have your groceries delivered to you within 30 minutes, if you live within a 3 km radius. Some stores have on-site restaurants, where you may be served by a robot waiter.[5] These innovations are all driven by technology rather than consumer need, in the sense that I don't think any consumer specifically asked for robot waiters and it's not clear how robot waiters benefit the consumer apart from the novelty value. Despite this, we can see that Freshippo aims to dazzle shoppers with exciting futurism and is, in fact, a good example of what Jack Ma called 'New Retail', back in 2017,[6] before he disappeared from public view.

## The unique perspective of semiotics

Here's why I'm telling you about Freshippo, even though your business might be on a tighter budget and less high-tech. Most retailers, the kind I work with every day, are using *legacy* business models. The result of this is that traditional ways of shopping are top of mind and hard to dislodge, while newer aspects of retail, such as paying attention to customer experience, are bolted on as an afterthought. The practical consequence of this is that **the experience supports the shopping**. The 'experience', such as it may be, whether in the form of seasonal decorations or a brand rep handing out tiny food samples, is added on to the core behaviours and transactions that we call shopping, in the hope of stimulating more shopping.

I don't think that Freshippo is doing everything perfectly, at least, not yet. For now, it is very driven by technology and not by consumer need, which can ultimately feel a bit cold (robot waiters are novel but not as emotionally warm as their human counterparts). However, it does lead me to think that if we want to compete with these innovative retailers, we might have to reverse the usual equation, so that **the shopping supports the experience**. If you watch any of the Freshippo videos on YouTube, you can see how spectacular it is. The experience is front and centre, and the only way the customer is going to be able to enjoy to the fullest Freshippo's novelties and delights is by making purchases.

It reminds me also of things like gift shops at museums and other attractions. It is not that the experience supports the shopping – if I wanted a toy dinosaur, I could order one from an online store, I don't need to go to the Natural History Museum to get it. Rather, the shopping supports the experience. The Natural History Museum in London is a pretty exciting place. I can learn new things and see things there that I cannot see anywhere else. It's a fun place to visit, and my enjoyment is rounded out by using all the facilities, such as eating a meal in the café and buying something from the gift shop. A toy velociraptor is sitting on my desk as I write. I didn't need it, but I enjoy it now it's here, and it added value to my day out.

I know, your high street store may not be a world-class entertainment destination. But smaller, traditional stores can still benefit from thinking about how to make shopping support the customer's experience, rather than the other way around. Tips are coming right up.

## Actions for retail marketers

Here are seven suggestions that you can try in order to introduce an in-store experience that is supported by shopping.

1 **Store exteriors and entrances** can be a good spot for children's entertainment, such as those rocking-horse rides that sit atop a large spring. We should make adult-sized ones. It would be very Instagrammable.
2 **Supermarket trolleys** are disliked, anonymous and dysfunctional. But boats have names, and park benches are often dedicated to someone. Kids attach streamers to their bicycles and customize their school books with stickers. Customers will do this for you, if you let them.
3 **Service counters** are often the most profitable areas of stores and have great potential for fun, because of the element of theatre. Italian food brand Sacla amazed consumers by placing opera singers disguised as staff members in supermarkets and even school cafeterias.[7]
4 **Zones, aisles and in-store signs** need not be limited to navigation. They could additionally function as checkpoints: when I arrive at the breakfast cereal aisle, I could scan a QR code or take a photo of the sign to mark

that I was there and collect a token or reward. Maybe there's an extra reward attached to visiting all the aisles or departments.

5 **Very small spaces** such as kiosks could offer improved customer interactions. Shopkeeper Rajith Manikath has a traditional kiosk (an open-fronted hut) in central London. He sells snacks, tobacco and water but he gives away yoga advice (Worthington, 2019). A newer definition of 'kiosk' is the over-sized touch screen you see in fast food restaurants. Have you ever noticed that they aren't very accessible (Hyowon, 2020)? Adding accessibility features differentiates your brand.

6 **Furniture** such as fixtures, bins and tables always offers chances to do something fun and different. When was the last time you visited a pick-your-own fruit and vegetable farm? Parkside Farm in the UK grows strawberries at table-top height to save people from bending down (Sims and McCabe, 2021).

7 **Packaging** and even **shopping bags** can be precious objects in their own right, when they are done well. At my house, some of these items are saved or are kept handy because they stand out from the crowd. There are a couple of particularly attractive hessian bags by my local supermarket, with seasonal designs, and for ages I kept a small carton that some fudge came in, because I loved the ingenious folding mechanism in the lid.

Just one of these things on its own could win affection if it is done well. A store that managed to do all of them would be genuinely offering an experience that is supported by shopping.

---

**EXERCISE**

Take a look around your store, in person, not on a spreadsheet. Do some shopping. Park your car, get a trolley, find some groceries, queue for the till. At each stage, rather than asking, 'What positive customer experience could we bolt on to this shopper journey?', ask, 'What shopping opportunities can we make available that will enhance the experience of attending the store?' If you are serious about competing with next-generation stores such as Freshippo, this perspective may help you to think creatively.

## 'I am branching out with a digital presence'

### A short introduction

Perhaps you have a physical store, or chain of stores, and you know that you need to get online, if only because everyone else is doing it. This section offers some practical tips for operating conventional e-commerce successfully and adds a few creative challenges in case you are feeling ambitious.

### A little more depth

The story I am going to tell you in this section has two parts. One part is the story I believe you want, because people keep asking me about it. There's a common set of questions that goes like this:

- Which words, images or other semiotic signs should we use on our website?
- We want to make 15-second videos for use on social media platforms such as Instagram. What should be in them?
- Digital packaging: how can we make ours look as good as possible for Amazon?

These are all questions that have answers, and we can discuss them. But they may not be the most future-facing questions. The fact is, most retail websites function reasonably well, because they are nearly all built according to the same design principles. They are very similar in architecture. The standard architecture, by convention rather than necessity, mimics a physical store. The landing page is the shop window. The listing page is exactly like looking at a supermarket shelf or fixture. Pack shots are arranged in neat rows, encouraging the consumer to choose the brand they always choose, by visually scanning through thumbnail images. The product page is about reading the packaging, even though few shoppers do this in physical stores. Then there is checkout, which is modelled on the traditional store in a very obvious way, complete with a basket and a pain point when you have to pull out your credit card.

    E-commerce sites are also very similar in appearance. There are websites with attractive photography and pleasing animations, yet I don't buy from them because the attractiveness of the website doesn't make the product more interesting. On the other hand, there's one UK company with whom I've probably spent a few hundred pounds over the last couple of years and their website looks bad. The main problem is that the landing page is cluttered and ugly. Despite this, I keep giving them money. The brand story is pleasing, customer service is excellent, and there are always new products to discover. In fact, the company has been one of the retail success stories of the pandemic. I will not name the company here; I simply invite you to notice that there's more to successful e-commerce than conformity.

If you would like to avoid discussion of this situation and its alternatives, instead getting some simple and direct answers to the above questions, please skip to the heading 'Actions for retail marketers'. But if you are interested in doing things a little differently, read on.

## The unique perspective of semiotics

Semiotics obliges us to ask *why* we are bolting on a digital component. Reasons that clearly serve the brand and consumers are better than doing it out of a feeling of needing to fall in line with competitors. Here are some examples of how that works.

### 1) GIVE SHOPPERS ACTIVITIES THAT FEEL MORE COLLABORATIVE THAN PASSIVELY VIEWING PRODUCTS AND PLACING THEM IN A BASKET

I recently ordered a PC from a British company called PC Specialist. It is not as difficult as you might think to make computers look sexy and the website's landing page has its fair share of colourful images. But the centre is reserved for a set of buttons showing things that the shopper can *do* on the website, that goes beyond passively viewing. Options include 'Configure a laptop' and 'Configure a server'. Of course, the process ends with a sale and the 'configure' buttons take the shopper through a question-and-answer process that replaces the conversation one might otherwise have with a live sales assistant, but, despite this, it feels quite creative and is idiot-proofed so that those of us who don't build PCs every day are saved from making bad technical decisions.

### 2) TELL A STORY

Most e-commerce sites don't do this, because as Zakkour and Dudarenok (2019) point out, 'all e-commerce today is search, but you can't find a story by searching.' Humans are inherently interested in stories – some anthropologists think that storytelling is our defining feature. A good story will keep people returning to your digital store.

In the previous chapter, I talked about Loved Before, which has a terrific human-interest story wrapped around second-hand soft toys (which would otherwise be difficult to sell). Another example of a storied digital store is the merchandise stores of content creators who are all individuals and therefore 'real people', to use everyday language.

A friend of mine is an avid chess fan and follows a particular chess content creator on YouTube. He has never 'donated' or 'tipped', although the creator accepts these types of payment. However, when directed to the creator's merchandise store (created on Shopify), he purchased a T-shirt and a mug, priced beyond what he would have paid for more weakly branded items sold in a supermarket. In his words, buying a T-shirt 'felt different' than simply tipping or donating. It embodied the feel-good factor of supporting a loved creator but at the same time felt like a 'real' and 'genuine' transaction.

Here we have stories and products working together to boost each other's value. People will not always hand over cash *just* for a good story, but if you have a good story *and* some products, the story sells the products and keeps people coming back for more.

3) TAKE THE STORE TO THE CONSUMER RATHER THAN WAITING FOR THEM TO COME TO YOU

A good example is the 'Shop Now' button that you can install on your Instagram posts, making them 'shoppable'. People spend time on Instagram because they like Instagram. They are not trying to shop or 'go shopping'; they are there to enjoy themselves. Your job is to catch them in a moment when they are feeling happy, and make purchasing (usually of a specific item) available to them. This is a philosophical shift. As digital culture grows and spreads, shopping ceases to be a discrete activity and becomes a built-in feature of daily life. It's not something you perform, it's something that is independently and constantly present, like time or weather.

## Actions for retail marketers

If the part you've been waiting for in this section is some simple, easy-to-apply rules that will help you succeed in a conventional way, according to the 'normal' rules of e-commerce, here they are.

CONVENTIONAL E-STORES

These are digital replicants of an idealized physical store. Your landing page is the shop window. You wouldn't clutter the window of a physical store with piles of random packages. Shop windows are usually reserved for a simpler display that captures the brand's personality or conveys a message about how the customer will feel when they enter. I earlier mentioned the food brand Sacla. The landing page of their US website demonstrates this perfectly. The brand mark is large and clear. The colours are inviting. The vegetables successfully convey what's appealing about Sacla products. The products themselves are limited to just two items – not the entire range. The overall balance of the composition is designed to stimulate the viewer's appetite and emotions, not to bombard them with information.

### LANGUAGE

Throughout your e-commerce site, try to use **natural language** (and this applies to physical stores as well). Use words and phrases that shoppers use, rather than professional marketers. A well-known confectionery brand plastered its e-commerce site with corporate language that consumers simply don't use, such as 'bagged sweets', 'gift packs' and instructions to 'mark an occasion' and 'celebrate with loved ones'. For those of us in marketing and retail, phrases like 'bagged sweets' and 'occasions' eventually affect the way we think and speak, but this puts distance between our brands and the public. Close the gap by thinking about what your customers want from your products and how *they* think and talk about these things. People don't care too much whether sweets come in bags, a tube or some other mechanism when what's really affecting their decision is the difference between mints, fudge and chocolate. Similarly, 'gift' is fine but 'gift pack' is a business concept. 'Happy Diwali' is better than 'Celebrate an occasion'.

### PRODUCT PAGES

My best advice to you concerning product pages is to use the space to tell people about the aspects of the product that you know they care about, based on customer feedback or market research. Amazon does a great job with its 'True to Size' tag on clothing pages, letting customers know that the sizes listed on the page reflect customers' real-world expectations of sizes. Clicking on the tag uncovers a bar chart showing exactly how many customers agreed that the product is 'true to size', accompanied by helpful quotes. This overcomes a common problem that consumers encounter when buying clothes online. Other problems that people regularly encounter: less-than-reputable manufacturers give misleading information about the fabric content of clothes ('cotton' garments turn out to be nylon); digital books are 'stuffed' with irrelevant content (Flood, 2019); shoppers are landed with unexpected and unpredictable customs charges when ordering from overseas.

## VIDEOS

Are you thinking of making 15-second videos for social media? It might sound obvious, but one thing that video is good for is capturing things that move. Begin by showing the end result (a plate of food, a person decked in hand-made jewellery, a dazzling drawing), then use most of your 15 seconds to show how the item is made or used. Make it look easy – you are selling the process just as much as the end result. At the very end, return to the image you started with.

## PACKAGING

Digital packaging needs to be bright and clear, for easy recognition. This much you doubtless know already; I will simply add that there are culturally variable opportunities to do things differently. While it is the norm for listings pages on Western sites to simply show a series of pack shots, each surrounded by white space, on Chinese sites such as Tmall, it's common to surround that pack shot with a coloured frame, often including text. The text often refers to a price discount, or conveys other attractive information. This is possible on sites that use Simplified Chinese (and Japanese Kanji, and Korean Hangul) because characters convey a lot of information while taking up hardly any space, in strong contrast to the Roman letters and English words that you are reading now. Where this advantage exists, use it.

You can read more about e-commerce design in Chapter 11.

---

### EXERCISE

If you have a conventional online presence or are planning to open a digital store using a ready-made architecture such as Shopify, go through your site or your plan and make sure that you have:

- an inviting front page that uses colour and simple images to tell people how your brand will make them feel;
- words and phrases that are used by your customers, not by the business community (unless you are selling B2B);
- product information that overcomes shopper fears and pain points.

Use video to capture things that move (which might seem obvious but needs saying) and make the most of local, cultural variations in design norms.

If you plan to be more ambitious and creative, then get shoppers involved as collaborators, tell a good story, and take shopping opportunities to consumers where they are, not where you want them to be.

## 'I want to design a fully integrated and innovative customer experience'

*A short introduction*

This section will interest you if your retail business is not held back by legacy business models, physical stores for which you need to identify some purpose, or other inherited assets. This could be because you are an ambitious start-up with nothing to lose or because yours is a wealthy organization that is ready to challenge the world's biggest retailers.

*A little more depth*

There are so many topics I could alight on here, but let's talk about live streaming as a tool for e-commerce. Taobao Live launched in 2016. Live-streaming influencer Austin Li made the equivalent of $10.8 million for himself, on Singles Day (now known as Double 11) 2019, and that's if we go by a conservative estimate that he received only 7 per cent of the GMV of the products he was selling (which is unlikely as he is hugely famous, 7 per cent is entry-level and in theory there is no upper limit to the percentage that a Key Opinion Leader can command – see Bund2Bro, 2020).

If you are a Chinese retailer, you are doubtless aware of this already, but the West is a region where businesses – even big ones – are still playing catch-up. McKinsey and Forrester both published reports explaining live streaming e-commerce in 2021; a move that would hardly have been necessary if their English-language readers weren't five years or more behind China.

If you've never seen Austin Li's broadcasts, there is plenty of recorded footage of him on YouTube. If you're a typical Western retailer or marketer and are already shocked by the thought of a social media influencer making $10.8 million in one day, you'll be even more shocked when you see the footage. While writing this chapter, I watched Austin Li sell mosquito repellent. At first glance, he's not *doing* very much. He's sitting at a table, in front of some cameras, talking about mosquito repellent. If you're wishing that you could earn that kind of money for doing next to nothing, so do a lot of people. So do a lot of consumers who partly follow KOLs because they desperately wish they could become them.

To properly understand how the most successful influencers earn their money and their huge followings, it's always useful to look at a contrast case. Late-coming Western copies of Taobao Live (I will not name them) put people in front of cameras and expect similar results, but are disappointed, in the same way that members of the public who make amateur 'unboxing' and 'haul' videos for YouTube, in which they unpack their shopping on camera, are disappointed when they don't become celebrities. The following are some of the features that Li has going for him (insights are based partly on Chinese commentators (Bund2Bro, 2020), on Li, and partly on my own work for brand owners and retailers):

- Li is confident in front of the camera. He is unabashed. He gives the camera (and hence the viewer) lots of eye contact. His Western counterparts spend relatively less time looking directly into the camera, which can make them seem awkward and shy. His 'chat' is fluent and he doesn't struggle for things to say or stumble over his words.
- A graphical user interface overlays Li's streaming video. One of the icons allows viewers to vote on how much they 'like' Li and his performance, and see how many other users feel the same (tens of millions). Ostensibly a measure of popularity, the heart-shaped button is substantially a vote for his physical attractiveness. Many Western streamers, especially those in e-commerce rather than entertainment, are not particularly groomed or polished and this is also true of the settings from which they broadcast, which are frequently scruffy and/or irrelevant to the video content.
- It almost goes without saying that Li has professional-quality lighting and cameras, and the stream is uninterrupted by technical problems. In contrast, the American streamer who I am watching right now is blurry and the video frequently cuts out, interrupting her broadcast.
- Chinese e-commerce streamers are very skilled at acknowledging and responding to viewers' comments (which scroll across the screen in real-time). In contrast, the US streamer who is currently trying to sell me a mattress has no comments to respond to, and this is perhaps linked to the fact that I am one of only four viewers. I must emphasize that I did not pick on this unfortunate woman because she looked unsuccessful, but because she is one of only six equally poor options: this is the livestreaming menu offered to me by one of the Western world's largest and richest e-commerce platforms, at 13:00 on a Saturday in London.

## The unique perspective of semiotics

All my comments so far on Chinese and US live streamers are technical and rational observations. If it is worth saying that live streaming doesn't sell a lot of product when presenters are awkward, sets are shabby and cameras are out of focus, it is only because these exact mistakes are made every day in Western e-commerce. Until they are repaired, Western live streaming for e-commerce will fail to compete with China.

At this point, I want to add some semiotic commentary that digs a little deeper into how a well-produced live stream benefits both consumers and retailers. The reason why we are taking (successful) live streaming as an example in a section that explains how to design a fully integrated online/offline experience is that live streaming does particularly well at demonstrating how online and offline can bleed into each other. Remember, the Chinese tech giants remain undisturbed by legacy concerns such as 'channels', and they have this in common with consumers. People – your customers – just want to live their lives, which means consuming entertainment, making choices, enjoying social relationships, developing skills, escaping their worries and responsibilities, and having a new pair of shoes materialize in their hands as quickly and seamlessly as possible after the moment that it occurs to them to want shoes. They do not care about channels. We retailers and marketers need to design shopping opportunities that do not force them to care or even to become aware of the difference between online and offline.

Here's how a good live stream merges the two:

- While live streaming, Austin Li is within reach of the consumer in a way that cannot be matched by something like appearing on TV or in a display ad. You ask a question, he responds. He's a very desirable person (attractive, famous) and live streaming is a chance for fans to receive individual attention, however briefly. He becomes, momentarily, part of the consumer's real world. This phenomenon is also seen in the adult-entertainment type of live streaming, where fans will pay cash tips to hear admired performers thank them and use their name. Many experts on consumer culture describe these one-sided relational experiences as another example of parasocial relationships, discussed earlier in the context of toys and avatars.

- Live streaming happens in real-time. This, too, brings the consumer closer to the performer. Consumers are encouraged to 'follow' specific performers of whom they have become fans. Following a live streamer means that you will receive a notification when they start broadcasting. If you, the reader of this book, have not had the experience of joining the live stream of someone whom you have reason to admire, I urge you to try. It is completely different from watching a recording. Live broadcasts have a spontaneity to them that can approach real human intimacy, especially when cameras are close up and you are viewing the broadcast in a semi-private virtual room that is occupied only by the performer and their fans (in other words, a completely different experience from watching live TV).

- The best, most successful live streaming takes place within a well-developed ecosystem. This means that the customer should be able to view product details and make their purchase without ever leaving the system. There should be no need to leave the 'room', go to a different website, or enter passwords or credit card numbers. The job of the streamer is to inspire desire and the job of the retailer is to make the wish come true with the minimum of fuss or delay.

At this point in the evolution of consumer culture and global capitalism, I don't think it is a stretch to say that many consumers would far rather be online than offline. Online is clean, bright, comfortable, arousing and studded with the bright stars of admired celebrities and seductive products. It involves near-zero physical effort. It only requires a working bank account or credit card. When physical goods and products materialize as a result of simply being alive in an online space, integration has been achieved.

## Actions for retail marketers

Whether or not live-streaming is going to be your 'thing', here are some actions that will fulfil the same or a similar function for consumers.

- Blur the difference between online and offline. If your retail offering is primarily offline, think how you can use technology and digitization to enhance it. The following chapter includes a section on smart cities, where we'll explore topics such as the power of augmented reality. If your store or retail offering is primarily online, consider that giving it some physical manifestation can be exciting for consumers. We can see this in Amazon Go stores, which turn the otherwise digital platform into physical spaces that one can visit 'in real life'. A similar phenomenon is found in theme parks, in which intellectual property such as Harry Potter and the Simpsons can be 'brought to life' in physical forms of entertainment such as roller coaster rides.
- For many people, shopping is at its most enjoyable when it is social. Think about how you can provide live experiences and even intimate experiences. This could mean using technology to help people shop

together, dine together or explore together even when they are physically separated. It could mean staging live events that take place simultaneously in your physical and digital stores. It could mean giving your consumers chances to get closer to events and places that seem otherwise unreachable. In his book *Resurrecting Retail* (2021), Doug Stephens explains how Burberry managed to have 40,000 consumers attend a live fashion show in the middle of a pandemic. Burberry used Twitch, an Amazon-owned streaming platform that used to be solely about gaming and is now catching the attention of non-gaming brands, thanks to its 140 million unique monthly users.

- Look for opportunities to create 'immersion'. This is another concept that is familiar to gamers but new to most retailers. Immersion means total mental absorption, a voluntary loss of awareness of anything existing outside of whatever bubble one happens to be in. In fact, traditional retail outlets such as supermarkets embraced the concept of immersion when they collectively decided to omit windows, natural daylight and clocks from their interiors. Doing this helps the shopper to forget that there is a world outside the store. If this seems manipulative, I would agree, given that shoppers did not ask for stores to be designed this way. However, when immersion is voluntary, it is a different matter. Consider that many players of games, readers of books and creative artists are in search of immersion, in which outside distractions melt away. Assuming that the bubble of shopping, gaming or reading is itself pleasant and voluntarily chosen, immersion means total escape from whatever sharp edges of reality one went there to avoid.

### EXERCISE

Here's my big challenge for you, to end this section on integrated experiences, and this chapter. As a temporary thought experiment, if nothing more, try abandoning the concept of 'channels'.

If you or your business have used up time and resources puzzling out how to reach shoppers through multiple online and offline channels, such as physical stores, kiosks, third-party resellers, branded e-commerce websites, and shoppable ads, take a day off. After all, your customers don't spend their time thinking about channels. Use your day off to reflect on what consumers are, in fact, occupied with, such as satisfying relationships and escape from the pains of daily life.

> When you are clear on what *they* want and what they are trying to achieve, ask yourself how your brand or your retail offering can best serve them. If you can succeed at the part of retail that involves meeting consumer needs, you might find that concerns about channels resolve themselves.

## Endnotes

1 **and 2** See Lillian Li's excellent blog, *Chinese Characteristics*, especially the post 'What I talk about when I talk about Chinese tech' (28 January 2021): https://lillianli.substack.com/p/what-i-talk-about-when-i-talk-about (archived at https://perma.cc/5BHH-Y3UB)
3 For example, https://techjury.net/blog/shopping-cart-abandonment-stats/#gref (archived at https://perma.cc/EWL3-XLUT)
4 Etsy's press release is available at: https://investors.etsy.com/press-releases/press-release-details/2021/Etsy-to-acquire-global-fashion-resale-marketplace-Depop/default.aspx (archived at https://perma.cc/W3AE-556Z)
5 See Freshippo's Robot Restaurant 2.0 at: https://youtu.be/FFCPKmLAZb4 (archived at https://perma.cc/B335-KZMW)
6 See 'Alibaba's "new retail" explained at: https://youtu.be/336YkwayCD4 (archived at https://perma.cc/L74H-J5JE)
7 'Sacla stage Shopera in London foodhall' at: https://youtu.be/44UC6muN8KY (archived at https://perma.cc/QP9E-QRSD) and 'Sacla stage a surprise opera in a school lunch hall' at: https://youtu.be/JNgCM7zp30M (archived at https://perma.cc/4WLK-P6W7)

## References

Bodoni, S (2021) Amazon gets record $888 million EU fine over data violations, *Bloomberg*, https://www.bloomberg.com/news/articles/2021-07-30/amazon-given-record-888-million-eu-fine-for-data-privacy-breach (archived at https://perma.cc/NKN3-KPVU)
Bund2Bro (2020) *Hidden China* ep2: China's vibrant livestreaming sales – Is rest of the world missing out?, https://youtu.be/enKwJrC7qpU (archived at https://perma.cc/G726-BF7A)
Flood, A (2019) Plagiarism, 'book-stuffing', clickfarms … the rotten side of self-publishing, *Guardian*, https://www.theguardian.com/books/2019/mar/28/plagiarism-book-stuffing-clickfarms-the-rotten-side-of-self-publishing (archived at https://perma.cc/6UAM-7S5V)

Forrester (2021) Shoppertainment is landing in Europe, https://osssource.alizila.com/uploads/2021/02/Shoppertainment-Is-Landing-In-Europe1.pdf (archived at https://perma.cc/7PLH-3QMM)

Hyowon, S (2020) Kiosks, are they really convenient?, *Voices of Youth*, https://www.voicesofyouth.org/blog/kiosks-are-they-really-convenient (archived at https://perma.cc/7XVX-P8SH)

Malik, O (2013) Meet the man behind New York's other billion dollar internet company, *Gigaom*, https://gigaom.com/2013/08/23/meet-the-man-behind-new-yorks-other-billion-dollar-internet-company-this-one-makes-money/ (archived at https://perma.cc/9Q5L-SMAB)

Mckinsey Digital (2021) Live commerce is transforming online shopping, https://www.mckinsey.com/business-functions/mckinsey-digital/our-insights/its-showtime-how-live-commerce-is-transforming-the-shopping-experience# (archived at https://perma.cc/R7VZ-CCV5)

Sims, A and McCabe, K (2021) 7 perfect pick-your-own fruit and vegetable farms in and around London, *Time Out London*, https://www.timeout.com/london/things-to-do/londons-best-pick-your-own-fruit-and-vegetable-farms (archived at https://perma.cc/RRV6-WVH6)

Statista (2021) Alibaba: number of Freshippo stores 2021, https://www.statista.com/statistics/1232366/alibaba-number-of-freshippo-stores/ (archived at https://perma.cc/S4GK-KLR7)

Stephens, D (2021) *Resurrecting Retail*, Figure 1, Vancouver

Worthington, D (2019) City Road kiosk is a small store that has a big impact, *betterRetailing*, https://www.betterretailing.com/store-profiles/city-road-kiosk-london/ (archived at https://perma.cc/9TYE-H2PT)

Zakkour and Dudarenok (2019) *New Retail: Born in China Going Global: How Chinese tech giants are changing global commerce* (independently published)

# 10

# The future of everything

> **WHAT'S COMING UP**
>
> This is the last of four chapters that concern the future. We've already tackled some big topics, such as the behavioural futures market, decentralized economies, parasocial relationships and digital ecosystems. These items are 'of the future' in the sense of being at the leading edge of changes to retail, but they are also things that exist here and now.
>
> In this final chapter in our set of four, we are going to take a long-range view and discuss things that are only beginning to emerge. They may seem daunting or exciting, depending on your view, but they are all necessary for forward planning. By the end of this chapter, you will be able to:
>
> - envisage who could be working in the retail stores of the future, and how you can make best use of them;
> - anticipate what is coming for retail when smart cities stop being an exception and become widespread;
> - see how humanity itself is evolving and anticipate ways for retailers to meet the needs of future humans.

## Talent

### A short introduction

We all know that traditional retail is contracting. In the West, department stores have gone out of business. When large stores go, small stores, which rely on their bigger neighbours to attract customers, close in their wake.

High streets and town centres are starting to look empty. North American malls, which were once a hub of mass culture in the 1990s and early 2000s, have in growing numbers become abandoned. There are many reasons for this, including but not limited to the rise of e-commerce.[1] Western business writers have called it a 'retail apocalypse'. The situation has not been exactly the same in Asia because of factors such as tourism and larger segments of populations continuing to shop traditionally and outside of e-commerce.[2] Despite this, there are few locations around the world where traditional retail has not been affected. Inevitably, this results in job losses, at least until the future of retail has been fully determined.

In the previous chapter, I suggested some things you can do with your physical store to attract customers. This section is about staff – who you will need and what kinds of work they could be doing.

## A little more depth

Klaus Schwab, founder and executive chairman of the World Economic Forum, is the author of *The Fourth Industrial Revolution* (2016) and *Covid-19: The Great Reset* (2020). In discussing the march of technology, he does not flinch from the issue that is making working people nervous. Digital culture brings with it automation, and that means job losses, including in retail. It's easy to see how. Amazon Go grocery stores need no cashiers. The tasks of shelf replenishment, managing a department or category, managing the shop floor, can all be partly or fully automated. In the future, retailers will employ many fewer staff. Those who remain will need to be adaptable and multiskilled. Employers will look for talent, which Schwab calls 'one of the most important, emerging drivers of competitiveness' and 'the dominant form of strategic advantage' for businesses in a rapidly changing world.

Futurist and writer on retail Doug Stephens (2014) envisages a new generation of retail workers who are brand ambassadors. They will be 'super-users of the brand's products, devout believers in the brand's creed', experts at building rapport and at using the latest technology to dazzle and amaze shoppers. The physical store of the future is a showroom and an entertainment centre and the staff are performers. The part of his vision that gives me pause is where he predicts that these workers will be 'paid handsomely'. As we saw in the previous chapter, Austin Li (Huang, 2020) made upwards of $10 million on Singles Day in 2019 because he was able to reach an audience of tens of millions of consumers. This kind of reach cannot be achieved by a sales assistant in a physical store who is expected to connect with customers individually.

It appears that the challenges for retailers-as-employers are these. First, you need to attract talent: confident, personable multiskilled people who love technology and are convincing evangelists for your brand. Second, you need to retain them. It's more expensive to replace a highly knowledgeable and skilled member of staff than it is to replace a person whose whole job was cleaning up on aisle three. Third, and this is the kicker that I don't see other writers discussing, you need to compensate them for the opportunity cost incurred when they agree to work in your store. That is, if they are as brilliant as Stephens proposes, we have to ask why they are working for you in your store in a medium-sized city when they could be outside or at home, building their own careers as digital content creators. How are you going to make it worth their while? And how is that going to stack up against the amount of revenue they can generate for your business from in-store sales?

## The unique perspective of semiotics

I want to propose that in the current industrial revolution, that is the fourth industrial (digital, technological) revolution described by Klaus Schwab, there is dehumanization of retail work and also of retail customers.

Retail work is dehumanized in an obvious and literal way whenever humans, such as supermarket cashiers and shelf stackers, are replaced by automated alternatives. Less obvious but just as real is the dehumanization of the customer. In the previous chapter I talked about Chinese grocery store Freshippo. In some of these stores, you can sit down and eat a meal delivered to you by a small robot waiter. Right now, this has immense novelty value and will attract customers to Freshippo wherever it can be rolled out. The challenge for the business is that novelty soon wears off. The challenge for the customer is that the loss of human contact eventually starts to be felt as a loss. Imagine that yours is a single-person household, you spend all day at home doing ghost work such as content moderation or proofreading (Gray and Suri, 2019), and, within this austere regime, eating at the grocery store restaurant is your trip out for the day. The robot waiter, alluring as it is, has replaced your last point of face-to-face human contact.

In fact, we've been building up to this for a long time. Customers suffered many indignities and frustrations as a result of the industrialization of shopping in the previous cultural upgrade. Herb Sorensen (2016) points this out: people visit stores where they don't know the owner, staff leave and are quickly replaced, they are required to pick their own products from the shelf, and now cash out themselves at automated tills. Some people who are old enough to remember what shopping used to be like are especially prone to experiencing the warehouse model of shopping as a bad thing.

I therefore propose that, alongside designing fancy augmented-reality and virtual-reality experiences for adults who have no special needs and are entertainment-hungry, we could be designing staff roles that reintroduce the best, most human elements of the way retail used to be. The challenge for the retail industry will be to achieve the delivery of human services that meet human needs without discriminating against less-than-ideal customers.

As working from home increases, people's need of somewhere to take their children becomes more acute. And as the gap between rich and poor widens, cities evolve no-go areas, often surrounding long-time residents. Street crime increases: for example, there is rising knife crime in London and Birmingham in the UK. Elderly people become afraid to go out. This is why wealthy people live in gated communities. I wonder how long it will take smart cities to become gated cities.

I once conducted a programme of ethnographic research for Titan Outdoor Advertising, since taken over by JCDecaux, another long-time client of mine. The aim of the study was to discover the value of advertising space in shopping centres, contrasted against outdoor roadside ad spots, for example at bus stops. I spent a lot of time traversing malls and high streets with consumers. One woman spoke for many when she eloquently described how safe she felt in the mall. 'I'm not afraid to take my best handbag,' she said. There were cameras and security staff. The mall felt like a secure environment.

It's possible that in the future we will see malls that are tightly secured (which becomes more affordable as technology advances) and socially exclusive. In an extension of China's social credit system, people may be barred from entering if they fail to meet pre-set standards for behaviour, trustworthiness and economic stability.

### Actions for retail marketers

As an alternative to replacing all your human retail workers with robots, or simply waiting until that becomes financially attainable, let's think differently by looking at what was and wasn't working about previous generations of retail. This will help you to add value for customers now, rather than becoming distracted by trying to jump three steps ahead into the future. What was good, and what was not so good about shopping in physical stores as we used to know them?

- **Good.** The shopping centre, market or traditional high street was both a place and a collection of ready-made activities. People would go there to spend social time together, as friends, family groups and couples. Some theme parks and resorts do well at facilitating this use of space: staff spot people who look lost or in need of an activity and guide them to the right spot. Note that this is not the same as compelling people to buy things.
- **Not good.** Shopping with children can be stressful. As Sherry Turkle (2017) remarks, 'kids are always on, and always on you.' This is very trying for parents. Retail staff who are vetted and trained to work with children could make a lot of difference to the shopping experience, which could then compete well with online shopping.
- **Good.** Malls were places where parents would let teenagers go unaccompanied, it was a relatively secure environment with just enough freedom and space for shoppers who have not yet reached adulthood to explore and exercise choices. Recreating this facility could benefit both parents and teens. In particular, there could be roles for visible security staff who are trained to spot adults behaving suspiciously around minors.
- **Not good.** In the old-fashioned 'warehouse' stores, shopping is boring, repetitive and effortful. People are their own pickers and cashiers. Automated tills reduce queues but add frustration in their own way by regularly breaking down. Many people prefer human service and didn't ask for it to be taken away in exchange for shorter queues. Here's a question: why can't the automated till be stored in a staff member's hand-held device? Why can't we check out customers in any part of the store, as soon as they indicate that they are ready to leave?
- **Good.** It was once possible to form a relationship with store owners and their staff. This capacity is lost when shopping becomes remote and automated. Meanwhile, there is a huge amount of loneliness and isolation in individualist societies, especially among older people. I know from my work with the UK supermarket chain Morrisons that older people really appreciate the chance to chat with a staff member. I even met a few who fabricate reasons why they need help. Achieve these relationships by retaining and rewarding staff who know both your customers and your business.
- **Not good.** Accessibility can always be improved. Stores can be overwhelming, confusing and hard to use for all sorts of customers. This applies just as much to digital stores as to physical stores. Consider that

your business and brand could benefit if your future retail staff include some 'accessibility champions', so that we do better in the future than we have done in the past.

> EXERCISE
>
> In the future, your retail business will employ fewer people because more of the work that takes place on the shop floor can be automated. Automation and increased efficiency save your business money, but carry a cost, which is a loss of humanity. Your customers are humans and depend for their survival on social contact with other humans.
>
> Make a list of all the ways that your customers benefit from interacting with *real people*. Use market research if necessary. Don't forget to ask your staff what they know about customer needs. Identify how you can introduce or retain some of these interactions in your business model without breaking the bank on superhero wages for superhero brand ambassadors.

## Smart cities

### A short introduction

Smart cities are evolving around the world. Eventually, in the long term, they are likely to become the norm. They have a lot in common with advanced digital retail stores such as Freshippo and ecosystems such as Alibaba because they collect human behavioural data and involve networks of internet-connected objects. They differ from these systems in that they are relatively more government-controlled and involve public services, such as transportation, utilities and law enforcement. The rise of the smart city will change the cultural and economic landscape in which retail happens, so retailers need to be ready for it.

### A little more depth

Smart cities vary between the exotic and the everyday. The exotic cities are opportunities for wealthy tech companies to showcase innovation and are very exciting to the public as well as to the business community. One example is the Toyota Woven City[3] in Japan, currently under construction. Often, these exotic cities are smart because they are new. They are themselves ecosystems and may be part of larger ecosystems, as when there are parent companies and investors, or partner organizations. This kind of city is exotic because it is technologically advanced. It excites consumers and is therefore something we marketers and retailers want to think about how to adapt to.

The Woven City, when finished, will initially house around 360 people and later rise to 2,000. Residents will be mainly Toyota employees and their families as well as other invited participants. Designed from the bottom up, technologically advanced features and services are built into the city's infrastructure. Underground space is custom-made to serve as a conduit for ('clean' hydrogen) energy, water and delivery of goods. Above ground, transportation has been reimagined with three different kinds of roads, driverless vehicles and a lot of trees and greenery (these improving health and social cohesion as well the atmosphere). Homes are light, airy and temperature controlled. They are both dwellings and testing centres for new technology. The health of residents is monitored. Chores such as taking out refuse and obtaining food are automated, as far as possible.

The more everyday kind of smart city might be one where you live. Perhaps you already pay for your parking or public transport using a smartphone. Perhaps you admit yourself to your local library, apartment building and gym using an ID card or code. Perhaps there are areas of your city where motion sensors make lights come on; when translated to public street lighting, there are opportunities to save energy.

This kind of city is more everyday because, rather than being designed from the bottom up as a demonstration of technological superiority, the majority of smart cities are existing cities that gradually become smart. This cumulative process of becoming smarter happens when small changes are introduced concurrently, and the evolution to becoming a fully smart city happens when independent systems join up. Lots of examples of smart initiatives can be seen at smartcitiesworld.net, along with city reports concerning Seoul, Sydney, Chicago, Atlanta and Barcelona. The priorities of cities, as they become smarter, include things like disease control, attainable housing, reducing pollution and generally being more 'green', better transport, and cybersecurity – powerful systems on which a city relies must be able to withstand and resist cyber-attacks.

## The unique perspective of semiotics

Some writers and industry experts have severe reservations about whether the reality of smart cities is going to be the utopia that the public is being promised. It would be an oversight not to acknowledge those points of view here. If one wanted to be critical of the smart city as a feature of society and something we have evolved ourselves, it's not hard to anticipate problems. To begin with, enjoying all these benefits is going to require the individual resident and their family to submit to constant surveillance. These are the first, obvious negative impacts that happen at the level of the household (Poole, 2018). Then there are questions about who is really in control of a smart city when most of the investment is made by private companies that own the technology on which the city runs. What will be the political economy that emerges as city, state and national governments collaborate or conflict with privately owned businesses? (See Tegmark, 2017, for example.) Lastly, as smart cities grow, semiotics obliges us to ask who will be excluded as well as who is included. City walls may appear, which are digital but no less effective than physical walls at keeping unwanted visitors firmly outside, becoming oversized gated communities.

These criticisms are important because they help us to retain some distance from the object of our semiotic analysis. But they are a beginning for analysis, not an endpoint. To complete the task, we need to attend to cultural variation. Most or even all smart city initiatives claim to benefit society or benefit the community in some way or another. However, what is meant by 'benefit' can be quite culturally specific and is correspondingly revealing. Here are some examples.

- Japan is a collectivist society that has an ageing population. Professor Atsushi Deguchi (president of the Urban Design Center, Kashiwa-no-ha) describes it as follows (Buntz, 2020):

  Aging populations have caused complex social issues regarding mobility, health care and workforce productivity as well as the devaluation of local or suburban communities. [...] Society 5.0 emphasizes solving such social issues while harmonizing sustainability and economic growth.

- In Dubai, 'benefiting society' prioritizes law and order. The city is enhancing its law enforcement capabilities using 'Robocop' (Reuters, 2017). The machine has a humanoid appearance, wears the colours of the Dubai police and can perform a military salute. Its cameras and software let it

- compare faces to the police database, read and record licence plates and detect risk (that is, crimes that have yet to happen but are at risk of happening).
- In the United States, things are usually agreed to be better when they are more efficient. In many US cities, this often places traffic management at the top of the list.[4] Smart initiatives in cities like Washington DC, Pittsburgh and Boston use traffic-detecting tech to manage traffic flow and reduce congestion. This not only benefits individual drivers by having them spend less time stuck in traffic, it is also less polluting, because engines spend less time running while the vehicle is sitting still.

I point out these cultural differences here because it causes us to realize that 'benefiting society' or 'helping the community' are highly relative phrases. Retailers and marketers are in a stronger position to design and plan for the future when they realize that these ideas are local and contextual. Nations and regions want *their idea* of a better city.

## Actions for retail marketers

The way that retailers like Amazon and Alibaba usually conceive of smart cities and their benefits is expressed simply as 'making shopping easier'. This is the headline benefit to the consumer. Presenting this as simultaneously a benefit to 'society' or 'the community' helps businesses like these gain the co-operation of the state where it is necessary, for example, with regard to planning permission and licences to use air space. Where successful, this strategy potentially allows Amazon to bring to life designs it has patented, such as 'flying warehouses' (BBC News, 2016) and buildings modelled on beehives (Yurieff, 2017), which have a multitude of entry and exit points for delivery drones. Meanwhile, in China, a digital umbrella hovers over Freshippo grocery stores. Right now, that manifests as extra-fast grocery deliveries for anyone who lives within a 3 km radius of the store. The foundational concept, though, is larger. As described by China business strategists Zakkour and Dudarenok (2019), the concept is to have what Alibaba calls a 3km 'ideal living community', which is dependent on Alibaba's convenient, integrated services. The point is to drive the consumer deeper into the Alibaba ecosystem, which incorporates consumer finance, entertainment and many of the other systems that support daily life.

That said, here's my first recommended action. **Identify how you can make shopping easier,** using whatever technology and business partnerships you have available. We know where the pain points are for shoppers. They dislike waiting, unless they opted to wait; they abandon carts when they have to enter a password. Parking can be expensive and children are demanding. They miss out on things that they would like, if only they knew of them, and they take home things that are not quite what they wanted. On this count, I recommend exploring a more or less Japanese approach to the problem. Japan's newest city designs are sensitive to under-served populations such as people who have mobility problems and are not as socially or economically engaged as they could be. It's possible to take an ethical and socially responsible approach to 'helping people shop' in the sense that, at some level, people need things and not everybody finds the necessities of life easy to access. Accessibility is a theme that we've returned to several times within this book.

Here's the second action. **Identify the local meaning of 'better for society'** or 'helping the community' in the major cities where your retail business operates. Is it all about efficiency, with cost savings and smoother-running systems? Is sustainability important? Is it mainly about solving social problems such as health care and elder care? Is it about security and keeping the peace? Is it about opportunities for mass governance, such as Seoul's idea that 'every citizen is the mayor' (Smart Cities World, 2020)? Identify some way in which your retail business can, in reality, make a contribution to a better society, according to locally defined standards.

Now **pair your ideas and see how they fit**. Perhaps you had the idea that your FMCG brand could make life easier for shoppers by launching a low-salt variant of a food item and clearly flagging it up at the fixture so people can find it. If your culture values *efficiency*, display it in store with other low-salt products and explain what they do, for example that they are 'heart healthy'. If your culture values *sustainability*, cutting back the salt is also a great marketing opportunity for talking about healthy, locally sourced ingredients, perhaps in collaboration with a fresh produce market. If your culture values *harmony and social care*, put together a marketing campaign that shows how you managed to make your low-salt, heart-healthy product available to people who would like health to be a little more attainable. Messages like these can be repeated in store and out of store. The ideal situation, as Zakkour and Dudarenok (2019) describe, is to have online and offline working together to drive up awareness and reward the consumer as they engage more deeply with the brand, store or platform.

EXERCISE

Here are three semiotically informed prompts to explore as you continue to think about the place of your business within smart cities.

1. What could you put inside a vending machine that wouldn't usually be there? If we can do it with automobiles (Core77, 2016), we can do it with anything. Buying a car from a vending machine has obvious novelty and fun value that certainly makes shopping a more pleasant experience. **Don't hesitate to build a machine around something if you can see how that would make it more fun** to buy or use. Younger consumers in countries around the world collected Pez dispensers from the 1990s; rod-shaped plastic machines that dispense little sweets.[5] The machines exceeded the candy itself in their ability to capture the consumer's imagination, but the candy has to be purchased to fill the machine. My point is that you can benefit from thinking about car vending machines even if the only change you can realistically make is tweaking your FMCG packaging.

2. Niantic's *Pokémon Go* (2016) was designed to work with Google Maps, and in fact Niantic was owned by Google at the start of its life. *Pokémon Go* was a global sensation at launch. It is an augmented-reality product that populates the real world, or at least the version you see on your camera-phone, with cute, collectible creatures. The idea is that you go to various physical locations, guided by the app, to 'find' these animals and build your collection. Both a game and a highly sophisticated marketing tool, *Pokémon Go* drove consumers to 3,000 McDonald's restaurants across Japan, as well as sending them to thousands of US branches of Starbucks, Sprint and many other corporate sponsors. This is an important example to be aware of because of the way it uses physical space, which is one of the distinguishing features of cities. It treats **physical space and bricks-and-mortar stores as part of the solution, not part of the problem**. And it exemplifies a principle I highlighted previously, which is that **shopping should support an experience – the experience is not bolted on to support shopping**. If you have premises of any description, then you have a place where you can create marketable experiences, especially in collaboration with business partners who hold data about where people are and what they are doing.

3. In her critique of information capitalism, Shoshanna Zuboff (2019) tries to envisage a genuinely benign alternative to the dystopia that may precede it. She does not get into the details, perhaps because it is our job to invent

> these things, but she offers a wish list. The socially embedded information technologies of the future may inevitably reframe or rewrite supply and demand, but they should do so in ways that are compatible with **democracy** and which **facilitate an effective life**. There are so many ways that these ideas can be integrated into the small details of products, marketing and retail. Perhaps 'democracy' suggests that your retail platform could be more generous in sharing customer data with the customer themselves. Alternatively, perhaps it means giving customers more chances to own shares in businesses and more chances to 'be the mayor', like the citizens of Seoul. See how many responses to Zuboff's list you can generate. Turn to Chapter 11 if you are stuck for creative ideas.

## Future humans

### A short introduction

In this section, we are going to take a look at the biggest of all the big topics we have discussed over this and the preceding chapters. Where is humanity heading? Assuming the continued growth of big data, artificial intelligence, privately owned ecosystems, smart cities, cryptocurrencies and creator economies, how is all this going to change us as humans? In the immediately following paragraphs, I offer short descriptions of two of the most distinctive and challenging aspects of the future that are swimming into view, along with some key elements of language that help us give a shape to emerging reality.

After that I'll try to put a frame around the future by describing it in terms of what people need, what they want, what they are going to get, what they fear and what they are becoming. I'll then use the same frame to recommend actions for retail marketers. At the very end, where I set out an exercise, I'll be as clear and explicit as possible about what all this means for an ordinary FMCG brand and encourage you to apply the thinking to your own brand or retail business. In this way, we will move from very large, complex topics to details and specifics.

### A little more depth

#### THE METAVERSE

Recall our earlier discussion of ecosystems, an evolving phenomenon in which multiple, superficially unrelated businesses, sometimes owned by the same parent company, work together to create a system that attempts to meet all of consumers' daily needs: shopping, socializing, consuming entertainment, organizing their households and task lists, managing their health, doing their banking, even earning a living. A broad-based and well-functioning ecosystem gives the individual user few reasons to leave, and rewards them for staying logged in and handing over their attention and data. A metaverse is like a larger, more ambitious ecosystem. It is partly or wholly decentralized, having multiple owners, stakeholders and contributors. It allows users to retain a single identity and account that functions across all parts of the system. Like smart cities, metaverses are under construction. Visions of how they will be when launched usually include a large measure of virtual reality. Consumers always want to know when life is going to start to resemble *Ready Player One* (Steven Spielberg, 2018) and the metaverse is the official name[6] for an all-encompassing, digital or digitally enhanced reality that has become the place where most people spend all of their time.

There's one more very important point about the metaverse. This is not just about having better experiences in business meetings or while playing games, although both of those are on offer, as you can see from Mark Zuckerberg's interesting interview of July 2021 on the Verge podcast. There's much more to it than simply better functionality. The significant part, where the future of humanity is concerned, is that the metaverse is the next step in a historically unprecedented moment where humanity is forming a hive mind. It is not just that we, as a global community, are all able to talk to each other, although that in itself is an incredible moment. It is also that the tech tools we are building are fully present in those interactions and help to shape them. Take just one example: the new behaviour that we call 'sharing'. 'The ways of "sharing" enabled by hyperlinks are now creating a new type of thinking – part human and part machine – found nowhere else on the planet or in history' says Kevin Kelly (2016). '*The web has unleashed a new becoming.*'

### SINGULARITY
*Singularity* describes a tipping point in the evolution of AI, where it becomes uncontrollable. This uncontrollability could be because it becomes increasingly good at modifying itself, writing its own software and making independent decisions that humans don't understand. It could be a tipping point that occurs when technology simply outranks humans in everything that humans are needed to do, making humans redundant. This loss of control used to be, and still is, an anxiety expressed throughout science

fiction; it's a recurring theme in sci-fi books and movies and has been for many decades. What's new is that we've arrived at a point where out-of-control AI is not *merely* an anxious fantasy or a crackpot theory. It's now a realistic possibility. Elon Musk thinks we will arrive at one version of singularity by 2025 (see Dowd, 2020, for example). Ray Kurzweil (Reedy, 2017) expects another level of singularity around 2045.

Singularity is an important topic, whether it happens now or in 20 years, which will not take long to pass. It's important because it raises hard questions that we as a global community of humans must try to answer. These questions include:

- Are humans necessary? To put it another way, how sure are you that, in the future, your government, the business community or wealthy investors will be interested in sponsoring your survival? 'Some economists predict that sooner or later unenhanced humans will be completely useless,' says Yuval Noah Harari (2016).

- Is there anything that makes us distinctively human? Is there anything special about us, such as consciousness, or our range and depth of emotions, that AI cannot possess and that ought to be preserved? If so, how do we plan to preserve it? Jack Ma takes the view that people have 'hearts' and 'wisdom' and that we should concentrate on caring for ourselves and the Earth before trying to terraform Mars.[7]

Collectively, we are grappling with these questions because, to a large extent, the future is already here. As we try to reduce the unpredictability of the future, closing the gap between what we know and what we don't,[8] many of us draw on the short history of human civilization to form a sense of the way things are going. That is, we tell ourselves a story, thoroughly built and constructed from semiotic signs, which reflects our politics, taste and cultural background, and often includes a wishful belief that history has some direction or a sense of purpose. This belief is called **teleology**. Scientist and author David Brin gives a good discussion in *After Shock* (2020), in which he points out liberal and conservative varieties. Liberal teleology is a story of progress, in which things keep improving. The sunny marketing stories surrounding all smart cities reflect and encourage this belief that, largely thanks to human ingenuity, things are inevitably getting better and better over time, when one takes the long view. Conservative teleology is a darker story in which history keeps repeating itself, humans don't learn, wars keep happening, empires rise and fall. I include the concept of teleology here because it helps us as semiologists to preserve a bit of analytic distance between ourselves and the reality-shaping narratives that we are inspecting.

We ran headlong into some big concepts and uncommon words in these paragraphs. I'll now start to break this down into smaller and more practical chunks that retail marketers can use.

## The unique perspective of semiotics

### WHAT DO PEOPLE NEED?

The topics we've covered in this book include the metaverse, smart cities, and the psychological climate of today's consumers, which tends towards anxiety, dissociation and the quest for, and public manufacture of, identity. You can perhaps see how these things are linked. Of course people experience these symptoms when the defining features of humanity seem to be easily outranked by our own creations, or are at risk of dissolving into a string of zeroes and ones. In various places I've cited Shoshanna Zuboff and Yuval Noah Harari, and they are not afraid to say what people need. The shopping list, if we can call it that, is a blend of: economic security and survival, successful relationships, a sense of what is true, a feeling of growing maturity, and evolving wisdom and competence, all of which are a bit neglected in the more crass and commercial ends of digital culture.

### WHAT DO PEOPLE WANT?

The $138 billion games industry knows a lot about what people want, as does Steven Spielberg. First, they want all the fun aspects of games. These are well documented. People like feeling empowered and capable (being able to fly, ride a dragon, ride a horse across a vast wilderness, drive a tank, perform magic, use superpowers). They like discovery – give them a map to explore with lots of surprises and buried treasure. They like being sociable and use games as communication tools. They love being able to express their own creativity. The application *Roblox* isn't a game: it's a tool for making games. Roblox Corporation claims 164 million monthly active users.

### WHAT ARE THEY GOING TO GET?

To answer this question, we might need both the 'dark' and the 'light' sides of predictions of the future. The dark side of the story says that what people are going to get is an immense loss of privacy and a submission to surveillance that will impact on individuals and families and is also potentially a threat to democracy. As gloomy as this may seem, it has some plausibility as a continuation of events that are already happening.

On the light side is the story about the many benefits that will accrue. Life will become more convenient because of technology. There will be more time to do the things we enjoy and care about. This has always been the allure of consumer-facing technology. What's more, the human lifespan will be extended. People will eventually have more years of good health in better-managed environments.

## WHAT DO THEY FEAR?

The fear is of two kinds of redundancy. The first is a very literal kind: people are afraid of losing their jobs. There is some justification for this concern, as people in retail, warehousing and transport will find that jobs become scarce when tasks and functions become automated. Economies and labour markets will change shape and newer jobs and forms of work will proliferate, ranging from low-paid ghost work (Gray and Suri, 2019) through independent app-development start-ups to extravagantly paid celebrity influencers.

The other kind of redundancy that people are afraid of is linked to the remarks above about what, if anything, makes us human, and why humanity should be regarded as important. People are very negatively affected by the suspicion that they aren't needed, they aren't 'valid', and they don't matter. A brief review of today's consumers interacting on social media will reveal constant reassurances to this effect. Evidently, people are worried, as they keep giving each other advice about it.

## WHAT ARE WE BECOMING?

I earlier cited Kevin Kelly, a founder of *Wired* magazine, who spoke of sharing as a new form of thinking which is (a) collective and (b) has AI participating with humans in this shared cognitive process. I think this is an important insight because if our habits of thinking – not the content of our thoughts but the tools and techniques that we habitually use for thinking – are going to change, then the impact on human civilization will be profound and the change is unlikely to reverse.

Here I add one more kind of change that's just as important: change in the bodies of individuals. I am not talking about small and relatively mundane changes such as a person's general health being slightly improved by being able to get a doctor's appointment more quickly. I mean human bodies that have been significantly enhanced and engineered to avoid and resist breakdown and perform some tasks at high levels. We do not need to dip into science fiction stories of cyborgs to see how this plays out. Instead, I refer you to a report (2021) produced by the UK Ministry of Defence, a fairly sober institution. The MoD describes genetically engineered humans, soldiers with exoskeletons, sensory augmentation (improved sight, hearing, heat detection), technology that can interface directly with brains rather than going via a screen and keyboard, and virtual reality that eventually becomes reality itself, having subsumed the more physical variety. Human bodies are changing as society changes.

Now let me break this down a little more into things that you can get involved in as a retailer or marketer.

## Actions for retail marketers

### WHAT DO PEOPLE NEED?

Most people's number one need is money, because it buys food, shelter and all the things at the bottom of Maslow's famous hierarchy of needs. They need to get paid. Your business could compensate them for a range of activities from simply giving you their attention to actively encouraging their immediate social network – people who know and trust them – to participate in your time-limited brand or store event.

Beyond that, we've spoken of people's need to feel sure of themselves. There's a need to know what is true, to experience inner integrity, to know who one's friends are, to be able to manage relationships and attain maturity. This is a big need, and trying to fulfil it is the project of a lifetime. The insight I offer here is that people habitually try to rescue themselves, and even quite small businesses can get involved in facilitating that, by providing educational opportunities and confidence-building challenges and supporting community endeavours that get people working in teams.

### WHAT DO THEY WANT?

People want beauty, power, discovery, sociable experiences and chances for creative self-expression. There are so many ways for brands and retailers to support this. Make your packaging, your fixtures and the interior of your store as beautiful as you can. It doesn't need a vast budget – signs of care (thoughtful, creative attention) are worth more to consumers than displays of corporate wealth. At the level of your interior signage and fixtures, add trees, bluebirds, garlands of flowers. It doesn't matter what they are made of. They could be paintings made by your customers and their children. They could be professional illustrations which you turned into die-cut shelf dressings or wobblers. They could be a soundscape of gentle birdsong instead of the synthetic muzak that supermarkets and elevators were once famous for. It is the attention to detail that matters: this is what makes people feel cared for.

### WHAT ARE THEY GOING TO GET?

Situations will arise in which people are asked to deepen their investment when they trade their privacy and some of their civil liberties in exchange for being allowed under the digital umbrella to experience the newest, sexiest benefits of the technology-enabled future. Because they will pay a high price for access to exclusive services and lifestyles, there will be an expectation of fun and the feeling of being at the cutting edge of human civilization.

The global business community is becoming exceptionally good at delivering groceries and other shopping. Eventually, a ceiling will be reached in terms of how fast we can deliver items to shoppers. The job of your brand or retail business is then going to be providing unique and special experiences to customers. It is liable to become your point of difference. If you sell food, create more opportunities for people to eat together. If you sell clothing, give people somewhere to wear it. Lululemon in New York does a great job of this with a gym inside a clothing boutique, reversing the expected set-up of a small clothing store inside a gym (see Bloomberg, 2019, for example).

### WHAT DO THEY FEAR?

People are afraid that they don't matter, and they seek and give reassurance about the essential worth and value of each individual. Despite experiencing chronic uncertainty about important questions, such as who they are and whether they can count on the support of others, people are sure of one thing: that *feelings* are of the utmost importance. When people ask for and dispense reassurance that each person matters, included in that is the message that each person's feelings matter. Feelings may not always be rational. But they are capable of being experienced as natural, authentic and sincere.

We need to design brands, stores and marketing campaigns that acknowledge the primacy of feelings. People want to have emotional experiences and share their emotions with others. Additionally, identity groups who have reason to think that their feelings have hitherto been ignored would like to be recognized, acknowledged and welcomed into the future. We could work on giving people more opportunities to tell their stories. Airbnb became a more inclusive and attractive brand when the illustrator for their marcoms began to model each illustration on real hosts and guests (Pardes, 2018). These complex texts (collections of semiotic signs) feel authentic and there is a sense of a story waiting to be told behind each of them. In your marketing, create these kinds of links to real people, real feelings and real life.

### WHAT ARE WE BECOMING?

As we move into the future, humans will become more distributed. At the moment, we have individual humans working within increasingly decentralized economies. As society evolves, the individual themselves becomes decentralized, and an example of this is seen in Kevin Kelly's remarks about sharing behaviour. However, at the same time, augmented humans of the near future will have bodies that are stronger, less fragile, longer lasting and technologically enabled.

One of my favourite sayings is, 'Whenever a problem is solved, a new problem soon arises to take its place.' The development of the metaverse and the augmentation of humans address or attempt to solve a lot of problems. They make city living bearable. They eliminate tedious chores. They make human bodies last longer or imbue them with new abilities. All of this, as great as it may be, is going to result in new problems and new forms of consumer demand. Augmented consumers are going to want to customize and tweak their own systems and settings. Exoskeletons break and require maintenance. Virtual and physical pinboards, whiteboards, discussion groups, maker tools, publishing platforms and performance spaces are all needed as hubs to capture the output of people's collective and distributed thinking. Some futurists think that malls could eventually become vast wellness centres, where people go to work on their physical and cognitive projects. What is your brand or store doing to promote wellness and help people work on themselves?

I know that readers of this book may want very specific directions, so below I set out an example using a fictional soap brand, and you may choose to play along by testing the ideas on your own store or brand.

## EXERCISE

**What do people need?**

Let's say you have a soap brand. Need number one is money, usually obtained through work. Do you know the origins of soap operas (Ganninger, 2020)? Perhaps we should consider reinstating the soap opera as part of our brand's marketing. We can use a revolving cast in the style of a reality TV show and broadcast it in episodes on TikTok, Instagram or YouTube. Pay performers for their time, reward their popularity and/or give away a few prizes. This doesn't need a massive budget – the original soap operas were short radio dramas.

**What do they want?**

As much as anything, people want beauty. Let's hold a competition to find talented illustrators or locate them on social media. Give as many as possible the opportunity to create careful and beautiful packaging, shelf-ready packaging and in-store signage. This should be an easy win for a soap brand. If your soap is laundry detergent rather than facial soap, so much the better. Most laundry detergent packaging lags a long way behind consumers' rising expectations of aesthetics. Introduce some art and beauty into the laundry room.

**What are they going to get?**

Our competitors are going to make an effort to provide enhanced shopping experiences to consumers. We need to be mindful of this and make sure we have experiences to offer that are worth consumers' attention. As we have a soap brand, I recommend that we organize some live, participatory workshops where people can make their own soap or massage bars. Handmade bar soap with lots of inviting inclusions is an appealing product, it sells well on DTC platforms such as Etsy, it's fun to make, beginners can enjoy an experience where materials and guidance are organized ahead of time, and no one has to make a mess in their own kitchen.

**What do they fear?**

People fear that they don't matter and they might become redundant. There's also a fragmentation of the self and a search for identity. If we need to sell soap, it's worth recognizing that soap is very personal. Gillette ran an ad campaign (see CNN, 2019, for example) that showed a young transgender individual shaving their chin for the first time. The youngster's father shows them what to do and it is a bonding moment. The brand is present and plays a key role in the validation of the person's identity. If you think about the semiotics of soap, it is about hope, renewal, optimism. We can build this into design and in-store communications: it doesn't always have to be global ad campaigns.

**What are we becoming?**
I keep noticing insect metaphors in the talk of futurists, and even the Ministry of Defence, about the humans of the near future. There is the hive mind, the collective mind of all internet-connected humans and the increasingly intelligent technology that connects us. Then there is the beehive building patented by Amazon, a honeycomb structure designed for drones. Then there are exoskeletons, which the human mammal will borrow from insects and apply to its own body. Do you know how bees clean their hives? They line the interior of the nest with anti-microbial resin (Walker, 2009). It inhibits the growth of pathogens in the bees' home and reduces their exposure to disease. This resin, and its application by bees, is interesting to scientists because of its potential to combat viruses and bacteria that affect humans. If we are in the soap business, I think we should look at some new product development or at least marketing which helps people appreciate new ways to care for their homes that embrace ideas that are both topical and important, like disease control.

Try this exercise on behalf of your own brand or store. For each question above, look through the ideas I've gathered in this part of the book until you spot something that your business can do. Again, this doesn't require a huge budget. You can make it as simple or as innovative as you want. Sometimes, a little bit more beauty in pack and store design is all that's needed.

## Endnotes

1. More factors are listed here, albeit with an American focus: https://www.businessinsider.com/retail-apocalypse-last-decade-timeline-2019-12?r=US&IR=T?utm_source=copy-link&utm_medium=referral&utm_content=topbar (archived at https://perma.cc/K5ZA-WQGX)
2. For example, see this interesting feature on Thailand: https://medium.com/strategyinasia/why-we-are-not-seeing-a-retail-apocalypse-in-thailand-a306a5635f8d (archived at https://perma.cc/K6H4-N59T)
3. https://www.woven-city.global/ (archived at https://perma.cc/H5V4-3772)
   A video of Woven City's design can be seen here: https://youtu.be/ng3X39lenvg (archived at https://perma.cc/NJ2V-28U8) Photos and a detailed description can be seen here: https://mag.toyota.co.uk/toyota-woven-city-hydrogen-power/ (archived at https://perma.cc/U3PV-MLB8)

4  Many examples appear here: https://www.digi.com/blog/post/smart-cities-in-the-us-examples (archived at https://perma.cc/DL53-DKQZ)
5  See the history of Pez at: https://us.pez.com/pages/history (archived at https://perma.cc/AN8Z-NKGB)
6  This is the right moment to credit Neal Stephenson's 1992 novel *Snow Crash* (Bantam Books), a precursor to *Ready Player One*, in which the metaverse is both predicted and named.
7  See the video of Jack Ma and Elon Musk debating the future at the World Artificial Intelligence Conference in Shanghai, 2019 at: https://youtu.be/f3lUEnMaiAU (archived at https://perma.cc/CX5E-KFXK)
8  Here I quote Elon Musk from the 2019 Shanghai debate with Jack Ma.

## References

BBC News (2016) Amazon files patent for flying warehouse, https://www.bbc.co.uk/news/technology-38458867 (archived at https://perma.cc/2C4E-JRMV)

Bloomberg (2019) Lululemon opens workout studio where visitors can borrow clothes, https://www.businessoffashion.com/articles/news-analysis/lululemon-opens-workout-studio-where-visitors-can-borrow-clothes (archived at https://perma.cc/BFP2-B8TL)

Brin, David (2020) 'Are old-style humans obsolete? The many sins of faddish techno-prophecy' in John Schroeter, ed, *After Shock: The world's foremost futurists reflect on 50 years of Future Shock – and look ahead to the next 50*, Abundant World Institute, Bainbridge Island

Buntz, B (2020) In Japan, smart city projects have a social dimension, *IoT World Today*, https://www.iotworldtoday.com/2020/02/26/in-japan-smart-city-projects-have-a-social-dimension/ (archived at https://perma.cc/VXU9-J54B)

CNN, (2019) This Gillette ad shows a man teaching his transgender son to shave, https://edition.cnn.com/2019/05/26/us/gillette-ad-transgender-man-trnd/index.html (archived at https://perma.cc/RG5E-ZL8M)

Core77 (2016) Carvana Car Vending Machine, https://designawards.core77.com/Interaction/51472/Carvana-Car-Vending-Machine (archived at https://perma.cc/9SG3-QHBX)

Dowd, M (2020) Elon Musk, blasting off in domestic bliss, *New York Times*, https://www.nytimes.com/2020/07/25/style/elon-musk-maureen-dowd.html (archived at https://perma.cc/B4HH-T8MD)

Ganninger, D (2020) Why are daytime dramas called soap operas, *Knowledge Stew*, https://medium.com/knowledge-stew/why-are-daytime-dramas-called-soap-operas-ee052d9edf17#:~:text=The%20origin%20of%20the%20soap (archived at https://perma.cc/JMK3-PP7P)

Gray, M and Suri, S (2019) *Ghost Work*, Houghton Mifflin Harcourt, Boston

Harari, Y N (2016) *Homo Deus: A brief history of tomorrow*, Harvill Secker, London

Huang, A (2020) Who is millionaire Li Jiaqi, China's 'Lipstick King' who raised more than US$145 million in sales on Singles Day, *South China Morning Post*, https://www.scmp.com/magazines/style/news-trends/article/3074253/who-millionaire-li-jiaqi-chinas-lipstick-king-who (archived at https://perma.cc/WGP8-6R3C)

Kelly, K (2016) *The Inevitable: Understanding the 12 technological forces that will shape our future*, Penguin, London

Ministry of Defence (2021) Human augmentation – the dawn of a new paradigm, https://assets.publishing.service.gov.uk/government/uploads/system/uploads/attachment_data/file/986301/Human_Augmentation_SIP_access2.pdf (archived at https://perma.cc/FFT4-B55T)

Pardes, A (2018) Meet the illustrator diversifying Airbnb's image, *Wired*, https://www.wired.com/story/jennifer-hom-illustrations-airbnb/ (archived at https://perma.cc/BG9N-65QM)

Reedy, S (2017) Ray Kurzweil claims singularity will happen by 2045, *Futurism*, https://futurism.com/kurzweil-claims-that-the-singularity-will-happen-by-2045 (archived at https://perma.cc/2AGD-BK89)

Poole, S (2018) The truth about smart cities: 'In the end, they will destroy democracy', *The Guardian*, https://www.theguardian.com/cities/2014/dec/17/truth-smart-city-destroy-democracy-urban-thinkers-buzzphrase (archived at https://perma.cc/DLU5-TKA2)

Reuters (2017) Robocop joins Dubai police to fight real life crime, https://www.reuters.com/article/us-emirates-robocop-idUSKBN18S4K8 (archived at https://perma.cc/FQB7-SBJ8)

Schwab, K (2016) *The Fourth Industrial Revolution*, Portfolio Penguin, New York

Schwab, K and Malleret, T (2020) *Covid-19: The Great Reset*, Forum Publishing, Geneva

Smart Cities World (2020) Seoul's smart city platform based on 'citizens as mayors' philosophy, https://www.smartcitiesworld.net/news/news/seouls-smart-city-platform-based-on-citizens-as-mayors-philosophy-4912 (archived at https://perma.cc/38N2-KXAB)

Sorensen, H (2016) *Inside the Mind of the Shopper*, Pearson FT Press, Upper Saddle River

Stephens, D (2014) The future of retail: Death of a Salesman, *Retail Prohet*, https://www.retailprophet.com/the-future-of-retail-death-of-a-salesman/ (archived at https://perma.cc/3Y5A-TNCL)

Tegmark, M (2017) *Life 3.0: Being human in the age of Artificial Intelligence*, Penguin, London

Turkle, S (2017), *Alone Together: Why we expect more from technology and less from each other*, Basic Books, New York

The Verge (2021) Mark Zuckerberg is betting Facebook's future on the metaverse, https://www.theverge.com/22588022/mark-zuckerberg-facebook-ceo-metaverse-interview (archived at https://perma.cc/G59U-CH4M)

Walker, M (2009) Honeybees sterilise their hives, *BBC News*, http://news.bbc.co.uk/earth/hi/earth_news/newsid_8152000/8152574.stm (archived at https://perma.cc/A954-GZ2V)

Yurieff, K (2017) Amazon patent reveals drone delivery 'beehives' *CNNMoney*, https://money.cnn.com/2017/06/23/technology/amazon-drone-beehives/index.html (archived at https://perma.cc/Z33D-B9ZX)

Zakkour and Dudarenok (2019) *New Retail: Born in China Going Global: How Chinese tech giants are changing global commerce* (independently published)

Zuboff, S (2019) *The Age of Surveillance Capitalism*, Profile Books, London

**PART FOUR**

# You can do semiotics: tools for retailers

# 11

# Fast answers to everyday questions

The earlier chapters of this book explore the practical wisdom of semiotics and its applications to retail marketing in considerable depth – as much depth and detail as I could fit into one book. This chapter is different. It gives practical and snappy answers to the questions that clients ask me most often. If you turned straight to this chapter before or instead of reading the whole book, you probably have a question in mind, and there's a good chance it is listed here. Each answer or solution is accompanied by a specific example that you can use as a reference point.

> **WHAT'S COMING UP**
>
> This chapter helps you solve marketing problems when you need new ideas and creative solutions right now. By the end of this chapter, you will possess a bunch of tips and rules of thumb that help you with:
>
> 1. attracting shoppers and getting their attention;
> 2. engaging shoppers;
> 3. selling;
> 4. merchandising and category management;
> 5. navigation and signage;
> 6. in-store experience, including pleasure;
> 7. communicating brand values;
> 8. communicating brand architecture and range;
> 9. e-commerce;
> 10. global marketing.

# 1. Attention and attraction

*Questions*

Here are the two most common questions that retail marketers ask me about how to get the attention of shoppers. These questions usually refer to physical, bricks and mortar stores.

- 'How do we achieve on-shelf standout or cut-through with our packaging?'
- 'How do we get people to snap out of autopilot in the store or at the fixture?'

Certain things are a given in traditional stores. Packaged goods are noisy, each one trying to shout louder than its neighbours. The result can be hard-to-navigate fixtures that look chaotic even when they are kept tidy. Shoppers rely harder than ever on their ability to recognize familiar packs, which dissuades them from noticing new products and promotions. Additionally, people don't necessarily want you to disrupt whatever shopper mission they are on. This impatience is well documented.

*Answers*

There are solutions to this problem that can be achieved through design of both packaging and fixtures. The underlying principles are the following. The best way to get people's attention in a store is to show them something unexpected. This can be surprisingly easy to achieve, given that supermarkets in particular and chain stores in general lean towards strong and repetitive conventions, where packs are rectangles and aisles are set out to form grids. Because of this linear, boxy aesthetic, focus particularly on shapes. Unusual packaging formats and three-dimensional decorations at fixtures are great for breaking up a loud but rigid and conformist visual landscape.

Once you have people's attention, you need to compensate them, otherwise all you have added to their shopping experience is distraction. Design packages and fixtures that attempt to deliver a rewarding experience and leave the shopper feeling good. Here are a few checkpoints:

- **Use semiotic signs that connote happiness**. This is often overlooked, but nearly everyone likes sunshine, sunrises and sunsets, beaches, flowers, lakes, mountain vistas and animals.

- **Show your humanity.** Display a sense of humour or give your customer some evidence that you understand their lives and experiences.
- **Find and own your brand.** If you are clear on why your brand exists and how it makes people's lives better, you will be more confident with simple and bold design, saving you from trying to cram too many messages on a pack.

*Example*

Here's one concrete example of what to do. Add some trees. There's a company called Custom Made Palm Trees in Ohio and their website has loads of colourful photos of hotels, bars, pools and retail fixtures that have been given an instant facelift by the addition of some trees. The company's products range across preserved natural trees and fabricated trees.

As I write this, I am looking at one of their photographs, in particular. It is a free-standing fixture for use in a retail setting. A fabricated palm tree curves upwards from a shiny, red, circular base. The rather elegant curved trunk has three circular shelves set into it; they might be glass. The shelves are stocked with bottles of Grand Marnier liqueur. A sunny yellow backdrop reinforces the brand name without overpowering the main attraction, which is the tree. Above head height, the tree bursts into fronds of green leaves. An oversized, juicy-looking slice of lime is placed so that it appears to dangle from the branches of the tree. It bears the text, 'A better margarita'.

The more closely I look at it, the more my effort is rewarded, which is crucial if you are planning to interrupt people's shopping. It's not just a happy-looking tree and a novel, unexpected object to encounter in a retail setting. It's also very Art Deco. With its trio of round shelves it resembles a 1930s cocktail cabinet. The 1930s theme is carried throughout, in the colour palette, the reference to the Margarita cocktail, which is a 1930s creation, and the tree itself. It appears to be a Mexican fan palm and alludes to the cocktail's origins and more widely to the tourism trends of the 1930s, in which wealthy travellers could not get enough of Mexico, Egypt and Fiji, which were all seen as exotic destinations. This aesthetic results in more than a novelty tree: the tree is the attention-getter that then draws the viewer into a fantasy of 1930s glamour.

See Chapter 3, 'Desire', for more ways to attract shoppers with pleasing packs and displays.

## 2. Engagement

*Questions*

You are confident that you can design packs and fixtures that stand out from the crowd, but then **how should you drive engagement**? At this point, you are asking for even more of the shopper's attention, and you additionally want them to take some sort of action that deepens their knowledge of the brand, increases its salience and helps them to promote it to others.

This is a question that applies about equally to traditional, physical stores and their digital equivalents. In my experience, though, it is the physical stores that generally need more help in this area because it is less obvious to marketers what they could be doing and there are usually a lot of constraints in a physical setting.

*Answers*

People are aware that their time and attention are valuable commodities. Above, I argued for rewarding and compensating people for our attempts to attract and distract them by giving them something interesting to look at. When we try to deepen engagement, it actually becomes easier to fulfil this unspoken contract. If you supply people with some interesting activity or a practical consequence of having paid attention, you've increased your chances of people thinking that their investment of attention was worth it.

Here are three quick wins, then a real-world example.

- **Inspire experimentation** in whatever way you can. Sell a new cocktail, a new dessert recipe featuring ice cream or a new way to decorate the laundry room and make it a cosy nook, featuring your attractively packaged products.
- **Interactivity** has high potential for being engaging. It's a truism that written ad copy should end on a call to action and I think this is also true of our attempts to get the attention of shoppers in stores. Give people something to do.
- **Games and game rewards** have the potential to keep people interested over multiple visits. In my opinion, we should give people loyalty points or virtual coins as a reward for opening our apps, showing up at our stores and interacting with our displays, and indeed your competitors may be doing this already.

*Example*

Here's one concrete example that is easy to scale depending on your budget and type of store. How about installing a **flower wall**? The thing about flower walls is that people love to have their photos taken in front of them: they are great Instagram opportunities that will let your brand enjoy the benefit of your customers' interest in sharing content with their social networks.

I wrote about flower walls in my first book, *Using Semiotics in Marketing* (2020). At the time, they were a fairly new feature of weddings, which kept expanding in budget, scope and theatricality, in line with the rise of social media and the aestheticization of everyday life (the rising need for everything to look its best and be photographable for Instagram). Flower walls instantly connote a sense of 'a special occasion', perhaps because they are contrived pieces of artistry that draw on nature but do not occur in nature. They instantly solve the problem of 'what should be in the background' that plagues every consumer who regularly takes selfies for social media.

Flower walls are much cheaper than they used to be and are now sold as garden furniture at some stores, meaning price shouldn't be a big obstacle if you want to introduce one in a store or at the level of the fixture. There are also lots of ways to be creative with the idea of a flower wall; a good example is seen at the Singapore flagship store of clothing retailer Love, Bonito. Individual blooms are spaced widely apart, creating an original and photographable wall for shoppers to pose next to.

Here's the underlying principle: show people something unexpected and, ideally, beautiful, then give them something to do.

You can learn more about interactivity, games and play in Part Three of this book, especially the 'Play-to-earn' section of Chapter 7.

## 3. Selling

*Questions*

The traditional marketing funnel says that attention and engagement should be followed by purchase. My clients in retail marketing want to know:

- 'How do we convert attention and engagement into purchase?'
- 'What is the best way to communicate promotions and VFM messages?'
- 'How do we make fixtures easier and more pleasant to shop?'

I assume that we want to have an ethical and wholesome relationship with the consumer where we are not tricking them into buying things. Therefore, the solutions I offer here are focused on giving the customer a worthwhile experience and acknowledging their patronage.

## Answers

I think that shoppers know they are doing us a favour when they choose our store and our brand rather than competitors. They are not oblivious when we ask them to take risks, such as ordering from a new supplier, selecting a product they don't know much about, or serving some new dish for dinner that isn't an established family favourite. We can help them out by **mitigating risk** – reassuring them that they are achieving value for money – and **reducing friction** or physical barriers to purchase, as when people have to take their item to a till, where they join a queue.

Mitigating risk can be done by offering social proof. There are lots of ways to do this: being a household name certainly helps; confident branding, in the manner of a brand that is or soon will be a household name; explicit social-proof messages such as 'Philadelphia's No. 1 Favorite' and 'Good Housekeeping Award'; and clever use of relatable influencers.

Value for money can be delivered in lots of ways too, but there are some semiotic signs you can always lean on, such as red-and-white colour schemes for promotions, as well as more subtle moves such as placing your brand in contexts where value for money is a given. Reducing friction can mean giving people more and easier ways to pay, as well as making stores and their furniture more accessible.

## Example

In 2017, one of the big stories in US retail concerned CVS Pharmacy, the retail arm of CVS Health. It announced the introduction of vending machines to its stores. At first glance, a vending machine might not seem like a very exciting concept. It is hardly new technology. But when one examines these exact vending machines, they reveal themselves as fun and quite rich in meaningful semiotic signs. They also tick all the boxes for 'how to sell'.

- A bold red-and-white colour scheme says 'low prices' and 'value for money'. These are the colours of discounts and promotions in retail. The vending machine itself, as a concept, also promises low prices. Consumers have learned that small necessities come from vending machines, not jewels or things that take a lifetime to pay for.

- Bold and confident branding says 'this is a brand you know and trust'. Even if I'd never heard of CVS, the fact that it relies on its acronym alone to do nearly all the work of conveying factual information to the consumer would tell me that this is a brand everyone else knows.
- The self-service vending machine always implies immediate service: you don't have to queue for a till – you can pay and leave. You can also buy products anonymously and in relative privacy.
- Here's the clever part. Having taken care of VFM, trust and friction, CVS is also poking fun at old-fashioned vending machines. If these machines are often neglected, a little grubby, places to buy chocolate and cigarettes, then the CVS machine stands in shining opposition to all of that. It is large, modern and it sells healthy snacks as well as the dozens of other small items that pharmacies trade in. It's not just *any* vending machine; it's a wellbeing machine.

You can read more about value for money messages in Chapter 4, 'Meaning'.

## 4. Merchandising and category management

### Questions

Supermarkets can be challenging environments for shoppers and retailers alike. These kinds of stores often confront shoppers with vast walls of products that are hard to navigate, especially when every brand is shouting as loudly as possible with its packaging and the products are crammed together. What's more, when retailers do have a little space for merchandising, they aren't always clear on how best to use it. That's why I'm often asked these questions:

- How do we make aisles or large fixtures easier to read?'
- 'What's the best way to visually segment a category?'
- 'Can semiotics inspire better merchandising?'

### Answers

For aisles and large fixtures, whose arrangement may be completely lost on the confused shopper who only knows how to look for 'their' brand, I'm an advocate of shelf banners.

Shelf banners are good at getting attention. They are often unusual shapes and help to break the overpowering grid aesthetic that dominates most supermarket aisles. They provide a little visual relief and a sense that at least some brands are capable of breaking out of the orderly ranks.

Banners work best when they are positively doing something. In line with the advice I've given above, they do not merely distract the consumer or add to environmental noise. They perform some useful function. You can use shelf banners to:

- help shoppers distinguish products within a large range, such as 'fudge' versus 'chocolate' or 'snacks' versus 'meals';
- draw attention to some item of news, such as a new product. If you do this, try to link it to a promotion that offers special value, as the launch of your new product all by itself is not as exciting to shoppers as it is to brand owners.

If you're thinking of arranging items on tables or pedestals in stores, my advice is to choose arrangements that create some visual interest, to break up the grid, but don't let them become over-complicated or vulnerable to falling into disarray. You want people to engage by walking over to take a closer look and perhaps picking things up, but people will avoid the display if it looks like you don't want them to approach it, or it might fall over if they brush against it.

*Example*

There are a lot of shelf banners and companies that make them, but the one I'm looking at as I write these words was made by ActMedia,[1] a leading retail marketing company in Southeast Asia. It announces a new product: a 'sparkling' variant of Lipton Ice Tea. It is attached to a typical supermarket fixture that is made of a light metal frame with shelves, upon which bottles of the tea sit in neat rows, behind a low metal fence that discourages them from falling off.

The banner has an unusual shape, formed to resemble bubbles. Added to this, it's quite large, probably around a metre tall. The combined effect is to break up the visual uniformity of the aisle and is an easy way to get attention. The colours are light and fresh: apple green, sky blue. This is important when we take into account that most stores are quite dark, even though the lighting is always bright and appealing in marketing photos.

In a perfect world. I would have liked this banner to compensate the shopper for grabbing their attention. It would have been a good spot for a QR code, which shoppers in Southeast Asia know can be the source of coupons, samples and small gifts. Another way to use banners like these is as checkpoints: you can guide shoppers around the store by giving them virtual coins, stamps or small rewards to collect as they travel.

If you are thinking about shelf banners and segmenting categories, you will probably also like the questions that appear later on as group 8, 'Communicating brand architecture'.

## 5. Navigation

### Questions

I've had the pleasure of working with numerous retailers, including one successful UK chain that decided to open a flagship store in the north of England as the business grew larger and the brand more prominent. I was hired to consult on various aspects of interior design including in-store signage, and it was an exciting project because we were designing the store from the bottom up. The client had a number of interesting and practical questions that have become a recurring theme in my work with the retail sector.

- 'What signage should we place in store? What functions should it fulfil and how should it look?'
- 'How do we tell people about our low prices and reconcile that with the generally premium feel of the store?'

Sometimes, brand owners also have this question:

- 'How do we drive traffic towards our aisle or area of the store?'

### Answers

I wish I could show you some examples of bad in-store signage, but in the interests of diplomacy, I will ask you to find some yourself. Skip past Google Images, which is prone to showing you professionally taken photographs and head to an image-sharing app that's mainly used by the public, such as Flickr. Type in the names of some stores that you know. You'll see real interiors. Instinct will lead you to spot the 'bad' ones. There will be signs that are garish and lack any aesthetic quality, often the signs that announce low prices. There will be signs that have too much text. There will be signs that make claims, such as 'quality' and 'fresh' but lack any creativity or joy, which rather undermines their intended meaning.

When in-store signage goes wrong, it happens in line with an underlying tendency, which is for the store to revert to being a warehouse. Its mask slips and the shopper is forced to confront the fact that they are inside a warehouse, a place that isn't supposed to be attractive, and they are doing unpaid warehouse work. Many shoppers are trying to avoid noticing that, so they can have a more pleasant experience in store. They want to feel cared for. One way to meet that need, while at the same time guiding people around the store to their desired destinations, is signage that looks like someone once loved it.

*Example*

Perhaps you know Wegmans, the famous US grocery store. I've been enthusiastically taken to Wegmans by market research respondents whenever I was in the US for semiotic field trips or ethnography. It's a store that people are proud of. One thing that I always notice is its in-store signage. You can see some examples for yourself in the wegmans.com photo gallery, and perhaps your eye may alight on a photo taken in the fresh produce area, announcing organic vegetables.

Now that we've made a list of what signage does badly, we're in a better position to see what Wegmans is doing right. Here are its techniques:

- The signs that say 'Wegmans Organic' are mass-produced, but the typeface of 'Organic' looks like it was originally painted by hand, with a brush. The 'organic' signs are a fresh shade of green that does not offend the eye. These signs, which look at first glance like painted wood, are cut into a leaf shape. All these details are semiotic cues for 'someone cares about this food', 'quality' and 'fresh'.
- At the same time, Wegmans has price messages to communicate. It is not going to let 'organic' get in the way of value for money. There are signs at the back of the store ('Bananas, 0.69lb') which use the red, white and yellow colour-scape of 'discount prices' but these, too, look as though they were hand-painted for Wegmans and the components are creatively arranged, so that the text curves like a banana. Speaking of text, there's

not much of it. Wegmans doesn't believe in burdening shoppers with too much reading. The emphasis is on simple yet creative signs that make the store feel inviting; transporting the shopper into an imaginative space where products and people are loved.

Good in-store signs are like little works of art and are capable of attracting people into areas where they feel that the retailer is being welcoming.

## 6. In-store experience, including pleasure

*Questions*

In the sections so far in this chapter, I have listed several ways to attract and engage shoppers and help them to feel that they are somewhere better than a warehouse. There's always more one can do, and shopper experience will only gain in importance if we want retail businesses to stay competitive. The client organizations I work with have varying budgets and resources available to commit to shopper experience. That's why their questions may take either of these forms:

- 'Should we do shoppertainment?'
- 'Are there any semiotic rules for store design that are economical and easy to apply, and make the store into a more pleasant environment?'

*Answers*

The short answer regarding 'shoppertainment' is that we want to avoid randomly bolting on gimmicks to an otherwise lacklustre shopper experience. You could put a pinball machine in the corner of your store and it might be entertaining, but it would not achieve its potential as a marketing tool unless the game were meaningfully improved by shopping and the presence of the machine enhanced the in-store experience for everyone, even those who didn't play.

Immediately below, I describe the case of Casper, a retailer of sleep products, which benefited from the expertise of architects HWKN in creating highly experiential stores. The insight I want you to take away from this example is that you actually do not need a concept store or a large budget to create a worthwhile experience for shoppers. HWKN skilfully implemented some core principles that everyone can use:

- Use store space to offer people an activity that they can't do at home.
- Offer services that don't require product purchase; offer products that enhance the lasting value of an in-store experience.
- Decorate walls and neglected spaces with semiotic signs for happiness, such as stars and other objects from nature.
- Show people unexpected objects (the bar is quite low here – shoppers have low expectations of being surprised while shopping).
- Realize that adult humans, much like children and animals, are drawn to objects and places that have their own interiors. This could be a shop within a shop.

All of these can be implemented at a small scale, down to the level of packaging, and do not require vast investment.

*Examples*

Casper is an interesting US company that sells mattresses and other sleep products, online and in physical stores. Like so many retail businesses, it had a hard time during the COVID-19 pandemic, but has nonetheless gained a reputation for innovative in-store experiences. You can see and read about these by looking up the Dreamery, a Casper concept store in Manhattan, and you can view images of Casper Sleep Shops on the company's website, casper.com.

The Dreamery caught the attention of the press upon its launch in 2018 (for example, Hartmans, 2019). Customers paid $25 for a 45-minute nap in one of several 'sleep pods', space-age circular structures made of wood, reconciling futurism and nature in one design gesture. Behind a curtain, one could recline on a Casper mattress, with the loan of a pair of designer pyjamas and the gift of various skincare samples. The pods themselves sat within a store with walls of midnight blue, studded with twinkling stars. The Dreamery was designed by NYC architects HWKN (see hwkn.com).

The same firm designed the Sleep Shops, which are more conventional retail stores. I'm looking at a photo of one now. The store itself has a conventional exterior with plate-glass windows and a steel-framed door. Inside the well-lit interior are several structures made of the same pale wood as the Dreamery sleep pods. They are miniature houses, like a child's Wendy house, but scaled up so an adult can fit through the door. The doorways are arched and the unglazed windows are round or square. It's like being transported back to childhood. You can enter the houses to experience the mattresses. They are surprising and intriguing objects; they are playful and they offer a chance to try a product with no obligation to buy.

To learn more about creating memorable and pleasurable shopping experiences, look especially at Chapter 3, 'Desire' and Chapter 9, 'The future of retail'.

## 7. Communicating brand values

*Questions*

If you make or sell FMCG, which is intensely competitive, then you have grappled with the following questions:

- 'How do we communicate brand values through our packaging?'
- 'How do we communicate brand values at fixture?'

Semiotics has answers to these questions. You have a lot of options available to you. I will try to keep my comments here concise.

*Answers*

Chapter 4 of this book, 'Meaning', is full of practical advice about how to use semiotic signs to convey meanings such as 'premium', 'modern', 'sensational' and 'natural'. My advice to you here concerns your brand. I am sure you love your brand, which you built carefully and which is therefore more than just a collection of off-the-shelf meanings that seem trendy or desirable. I urge you to form a clear idea of why your brand exists, what its worldview is, and how it is making your customers' lives better. This will help you in various ways:

- It will be easier to identify your brand assets.
- You will feel less need to crowd packaging and fixtures with multiple layers of badges, blocks of text and other information-giving devices.
- It will free your creative imagination. You'll have an easier time thinking of point-of-sale activations because it will be easier to envisage what your brand, if it were a person, would do in any situation.

No matter what you choose as your brand personality or core values, the foundational principal is 'show – don't tell'. If you are a friendly brand, don't simply state it, but invest your resources in being friendly. If you are an innovative brand, then show people an innovation rather than an award that says 'most innovative supermarket'. Here's an example, involving some happy avocados.

## Example

Next/Now is a Chicago-based digital experience design agency. It created a food truck for its client, Avocados from Mexico. The Avo-Matic food truck was made for a food festival. Any time you can attach your brand or retail business to an event, you have created a little extra sense of something special happening. Consumers will see that you are making a special effort for something that is available for only a short time.

The truck itself has lots of digital and interactive elements to engage visitors, which you can view and read about on the Next/Now website.[2] I focus on only one aspect here, so we can see the underlying principle. Avocados from Mexico knows its own personality and purpose. It is a non-profit marketing organization that promotes consumption of Mexican avocados in the US. This benefits consumers and also 29,000 small avocado growers. Avocados from Mexico is understandably very proud of its achievements. A glance at its website shows that its tone of voice is upbeat and it is clear on how it is making the world a better place. Even its brand mark is jolly.

Next/Now designed an attractive and witty avocado food truck where people could order tasty dishes using digital touch pads. To keep people busy while they were waiting for their dish to be dispensed, the app invites them to play a mini game where they 'win' by smiling as broadly as possible for a camera. Players are rewarded with photos of their own smiles for use on social media, plus various avocado recipes and tips. The key thing that I want you to notice is that Next/Now recognized a brand with happiness at its core, encoded that as a smile (a semiotic sign for happiness) and applied that sign *to the face of the shopper*, not just to its own static brand comms.

This is what I mean by 'show – don't tell'. You don't need a big budget for interactive toys – those are just nice to have. You can communicate your brand values cost-effectively on pack or at fixture by cutting out extraneous messages and demonstrating your values rather than announcing them. If you think you are a witty brand, make people laugh. If you are a caring brand, focus on making people feel cared for by showing how you are making a special effort for them.

## 8. Communicating brand architecture and range

*Questions*

I am frequently asked the following questions, which go hand in hand with anxieties about expressing brand values:

- 'How do we communicate brand architecture and range through our packaging?'
- 'How do we communicate brand architecture and range at the fixture?'

The architecture in question is usually horizontal; that is, there could be a range of products that are similar in price and quality, but vary in format, expected usage occasion and perceived consumer need, and within those tiers there could be flavour variants. Sometimes the company is unsure which aspects of the brand architecture are the key differentiators, and sometimes they are additionally unclear on what the brand stands for. This can lead to anxiety and crowded communications.

*Answers*

There are simple answers to questions of communicating architecture and range, and then there are deeper answers. If you are looking for quick and easy solutions, here are a few:

- Link pack formats to product formats. If you make breakfast foods, put cereal in a tube, liquids in a pouch and baked goods in a bag. Use the pack format consistently to help people detect differences within the range.
- If your products vary according to something like how long they take to prepare, then try grouping them at fixture with banners or shelf runners that say things like 'ready to eat', 'microwave 5 minutes' and 'oven bake'.
- You can also use on-pack text and icons to help people find their way around. Like many stores, my local supermarket offers a mechanism where customers can build a meal for two by choosing from quite a wide range of components. Items feature stickers that say 'main dish', 'side dish', 'dessert' and customers easily grasp the idea that they are supposed to choose one of each. They are charged a flat rate for the meal as long as they select within the range.

The deeper and better answer is to identify how your architecture benefits the consumer, exactly. Why do *they* need your brand architecture? The following is an example of a brand that seems to know.

*Example*

Happy Family Organics is a US company that makes foods for babies and young children. I single it out here because I was struck by the way it helps shoppers to navigate their way around a wide range of products with different specifications and purchases.

The main way that these foods are grouped for the assistance of shoppers is 'baby', 'toddler' and 'child'. Some pack formats such as pouches are found at every tier, so format is not a reliable guide to the intended consumer. This means that the company has to do all the communications work on pack, using visual signs and symbols. In line with my advice above, there's one immediately obvious strategy and one strategy that is deeper and more connected to consumer need.

The immediately visible strategy consists of slightly varying the brand name. It appears as 'Happybaby', 'Happytot' and 'Happykid', depending on the age of the intended recipient. The more interesting strategy is that the brand's architectural cues go beyond simply applying labels of 'baby', 'toddler' or 'child'. These labels are bits of confirming evidence, not the main event.

The main event is that the brand shows an intelligent awareness of the things that parents worry about with regard to feeding their differently aged children. Viewed from one angle, a large part of the experience of being a new parent is an education in what one should be worrying about, and when.

Thus, the baby foods within the Happy Family Organics architecture are named after specific vegetables, which, as semiotic signs, are a mix of traditional and wholesome (cauliflower, broccoli), and colourful and adventurous (purple carrots). Babyhood is as much a stage for adults as it is for infants themselves, and the special way in which socially conforming parents are supposed to comply with feeding their baby is by weaning it onto the correct foods, which means carrots, even if the parent is mainly eating Doritos. The consumer is presented with the opportunity to feel like a good parent by recognizing that one's job as a food educator is to persuade the baby to happily consume these wholesome-yet-exciting combinations of vegetables.

The toddler foods are different. The way the foods are named and described changes. There is less focus on simply naming familiar vegetables and much more focus on planned nutrition. The brand offers (the parents of) toddlers several 'super foods' pouches: the implication is that active toddlers need extra fuel for their newly acquired superpowers. This is a message that the toddler's parent can be relied on to have absorbed, along with other truisms, such as 'toddlers can make mornings chaotic' (so breakfast foods are labelled 'super mornings', because isn't that what every parent would like?). What's more, all parents learn or are taught that 'toddlers are picky eaters', hence the relevance of pouches marked 'love my veggies'.

The 'kid' food packs make big flavour promises, through extra-vivid colours and vibrant depictions of glistening fruit. Ingredients that are everyday for most American children, such as bananas and oatmeal, are mixed with more sophisticated ingredients usually reserved for adults, such as pomegranates and cinnamon, and there is the ever-tempting chocolate. At this point, the parent's dilemma, which they are relied on to know and recognize, is how to feed 'healthy' foods to strong-willed children who live for sweets and yearn to be treated as grown-ups.

I discuss this strategy, in which architecture is expressed through packaging, because of its close attention to what the parent or shopper is feeling. It understands the culturally driven concerns of parents of differently aged offspring and communicates the range by addressing those concerns directly. This is a much more sensitive approach than simply labelling things 'baby' and 'child' or presenting pouches versus bars.

When you can identify the reasons why your customers need your brand architecture, and you are also sure of your brand values, knowing which semiotic signs to include on your pack or fixture becomes a lot easier.

## 9. E-commerce

*Questions*

I have spoken about e-commerce at length in the four chapters of this book that concern the future of retail. There we encountered a future in which 'e-commerce' as a word and an idea, like 'omnichannel marketing' and 'shoppertainment' fails to describe how businesses will compete for a population of consumers who are online as much or more than they are offline, and who care nothing for 'channels', only novel experiences and instant wish fulfilment. If we are relying on e-commerce, channels and shoppertainment, we may be doing too little to save our businesses in the long term.

I am sure you know all this, and yet right now you still have outstanding questions that are located in the present day, such as:

- 'How do we design a good e-commerce website?'
- 'What should go in a 15-second video for social media?'
- 'What is a good pack shot or product shot, in the context of people shopping on hand-held devices?'

## Answers

Let's take these in reverse order. Of course, a good photo makes the product or pack clearly visible – that's its first job. If you have the opportunity to show more than one photo, then include a shot that gives a visual point of reference for the pack size, as this is where people often become confused. When choosing photos for specific world regions or e-commerce platforms, follow local norms. Western shoppers who are used to Amazon expect to see a 'main' product photo that has only one item in shot and plenty of white space around it. But on platforms such as JD.com and Lazada, it's quite common to add elements to the photo, such as lines of text, informing shoppers of discounts, or decorative frames. Don't over-think it. You don't need to decide which method is 'best'. Shoppers will tend to prefer the type of display that they are used to and it's not your job to reform their taste.

If photos are good for freezing a moment in time and capturing your product or pack at its best angle, then videos are of course about capturing things that move. Fifteen seconds is long enough to show how something in your consumer's world will change as they use the product. Many products, from oven cleaner to educational items, claim to transform the user; a 15-second video is your chance to show or imagine that transformation. Remember that through your video you are helping your consumer to enter a pleasant fantasy about how they will feel, so prioritize feelings over rational claims such as 'concentrated' or '20% off', which can be expressed with static text and images.

A good e-commerce website is one that is imaginative, creative and cared-for while still being easy to navigate and use. An example is coming right up.

## Example

Wannabe Toys is an Italian retailer that sells toys for adults; mainly action figures and collectibles. Its website has a conventional structure that is therefore easy to navigate. There is a landing page, a search function that returns lists, individual product pages and of course a page where you pay. This makes it very straightforward to use. But beyond this reliable and familiar structure, no effort has been spared to make the shopping experience into something as magical and tender as possible. No detail has been overlooked. For example:

- If you are using your desktop PC to access the site, as I am right now, your conventional arrow-shaped cursor will turn into a delicate halo, which is followed around by a shadow, so that you can see which area of the screen you are about to click on.
- There are no white backgrounds anywhere on the site. All the pages have a nostalgic, sepia background except for the payment and checkout page, which is black.
- At least one of the typefaces on the site, the one used for priority information such as headings, appears to be custom designed. Its elegant details are visible because the size of the letters is large.
- Product shots are also large, they take up a lot of real estate on the screen. Seemingly, the retailer feels no need to impress the customer by showing them hundreds of minute pictures of stock. They prefer to impress by showing them large and beautifully photographed close-ups of just two or three products at any given moment, based on the user's selections from a text menu.
- Text does not pop or flash into view. It rolls and glides at the leisurely pace of something manufactured a long time ago.

This site is not trying to be avant-garde with its design. Anyone could understand how to use it, at whatever level of technical proficiency. And yet every conceivable detail of the site design has been lovingly and imaginatively executed, producing a dreamy and almost euphoric experience, in which the brand draws you into its embrace. I urge you to take a look at it.

# 10. Global marketing

## Questions

Semiotic analysis results in a lot of practical advice about how to design, package and display things. Its recommendations are based on cultural insights. In practice, this means that as a buyer or user of semiotics, you will often receive advice or discover a way forward for marketing that is tailored to a specific region and a specific category. Marketing personal care items in France is inevitably going to be different from marketing pet food in California, so knowing about these cultural differences makes for better marketing communications and more successful brands. Eventually, though, nearly all client organizations arrive at these questions:

- 'Does semiotics reveal rules for marketing and retailing that apply globally?'
- 'Are there semiotic signs, such as words and images, that have universal appeal?'

## Answers

The short answer is yes, some strategies work everywhere and across most categories. I know of a couple of dozen, of which several are recurring themes in this book. Because you have come to this chapter looking for quick answers, here is a selection of semiotic signs and design strategies that will not let you down.

- **Curves** seem to be universally popular. There will be occasions when you choose to instead use sharp angles, perhaps if you are selling scientific instruments or another product or service that implies precision. But most of the time when you are selling goods to consumers, curves are a safe bet. They soften the harsh lines of supermarkets and make store entrances feel special.
- Cultures around the world appreciate **nature**, and indeed, this is one reason why people like curves. You can introduce trees, flowers, foliage, the sun and other objects from nature into marketing communications and at point of sale across most consumer-facing categories.
- Adults and children alike can recognize semiotic signs for **happiness**, such as balloons. What's more, they each recognize conventional colour schemes.

Children know that objects in primary colours are more likely to be for them, while adults recognize deep reds, blues, greens and greys as signifying an adult experience or occasion.

- Any and all signs of real **creativity, imagination and attention to detail** at the level of packaging, fixtures, merchandising and store design are capable of being interpreted by shoppers as signs of care, meaning that you the brand owner or retailer care about them and find their custom to be worth the effort of making things beautiful and comfortable.

## Examples

In this final section, I refer you to two examples. The first is a fine example of an everyday store making a big effort. It is a branch of Boots, the pharmacy chain that is part of the Walgreens Boots Alliance, an organization I have worked with in the UK. The branch is a flagship store in Indonesia and was announced in May 2021.[3]

The second example is a Dutch optician called Hofstede Optiek, with store design by architects Nowotny Atelier,[4] also in the Netherlands. It exemplifies the same principles, but takes them a little further and helpfully demonstrates what more can be achieved. If you follow the links in the endnotes to view these stores, you will see how they tick off the items I listed above.

- Both make good use of curves. Boots has a pleasantly curved exterior and adds cursive script and trailing decorations.
- Hofstede Optiek goes so far with curves that the interior of the store is positively organic, like being inside a cave or a bubble. There are lots of natural wood features in the interior fittings.
- Boots knows that balloons are a universally recognized sign of celebration; just right for a new flagship store.
- Hofstede Optiek is not a party destination, but its careful lighting almost creates the feel of an upmarket wine bar or nightclub.
- Both stores choose colours that appeal to adults. Boots opts for a sophisticated midnight blue that's similar to Casper's, discussed earlier, and Hofstede Optiek punctuates its natural cream and wood tones with splashes of glamorous purple.

FIGURE 11.1 Nowotny Atelier's design for Hofstede Optiek's store in The Hague

Reproduced with kind permission of Hofstede Optiek and Raoul Suermondt architectural photography

If you like what you see in this chapter and have not yet read the rest of the book, I encourage you to explore the earlier chapters, where all of these topics are discussed in more depth. If you're all caught up and keen to do some semiotic analysis of your own, please turn to Chapter 12. I have something for you.

## Endnotes

1 https://www.omg-asia.com/actmedia-asia.html (archived at https://perma.cc/Z6YX-PP9J) and see a banner at https://www.omg-asia.com/actmedia/_gallery/shelfvision-banner/slide6.jpg (archived at https://perma.cc/XJ8G-XJTG)
2 You can see the Avo-Matic in Next/Now's portfolio at: https://nextnowagency.com/project/facial-emotion-tracking-food-truck/ (archived at https://perma.cc/ZVP4-BMN7) and an article at: https://www.foodtruckoperator.com/articles/food-truck-with-touchscreens-educates-students-about-avocados/ (archived at https://perma.cc/P2WN-Q5TE)
3 See the press release at: https://www.walgreensbootsalliance.com/news-media/our-stories/boots-opens-its-doors-its-first-flagship-franchise-store-indonesia (archived at https://perma.cc/2WG2-YF3Z)

4 www.hofstede-optiek.nl (archived at https://perma.cc/5MFL-DVVH) and www.nowotny.nl (archived at https://perma.cc/8H6D-RL4X)

## Reference

Hartmans, A (2019) Inside Casper's Dreamery nap room in New York City, *Business Insider*, https://www.businessinsider.com/casper-dreamery-nap-room-nyc-review-photos-2018-7?r=US&IR=T (archived at https://perma.cc/89D6-EUUD)

# 12

# Tools for thinking: how to generate ideas using semiotics

Welcome to the final chapter of the book, in which I complete a quest that I set for myself in Chapter 1. There I promised to help you develop a semiotic perspective or point of view that you can apply to any brand, business category or quirk of consumer behaviour. In my experience, the best way to master this point of view is to work on a skill called **top-down analysis**. Let me briefly remind you what that is.

Top-down analysis is a very important activity in semiotics that, for me, amounts to at least half of my thinking time when I'm doing research. It involves taking a series of prompt questions and hypotheses and applying them to a market, category or brand. These are not small questions, such as 'Does green mean healthy?' or 'Should we use Times New Roman?', which are a matter for bottom-up analysis. They are big questions aimed at how society is organized and how we perceive reality.

Every practitioner of semiotics who carries out top-down analysis has a set of these questions at hand. The exact questions on the list vary from one person to the next, but perhaps only slightly, depending on their experience and research interests. My own personal list has a few dozen items and in this chapter I organize some of the most powerful ones into five themed groups, for your convenience.

Have fun with this chapter. The questions and prompts are challenging, but they deliver fabulous returns in the shape of new ideas that are strategic and sometimes game changing. All the prompts ask you to look at the world around you from a specific, semiotic point of view, and, if you keep at it, it is a skill that grows. After a while you will have a large collection of prompts that will enable you to generate original ideas concerning virtually any topic, and they will come to mind easily without having to pull a list out of your pocket.

> **WHAT'S COMING UP**
>
> In this chapter, I share a selection of the prompts that I use every day in my work as a semiologist. I use them because they kickstart creative thinking and reveal insights. By the end of this chapter, you will be able to:
>
> - quickly identify 15 unique prompts that will help you think afresh about any and all aspects of retail marketing;
> - follow the examples provided here and apply each prompt to a real-world business situation, such as the ever-present challenges of improving logistics and delivery, engaging shopper attention, pacifying loyal but discontented customers and responding to the non-trivial efforts of consumers to make better lives for themselves;
> - recognize opportunities for further, original semiotic research, if you are attracted by the chance to make a groundbreaking discovery in semiotics – five research pathways are shown here, with the prompts grouped under them.

## Reality is in crisis

### Insight

**'Reality is in crisis'** is a phrase that I do not use casually, even though it has some of the semiotics of an attention-getting headline. In recent decades, accelerated by the rise of digital culture, there is a widespread loss of certainty in ideas and institutions that once seemed reliable. There is an erosion of faith in traditional authority figures as well as science, mainstream religions and various social codes that used to be allowed to guide and shape behaviour, such as gender roles and ideas of character and citizenship.

The consequences of reality being in crisis are significant. On the one hand, it is linked to contemporary malaises such as anxiety, identity crises and disorienting encounters with fake news. On the other hand, the collapse of reality might not have happened if people en masse were not desperate to break away from it or break it up. Its positive benefits to consumers include more rights and freedoms than before to decide who they are. There are more ways to get paid than having a job, there is an upsurge in creative work and many aspects of digital space and culture are more sensational and exciting than the physical world that preceded it.

Below are three prompts that I use daily, all connected to this keystone hypothesis. Amazon, architecture and laundry detergent will supply helpful examples.

*Prompt*

**'There is nothing outside the text.'**
This phrase, common in semiotics, is the subject of academic debate. We need not tangle with it here. I invite you not to wrestle with this provocative phrase, but only to find it a useful hypothesis that might mean 'There is no access to the world except through human-made semiotic signs.' If that's not the whole academic story, it is quite enough to keep us marketers busy.

*Opportunity*

The opportunity here is to take the brakes off your imagination. If, for all practical purposes, nothing is outside of semiotic signs and their exchange in human communications, then everything is within that realm and is available for negotiation. Semiotics is an invitation to challenge and break assumptions that may have held you back until now, such as the seemingly obvious differences between babies, toddlers and children, or legacy ideas about retailing.

*Example*

Earlier in this book, I referred to a building design patented by Amazon, with architecture that resembles a beehive. It has many small entrances, far above street level, not easily accessed by humans. It is designed for drones. At first glance, it might seem inevitable or obvious that building design should place human accessibility first. But perhaps there is nothing outside the text; that is, there are no rules that are absolute necessities. If so, and we come to realize that buildings are limited mostly by our own sense of the way things are somehow *supposed* to be, it's then easier to design radical, new structures.

*Prompt*

**'Where have I seen this before?'**
It might have been tech writer Kevin Kelly who said that today's internet user, with all the many tech tools and imaginative opportunities available to them, ultimately pursues only one question: 'What is it?' People who try to answer this question, for example when they encounter your new product or store, begin with familiar reference points, because it's all they have.

*Opportunity*

Design products, brands and marketing communications that strategically use familiar motifs or metaphors, even if you are offering something new. They are easy for shoppers to understand and point their expectations in the preferred direction.

*Example*

'Where have I seen this before?' is a question perfectly anticipated by calling the Amazon building 'a beehive'. Even though the building is quite radical, even by the standards of industrial architecture, which can sometimes seem outlandish to the lay person, a beehive is something familiar, even cosy. It even makes drones seem nicer – bees are hard workers, they're eco-friendly and not a nuisance to humans. This metaphor highlights the wholesome, beautiful and creative aspects of the building.

*Prompt*

**'If something is true, the opposite of that thing is also true.'**
This is a hypothesis and the subject of a technique called 'truisms', detailed in my first book, *Using Semiotics in Marketing*. The short version is that you should identify a few foundational claims that 'everyone knows' are true of your category or sector. Find reasonable oppositions to each of those claims. Find the evidence and build the case that the opposite is true.

*Opportunity*

The big opportunity is to identify new and refreshing stances for brands. Laundry detergent Persil had a famous campaign, 'Dirt is good', which is based on an oppositional truth. It takes the conventional idea that dirt is bad and finds a creative but reasonable basis for inverting it.

### Example

I perceive oppositional thinking throughout Amazon and its competitors. Early on, online retailers embraced oppositional truisms such as 'People don't need to see an item before they buy it' and 'Of course people will trust us by putting their credit card details into a web form', which at the time were controversial. More recently, we see it when physical stores open in the form of Amazon Go, and Freshippo, just when it seemed that they were in danger of becoming history. Be oppositional. See where it takes you.

## Reality is under construction

### Insight

The prompts in this section are informed by a different take on reality as changeable, sometimes fragile and culturally specific. Rather than focusing on a crisis or collapse of reality, we may instead perceive one long, constructive process. Indeed, if there's one thing we can say about the shopper of today, it is that they expect to actively participate in the three-way relationship between shopper, brand and retailer. They want to be consulted and listened to, which is different from the early days of marketing when they were expected to trustingly absorb ad messages and fill out an opinion survey if they were lucky enough to be invited.

Even though consumers are sometimes dismayed by the fragility of things that they had confidently trusted as real, most are simultaneously gladdened by the perception that some power is finally theirs. It's exciting to think that the ordinary person has the chance to shape the future and change history. It's also exciting to think that even small changes in the way they use language, shop, work and play can contribute to individual freedom, larger social change and a better tomorrow.

Here are three of my most-used prompts that connect to the hypothesis that the construction of reality is an ongoing project, in which people like feeling involved.

*Prompt*

'Where there is choice, there is meaning.'
All communications, amateur and professional, are 'designed', and where there are design decisions, there is an expression of meaning, the possibility of communication, and actions that help to shape reality. If you manufacture some food item, and all of your competitors sell it in a rectangular pack while your version arrives in a container which is a pyramid, you have a design decision that has worked for chocolate (Toblerone), tea bags (PG Tips) and boxes of facial tissues (Kleenex) and which says, at a minimum, that you are trying hard to keep things interesting and a little sensational for consumers.

*Opportunity*

The opportunity is to realize that consumers actually want to experience your product or retail offering as meaningful, and that contributions to meaning can come from either your side or theirs. On your side, small changes to your graphic design or marketing copy can work to help consumers ascribe meaning to whatever you are selling, even if it's something simple, like 'this is premium and worth paying a bit more for'. On their side, every time your customers or shoppers exercise choice, for example by building their own bundle of products, choosing and naming a new variant or using their purchases to invest in social causes, you are giving them the opportunity to tell themselves a story about why they and their actions matter.

*Example*

One of the reasons why shoppers love products that can be *customized* is because their choice, their design decision, imbues the object with meaning. This is the difference between a car with personalized number plates that were specially ordered, versus a key ring that happens to have one's first initial on it, chosen from a rack of prefabricated items that features everyone's first initial.

*Prompt*

'How are commonplace and everyday features of reality constructed? Do they vary from one place to the next?'
When I use this prompt, I ask myself to consider what is particular about the semiotic design and construction of things that seem commonplace. One

good way to handle this is to ask how taken-for-granted aspects of reality manifest themselves in different situations. Some completely ordinary, uncontroversial ideas such as 'a family meal' or 'a supermarket' can be very variable, not just in their executional details but in the local and cultural values which those details embody.

## Opportunity

The opportunity is to develop a new appreciation of why certain versions of reality are valued. If you understand that, you understand a lot about your customers. A great way to get a handle on your topic is to look at how it is built up and constructed in different parts of the world.

## Example

Here's a real-world example that follows on from the Boots store that we looked at in Chapter 11. I recently had a very interesting conversation with a client about the semiotics of retail. One of us kept saying 'pharmacy' and the other favoured 'drug store'. At first, we treated these words as interchangeable, but soon realized that they differ for a reason. 'Pharmacy' describes the special licence and expertise of the pharmacist. Without the pharmacist, there is no pharmacy. It's not a surprise that *'pharmacie'* is the preferred word in France, which values expertise. 'Drugstore' describes a shopping opportunity. It may include a pharmacy counter that dispenses medicines but also provides hundreds of other daily necessities for the convenience of shoppers. It's not a surprise that this is the name of choice in the United States. When we understand how language connects to culture, we are better able to build the pharmacies – and drugstores – that people want.

## Prompt

**'What new versions of reality are we capable of imagining? What new versions of reality are being ushered in?'**
I asked myself these questions a lot as I was writing this book, because the research brought up a lot of challenging observations. For instance, I've been interested for several years in the way that play has morphed into work, first writing about the subject in a paper called 'Futurology through semiotics' (2009). At the time, it was a prediction. Now it is a reality in the

form of play-to-earn business models. It makes me consider a new prediction, which is that play will soon need to wrestle its way out of the grip of work and be rediscovered as a form of rebellion.

*Opportunity*

The opportunity offered by this prompt is to envision new futures, a daring act at the best of times, but one which can be given a boost of confidence when there are conceptual tools at hand. Over time, you will become practised at identifying 'versions of reality' and then identifying conflicts or variations between versions. When you can see how dependent reality is on contingent and changeable ideas, you will be able to imagine futures, including future business scenarios, which have not happened yet.

*Example*

As I write these words and return my attention yet again to the evolving relationship between play and work, I'm reminded of the playful and quite subversive project that was 'The Shed at Dulwich', a largely fictional restaurant created by British journalist Oobah Butler. In 2017, the Shed was briefly the highest-rated London venue on TripAdvisor, despite never having opened for business or served any customers. To celebrate its success, it opened for one night only, serving microwaveable ready meals to ten unsuspecting guests who were seated outdoors on garden furniture. Of course, the project has its serious side, as a critique of online reviews. But it was popular with the public because of its sheer frivolity and cheeky manipulation of reality. If your brand or store aims to be fun, this kind of seemingly unproductive non-work is where I would suggest looking for inspiration.

## Everything is a group effort

*Insight*

Here's a useful phrase: 'consensus reality'. It turns out to be surprisingly user-friendly to busy marketers, even though its academic origins might lead a person to expect heavy lifting. Consensus reality describes the reality you are inhabiting right now and hypothesizes that it exists by common agreement. Common agreement about what's real and what isn't seems a necessary foundation for most of humanity's notable achievements, by which I mean things like vaccination, flight, space exploration and the invention of the internet. It's like a set of rules for playing the game of life.

As you already know from our earlier discussions, different versions of reality exist and sometimes compete with each other, as when people have dramatically different views of the world, which are shaped by their politics. We can also see that some people are more or less outside consensus reality much of the time. These people include children, who say outlandish things because they have yet to fully learn and embrace consensus reality, and surrealist artists, whose job is to shake the foundations of consensus reality by revealing other worlds.

Consensus reality not only 'works' in the sense of supporting the ongoing march of human civilization, it also feels like a safe place to be for most people, most of the time. Not many people like being outsiders; there is comfort in togetherness. What's more, although today's digital culture has its brutal aspects, particularly in encounters on social media, it also brings an upswing of creativity and co-operation, as people spot chances to take pleasure in groups.

*Prompt*

**'Where do you see people invoking their own group memberships? What social functions are being fulfilled?'**

Where you can, observe the conversations of your customers. See how they form into groups and make statements about what kind of group it is, what version of reality it agrees with and what kinds of people are members. When people go to online discussion forums and classify themselves in graphic terms as anxious new mothers or oppressed workers seeking justice, they shape the community into exactly that.

*Opportunity*

The opportunity is to notice that people are aware of reality as a group project and are hopeful of their power to shape it. What's more, some of the things they want to do are best achieved in groups. Businesses could choose to respond to this more than they do presently.

*Example*

A simple example is to please groups who are unhappy about change by conceding to their desire for 'the way things used to be'. *World of Warcraft*, a game by Activision Blizzard, is one of the world's longest-running multi-player games, first launching in 2004. By the late 2010s there was a sharp distinction between 'original' players, who had poured effort into the game for 15 years, and recently acquired 'casual' players, who demanded ease of access and simple instructions. Blizzard responded in 2019 by launching '*Classic WoW*' which transports veteran players back to the product much as it was in 2004. It is a separate game from what is now informally known as 'Retail WoW', its modern counterpart. Activision Blizzard does not publish subscriber numbers and the company is not free from PR problems, but *Classic WoW* is widely agreed to be a commercial success and perhaps to have doubled the number of active users of *World of Warcraft* products.[1]

*Prompt*

**'Where do you see people investing in each other? What kinds of things attract investment?'**
When online communities form, or when offline relationships manifest online, people invest in each other as well as possibly investing in a larger group. Investing in each other, using money, time or affection is a form of pro-social behaviour, which is studied by psychologists. They usually find that pro-social behaviour makes people feel good – the people enacting that behaviour, as well as the recipients.

*Opportunity*

The opportunity is to give people more ways to build or cement their relationships with each other. Earlier in this book (Chapter 9) I spoke about creator economies and consumers being willing to support each other's creative efforts, through purchases of direct-to-consumer brands, donations, tips, votes, 'likes' and other mechanisms. Often, they are handing over money to strangers or to people they know only from a distance in parasocial relationships. Just as often, they are investing in relationships that exist offline. A friend of mine who attended a family party remarked that they 'needed' to get on Facebook and like a few people's photos, because not to do so would be failing to make an affectionate gesture where one was expected.

*Example*

Advice and support forums in which people can reach out to peers, are a great way to increase engagement with the right kind of brand. Noom is an online weight-loss programme where the main features of the product are digital tools for tracking exercise and food intake, lots of psychology tips, plus a certain amount of one-to-one counselling with a Noom expert who is assigned to your case. Added to this, Noom sensibly places users into peer support groups, and some users, particularly in the US, show great readiness to share information about their personal journey and get the group to gel. Similar behaviour is sometimes seen in the artificial and temporary online communities assembled for market research purposes. Where relationships are available, lots of people will invest.

*Prompt*

**'Where do you see heightened energy? What is the anatomy of excitement?'** I include the topic of excitement under this heading of group effort, because excitement reaches greater heights and is more sustainable when it affects groups. For me, one of the hallmarks of excitement is people making elaborate speeches to each other about how excited they are. When we considered the GameStop saga in Chapter 6, I quoted a Reddit user who made a passionate and eloquent speech, with motifs of courage, victory, nostalgia and belief in the future, among other rousing ideas. Whenever you see someone being excited, I encourage you to take a close look, because even trivial events may be wrapped in noble ideals and precious feelings.

*Opportunity*

The opportunity is to recognize when people are helpfully revealing things that are tremendously important to them. You then have the chance to build these ideals and values into your business and brand and show people that you know what matters. If you think about it, it is beyond the expectation of most market research focus groups that people would suddenly start making speeches about love, honour and how it feels to make history. In my own research as a semiologist, I therefore try to be alert to this sort of thing happening in the wild.

*Example*

Group events and their build-ups are among the best places to observe expressions of excitement. My honest advice to you as a marketer is to find organic sources of excitement and inspiration, and do what you can to encourage people in that situation. Help them celebrate their birthdays, for example. I noticed that, as people ventured out from the restrictions of COVID-19 lockdowns, they wanted some help making memories. At the same time, there are consultants out there who will tell you that you should strive to become the world's most inspiring brand. Based on the research that went into this book, I do not reach the same conclusion. I think it is over-reaching and is the wrong order of priorities. People want to own their joy and their ability to inspire others. They do not live in hope of your brand stealing all their human glory by being the world's most inspiring snack or razor. Support naturally occurring inspiration and let people own what they make.

## How to decode stories

*Insight*

This book has lots of content concerning storytelling. We saw in Chapter 5, for example, how six different kinds of stories fed into just one shopping spree; a relatively simple event that happened entirely online and involved a cast of only two characters. It is not my intention to repeat the whole of that analysis here, nor merely to state that I attend to stories because they are interesting; I want to convey *how* I approach stories, whether they occur in consumer talk or in marketing communications. In fact, there are a number of things that one can choose to look for in stories, like the way they manage tense, setting, pace and third-person versus first-person narration. Semiotics has long benefited from being an interdisciplinary project, so I regularly borrow techniques from discourse analysis and conversation analysis, which are both good with stories, and also from narratology, which is a branch of literary theory. These are all places where you will find treasure if you become passionate about decoding stories.

In this section, I offer three of my favourite story-decoding prompts. Stories address anxieties and fears, they make wishes come true, they can be very safe and comforting, and some of them offer delicious puzzles to be solved. Being able to appreciate the many valuable functions of stories helps marketers make best use of them.

*Prompt*

**'Is the story a myth?'**
Specifically, does the story act like a fairy tale in attempting to explain or relieve common anxieties? In my previous book, you can read about the details of an innovation technique called the Semiotic Square which uses myth, but here I will cut right to the chase. There are some anxieties that persist throughout history, such as the problem of deceptive appearances. Indeed, in an age of internet scams and catfishing, that old anxiety seems more relevant than ever. Myths and fairy tales like 'Snow White' and 'Beauty and the Beast' succeed because they allow us to explore our fears that bad things are sometimes seductive, and reassure ourselves that good things sometimes come in unconventional packages.

*Opportunity*

Myth is an aspect of stories that semiologists are very keen on, especially those serving the business community, because it is easy for brands to find a role for themselves as relievers of tension and solvers of problems.

*Examples*

Two great examples are found in this book. British cleaning influencer Mrs Hinch is a one-woman brand and self-made myth that resolves a problem resonant with lots of women who do their own cleaning: how to reconcile unpleasant and low-status chores such as cleaning the toilet with being the epitome of feminine glamour. That she manages to do this while simultaneously being quite self-aware and 'keeping it real' is a testament to her marketing abilities. See also the Robinhood investment app, which sold thousands of shares to day traders, no doubt based in part on its branding, invoking an enduring myth about a man who stole from the rich to give to the poor. You can read the rest of that story in Chapter 6.

*Prompt*

**'Inside every story is another, hidden between the lines, waiting to come out.'**
I find that today's consumers, perhaps because of their relative comfort with multiple realities, are happy when they can detect a story inside a story. When they want to, they can do this more often than not, and things only

go the way brands would prefer some of the time. If you tell a brand story about how caring your company is, people will try to detect ways in which it is not caring, which are hinted at or betrayed in the text. This is inconvenient for businesses, but we cannot blame consumers for being sceptical.

*Opportunity*

The opportunity is to create brands and marketing communications that have a prepared story within a story, which consumers may then have the pleasure of uncovering. I'm reminded of the 'golden age' of detective fiction, a Western phenomenon lasting from 1920 to 1945. Readers of the time couldn't get enough of writers like Agatha Christie, whose novels revolved around 'whodunnit' puzzles, usually concerning the identities and motives of murderers. For readers, the fun and the great triumph of these stories was their own victory in piecing together clues and solving the puzzle ahead of the story's detective and ahead of their friends.

*Examples*

People love uncovering the 'real story' behind things, and it works well for brands that have an eccentric founder or a sudden change of direction in their origin stories. Apple is more enjoyable as a brand because of its idiosyncratic founder, Steve Jobs, perhaps especially when one uncovers popular theories such as 'Jobs was attempting to live on an extreme vegetarian diet consisting of only fruit, so that's where the company got its name' (Byrne, *nd*). Mattel is a much more interesting brand when one hears that the founders tried to start a company making picture frames, but succumbed to an obsession with building dolls' houses, leading to the founding of a toy company. Rumours and theories need not be strictly true to work their charm. What's important is that people have the enjoyable sense of finding out for themselves.

*Prompt*

'Does the story contain a just-world hypothesis? Is virtue eventually rewarded? Does compliance with effortful social norms deliver success?'
Many people love rags-to-riches stories in which someone is catapulted into another life by winning the lottery or discovering that they are a wizard.

These stories are appealing because of the element of 'it could happen to anyone – it could happen to me.' At the same time, most people realize that they aren't going to win the lottery or receive an invitation from Hogwarts. They also aren't obsessed, genius inventors or mavericks. Most people are just trying to get by in a conventional way. They put in a lot of effort to do the right thing according to the local standards of their culture, and they like being reassured that it is going to pay off. Many years ago, I read an analysis of TV sit-coms, which said that they were always conservative in their final import. The events of the story upset convention in amusing ways, but order is always restored by the end. If it were not, the story might be more disturbing than funny.

## Opportunity

Your opportunity is to reassure people that they are doing the right thing by playing safe. Stories about unexpected strokes of luck are good, but potentially even better are stories in which justice prevails. Actions have morally appropriate consequences. People who adhere to widely agreed or conventional morals are rewarded and wrongdoers are eventually called to account.

## Example

I mentioned French pharmacies a few pages ago and have done quite a bit of work for beauty brands that are either French or want to emulate French values. If you have worked with European beauty, you'll know that French women often make conservative brand choices. They are not easily distracted by flashy colour cosmetics and glitter. They are, however, very interested in beauty, which is seen to proceed from great skin, which in turn proceeds from fidelity to traditional products, often sold by trusted pharmacists. Consumers who 'play safe' in this manner like hearing about the rewards and successes of that strategy. They even enjoy it when the story and morals are not of their own culture, which is why women who are not French excitedly stock up on pharmacy skincare brands when visiting Paris – because less-is-more French beauty is seen as elusive and mysterious, a perception that is enhanced by its reliance on traditional, understated pharmacy brands.

## How to track power

*Insight*

Power is important. It is never equally distributed and it is always present, even in the most banal act of shopping. There are shopping experiences where 'the customer is always right' and then there are experiences where people are made to feel that they haven't quite qualified as customers or haven't performed 'being a customer' correctly. Consumers are currently very sensitive to the power relations that exist between themselves, brands and retailers, so it's worth thinking about these matters now before they surprise you with it.

The other reason why I bring up power in this book is because consumers want power on a grander scale than feeling welcome in shops, so there's benefit to retailers and marketers in examining what kinds of power they want, how it is lacking and then what they plan to do with it. They sense that there is power in social media and in consumer activism, but they have yet to manifest their dreams.

*Prompt*

**'How is the topic or situation shaped by assumptions of gender, race, social class or sexuality?'**
The reason I like this question is not just because I'm personally interested in working towards a world that has equality and justice, which I take to be common values. I ask it because when I bring it to new topics, such as branding and retailing, it often results in unexpected insights. A great way to use this prompt is to apply it to above-the-line and below-the-line marketing communications. If you see a person depicted or implied and you suspect that stereotyping might be going on, use your imagination to slot a person of another group into the picture and see if the story changes, becoming more interesting or less reasonable.

*Opportunity*

This exercise has two useful outcomes. First, it helps your brand or organization to be more inclusive, which is of paramount importance to today's consumers. There's detailed discussion of inclusivity in Chapter 6, and in Chapter 3, where I speak about desire and how it feels to be excluded from shopping. Second, it reveals the tacit assumptions in marketing communications and lets you make informed decisions about keeping or ditching those assumptions.

## Example

In 2018, US personal care corporation Kimberly-Clark renamed a variant of its facial tissues, which was then called Kleenex Mansize (BBC News, 2018). First introduced in 1956, the bigger, thicker tissues were at first called Kleenex For Men, because the latter half of the 20th century was a time when marketing felt the need to constantly reassure men of the manliness of various products. One can see how 'Mansize' eventually came to seem a more confident, less anxiously macho way of targeting the same customer, using the rationale that, on average, men are physically larger than women. Eventually, consumers complained, in 2018, when society had changed in the direction of alertness to unwanted discrimination. Kimberly-Clark's response of changing to another new name was a good one, but the company could have stepped in *before* complaints emerged, by taking a semiotic perspective. Would they have launched a range of tiny, one-ply tissues called Womansize? Of course not, and that's why this prompt is useful, because it denaturalizes things that we may be used to, but could stand to be refreshed. The product is now called Kleenex Extra Large.

## Prompt

'Are there mechanisms through which power is managed and passed around?'

Restaurants, hair and beauty salons and even services like language schools walk the customer through a pre-set process. The service provider may border on the deferential, yet, once the process has started, the customer does not have very much power and is highly likely to follow the tramlines of the event to its conclusion, even when this results in poor customer satisfaction. I once conducted research on behalf of L'Oreal, which entailed accompanying young women on trips to the hair salon. One participant looked stricken as we sat in the pub after her haircut. Technically, perhaps, she had received the fashionable hairstyle that she had indicated she wanted. But power was taken out of her hands when the stylist started the process and stopped asking questions. Philosophers Deleuze and Guattari talk about machines, and it's a useful metaphor because we can see the hairdressing salon as a machine that makes haircuts and the supermarket as a machine where the product is something like 'the big weekly shop'.

## Opportunity

The opportunity is to realize that your customers, who you may have felt are in a relatively powerful position or are even being pampered, do not feel in control all the time. They don't particularly enjoy feeling that they have been sucked into a machine, even though they will submit to it when they perceive that there's no better way to achieve their goals.

## Example

Speaking of being sucked into a machine, in 2017, a Twitter user called Paul Franks tweeted Elon Musk with a specific request regarding the Tesla. Franks asked, 'Can you guys program the car once in park to move back the seat and raise the steering wheel? Steering wheel is wearing.' Within 30 minutes, Musk replied, 'Good point. We will add that to all cars in one of the upcoming software releases.' You might argue that promises are not reality and that Musk's time frame was vague. You might also take the view that a member of the public being able to speak directly with the CEO of any company is an unusual situation. But on this latter point, the unusual situation is something that the digitally empowered consumer is coming to expect. Moreover, if Musk can reply to this type of request within 30 minutes, then it is within the power of a salon hairdresser to check in with their customer in case they are feeling nervous or upset.

## Prompt

**'Who holds and retains power? What are the benefits of gaining and retaining power?'**
We ran into questions like these when I discussed decentralized economies in Chapter 7. Decentralized economies are somewhat of a paradox. On the one hand, they are an ideal to many people. They intuitively seem democratic. Yet it is usually the case that the tools and platforms that allow decentralized economies and creator economies to flourish are privately owned. The individual consumer's power is partly illusory, and the attempt to achieve it, for most people, remains unfulfilled.

*Opportunity*

One opportunity is to recognize people's thwarted ambitions. When you see a situation of unbalanced power playing out between organizations and consumers, ask how consumers would benefit from being in a stronger position. It could be about simply getting paid and enjoying economic security. It could be that they want more and better ways to control their personal lives, such as having the resources to realize their creative or business ideas. Many people would like to live an aspirational lifestyle and enjoy sensational and relaxing leisure time with friends. Our chance as marketers is to notice when there's something that people want but don't have.

*Example*

In May 2021, Ronan Harris at Google announced that its Career Certificates had reached the UK, from where I write. Google charges a few hundred pounds for certificated courses in project management, UX design and data analytics. Courses are competitively priced in terms of the time the customer is required to invest, as well as how much money. This could be regarded as somewhat of an incursion by Google into the education space, putting it in competition with universities (which have struggled during the pandemic), but is difficult to criticize from a purely marketing point of view. Nike, to take another example, did a great job through the pandemic lockdowns of 2020 by encouraging everyone to participate in its online training, growing and becoming strong, in front of the audience they've always wanted.

## Dear Reader: An end and a beginning

Dear Reader, we have reached the end of this book and perhaps the beginning of your journey in semiotics, if it pleases you to join me. I urge you to try out all the ideas in this book for yourself and watch them come to life as you apply them to your own brand or retail business. This book has been a serious attempt to go beyond sharing observations about retail marketing and giving advice. More than simply revealing *what* I think, I've tried at each step to reveal *how* I think so that you can pick up the ball and run with it. Like almost everything else, semiotics is a team sport.

Supplementary resources accompany this book, including photos, reading groups and tools for designing semiotic research. These are available on the website of the book's publisher, Kogan Page, and on my own website and social media. I also draw your attention to my first book, *Using Semiotics in Marketing*, also from Kogan Page, which is a popular how-to manual of semiotics for all marketers and market researchers.

**Thank you for reading.**

## Endnote

1   Measured at a point in time three to six months after the launch of *Classic WoW*, also reported as the largest quarterly gain in WoW's history. A typical news report can be found at: https://www.overclock3d.net/news/software/world_of_warcraft_subscriber_base_has_doubled_since_the_release_of_wow_classic/1 (archived at https://perma.cc/U3C2-HKMM)

## References

BBC News (2018) Kleenex bins 'Mansize' tissues, https://www.bbc.co.uk/news/uk-politics-45899784 (archived at https://perma.cc/6D6D-NQCK)

Butler, O (2017) I made my shed the top-rated restaurant on TripAdvisor, *The Vice*, https://www.vice.com/en/article/434gqw/i-made-my-shed-the-top-rated-restaurant-on-tripadvisor (archived at https://perma.cc/A5H6-PCPZ)

Byrne, M (*nd*) 22 true stories about the most famous brands, *The Coolist*, https://www.thecoolist.com/true-stories-famous-brands/ (archived at https://perma.cc/Z6Y2-QJKN)

Harris, R (2021) Google Career Certificates launch in the UK, https://blog.google/around-the-globe/google-europe/united-kingdom/google-career-certificates-launch-uk/ (archived at https://perma.cc/2WV2-XA5U)

Lawes, R (2009) Futurology through semiotics, https://lawes-consulting.co.uk/wp-content/uploads/2018/06/280643603-futurology-through-semiotics-full-paper-vfinal.pdf (archived at https://perma.cc/V33Q-N2VM)

Musk, E (2017) on Twitter, https://twitter.com/elonmusk/status/898713949125787650 (archived at https://perma.cc/RXL7-MEN8)

# ACKNOWLEDGEMENTS

This book benefited enormously from the kind co-operation of Unilever. I am beyond grateful to Vijay Raj, Executive Vice President CMI, for his generosity in permitting the Unilever parts of this book to go ahead. I'm extremely thankful for the kindness and generosity of Keith Sleight, Director of Global Shopping Insights, who invested considerable amounts of his precious time in helping this book to happen. Huge thanks also to Iris Cremers, CMI Global Shopping Insight Manager, and Corinne Trentadue, CMI Shopping and Commerce Insight Manager France, for allowing me to interview them and share our conversation within these pages.

Publishers Kogan Page have been as supportive and encouraging as one could possibly wish for. Thank you, Heather Wood and Stephen Dunnell for being both meticulously professional and super fun to work with. Thanks to Lawes Consulting staff and our staunch, loyal freelancers who carried the burden of work while I was writing: Elina Halonen, Joe Lawes, Naurin Rashid and Daniel Sherrard all played a role in making this book possible, for which I'm grateful beyond words.

Finally, thanks to my partner, Denny Marcus, whose patience and understanding sustained both of us through seven months of writing, at all hours, seven days a week. Sorry we had to put off our wedding. I expect we can get around to that now. Thank you for waiting.

# INDEX

academic books (semiotics of shopping/consumption) 20–21
Activision Blizzard 251
ActMedia 226
*After Shock* (Brin) 205
*The Age of Surveillance* (Zuboff) 158
Airbnb 210
Alexa 130–31, 159
Alibaba Group 130, 137, 172–73, 197, 200
    Coins 141
    Singles Day 72, 134, 135
    Taobao 72, 135, 147, 173
    YouTube channel 176
*Alone Together* (Turkle) 153–54
Amazon 91, 97–98, 103–04, 108, 130, 154, 173, 174, 183, 200, 212, 245
Amazon Go 193, 246
American Museum of Natural History (New York) 153–54
Andrex puppy 160
animation 37, 57
anxiety 94–95, 156
    social 159–60, 161
    spike in 151–52
Apple 79, 161, 255
Apple iPhone 151
art 86–87
ASOS 90, 114
attention span 152
authentic and traditional 75–76
    images/icons 77
    materials 76
    store furniture, category management, merchandising 76
    traditional yet modern 77
    typefaces 77
Avo-Matic food truck 232
*Axie Infinity* (online game) 140, 141
Axie Marketplace 140–41

Babybel 57
bargain bin 72
Barnett, Michael 92
Barstool 145
Barthes, Roland 10

Baudrillard, Jean 121, 154
BBC shopping report (2021) 90
beauty (aesthetics) 53
    domestic interiors 53–54
    Instagram posts 53
    outdoor space 54
    teeth, hair, skin 54
Beckham, David and Victoria 135
behavioural futures market
    and control 133–34
    in depth 130–31
    introduction 130
    make something of lasting value 133
    mould/shape reality 132
    own something 133
    perform magic 133
    retail marketers actions 132–33
    semiotics perspective 131–32
behaviourism 131–32
Ben Sherman shirts 90, 98
Bezos, Jeff 164
Bhaktiari, Kian 146
Black Friday 72
BOGOF promotions 55
Boots pharmacy 239, 248
bottom-up analysis 13, 14
Bourdieu, Pierre 20–21, 56, 58
brand
    ambassadors 193
    authenticity 75
    communicating architecture/range 233–35
    communicating values 231–32
    message 68
    own brand 221
branding 174–75
*Brandsplaining* (Cunningham & Roberts) 120
Branson, Richard 164
Brin, David 205
Build-A-Bear Workshop 123–24
business books
    business/academia nexus 19–20
    semiotics 19
    shoppers/shopping behaviour 18–19

buyer's remorse 63
ByteDance 145

*Call Her Daddy* (podcast) 145
Campbell, Colin 58–59, 63
Carrefour 83
Casper (sleep products) 230–31, 239
category management 69, 73, 76, 79, 80, 82–83, 225–27
category management Unilever 31–33
Charmin bears 160
Clinique 61
closing down sale 71, 72
collections, collecting 52
colour 56–57, 70, 72, 73–74, 78, 81, 84
commodity racism 113–14
communicative output 13
consensus reality 249–53
conspicuous consumption 119–20
consumers (relationships)
  in depth 158–59
  exercise 162–63
  introduction 157
  nurture 161
  parasocial 159, 161–62
  problem 158
  retail marketers actions 160–62
  semiotic perspective 159–60
  socially anxious 159–60, 161
  virtue 161–62
  what's going well 158
consumers (sicknesses of consumer culture)
  anxiety/depression spike 151–52
  creativity as limited/conservative 152
  in depth 151–52
  exercise 156–57
  global context 151
  introduction 150–51
  loss of empathy 152
  loss of value in reality 153–54
  problem of depersonalization 152
  responding to 155–56
  retail marketers actions 154–55
  semiotic perspective 153–54
  shrinking attention spans 152
consumption
  academic books on 20–21
  exclusions 54–55
  improving experience of 55–56
control
  behavioural futures market 130, 133–34
  collecting 52
  consumer 142, 143, 259
  creator economy 145–46

  loss of 204–05
  and power 82
  shopper needs/behaviour 91–95
  tech users 158
Cooper, Alexandra 145
corporate social responsibility (CSR) 162–63
Covid anxiety syndrome 93
*COVID-19: The Great Reset* (Schwab) 193
COVID-19 pandemic 253
  consequences of 151
  loss of jobs during 146
  shopping/spending during 89–91, 92, 93, 115, 117, 134
*Creating Value* (Oswald) 19
creativity 152
creator and decentralized economies 251, 259
  creators need an audience/platform 147
  currencies (Bitcoin, Ether, Dogecoin) 145
  in depth 145–46
  exercise 148
  facilitate/reward play 148
  introduction 144–45
  making content 147–48
  retail marketers actions 147–48
  semiotics perspective 146–47
cryptocurrencies 145, 146
culture 12
  global and mass agreement 54
Cunningham, Jane 120
Cushelle koala 160
Custom Made Palm Tree 221
customers
  attracting younger consumers 123–24
  company investment in keeping energy up 112
  experience 17–18
  finding new friends/banding together 112–13
  fully integrated/innovative experience 185–90
  version of reality 112
customization/personalization of items 123–24
CVS Pharmacy 224–25
cybersecurity 198

data analytics 131
Davis, Katie 152
Day, Felicia 124
Debenhams 98, 104
*Decentraland* (VR platform) 164
decentralized economy *see* creator and decentralized economies

Deguchi, Atsushi 199
dehumanizing of retail 194–95
Deleuze, Gilles 258
depersonalization 152
depression 151–52
desire 49
    activating 61–62
    aesthetics 53–55
    disappointments 62–64
    exercise 65
    motivational principles 50–53
    pain of exclusion 54–56
    pleasure and satisfaction 56–59
    rewards 64–65
    romantic 59–60
Diderot Effect 99
digital 81–82
digital ecosystems *see* ecosystem
digital presence
    collaborative not passive activities 181
    conventional e-stores 182–83
    in depth 180–81
    introduction 180
    language 183
    packaging 184
    practical exercise 184
    product pages 183
    questions concerning 180
    retail marketers actions 182–84
    semiotics perspective 181–82
    Shop Now button 182
    similarity of design/appearance 180–81
    tell a story 181–82
    videos 184
    *see also* e-commerce
Disney 153–54
Disneyland 155
*Distinction: A social critique of the judgement of taste* (Bourdieu) 20–21
diversity and inclusivity 113–15
    Katy Perry Collection example 114–15
    marketing tips 118
    Paperchase example 115–18
    semiotic insights into 115
Double 11 shopping festival 185
    build-up to 135
    co-operate with business partners 137
    effect of COVID-19 on 134
    exercise 138
    expansion/success of 135
    gamification 135
    multi-channel experience 135–36
    reality accessed in real time with real people 138
    retail marketers actions 137–38
    semiotic perspective 136–37
    show something not seen before 137
Dove Campaign for Real Beauty 124
Dudarenok, Michael 181, 200, 201

e-commerce 11, 16, 19, 68, 74, 193
    dropped basket phenomenon 173
    insights 34–35
    language 183
    live streaming 185–90
    practical suggestions 180–84
    questions/answers 235–37
    Unilever 33–37
    *see also* digital presence
Easterling, Addison Rae 145
eBay 72, 90
    Bucks 141
    Mastercard 141
ecosystem
    branching out with digital presence example 180–84
    checklist of questions exercise 175–76
    in depth 172–73
    designing fully integrated/innovative customer experience example 185–90
    introduction 171–72
    physical store example 176–79
    retail marketers actions 174–75
    semiotics perspective 173–74
El-Saleh, Tomm 86–87
empathy, loss of 152, 157
empowerment 116
    *see also* power
Energizer bunny 161
Epic Games 139, 145
Ericsson 165–66
Etsy 57, 174–75

Facebook 75, 93, 147, 151–52, 157, 251
families 155
fantasy
    activating desire 61–62
    as central to desire 59–60
    Disney parks 155
    product as entirely imaginary 60
    tragedy adds flavour/depth to 60
    travel as well as wealth 60
fast moving consumer goods (FCMG) 201, 202, 203, 231
Featherstone, Mike 53
feminism 116–17
FIFA World Cup 136
Flickr 227

flying warehouses 200
Foot Locker 82–83
*Forbes* magazine 133, 135, 146
Forrester Consulting 185
Fortnum & Mason 69
*The Fourth Industrial Revolution* (Schwab) 193
Franks, Paul 259
Freshippo 176–77, 200, 246
Fruit of the Loom 90, 98
future of business
    behavioural 130–34
    creator/decentralized economies 144–48
    Double 11 festival 134–38
    play-to-earn 139–44
future of everything
    in depth 193–94, 197–98, 203–06
    exercises 197, 202–03, 211–12
    introductions 192–93, 197, 203
    retail marketers actions 195–97, 200–201, 208–10
    semiotics perspective 194–95, 199–200, 206–08
future humans
    cognitive process 207
    dark/light predictions 206–07, 209
    in depth 203–06
    fear of redundancy 207
    feelings 209–10
    human body changes 207–08, 210
    introduction 203
    metaverse 203–04
    needs 206, 208
    practical exercise 211–12
    retail marketers actions 208–10
    semiotics perspective 206–08
    singularity 204–06
    wants 206, 208–09
future of retail
    branching out with digital presence 180–84
    designing fully integrated/innovative customer experience 185–90
    digital ecosystems 171–76
    traditional grocery store/small physical store 176–79
future-facing 77–78
    colours 78
    materials 78
    store furniture, category management, merchandising 79
    typefaces 79

games, gamification, games industry 139–44, 164, 202, 222

GameStop 108–09, 252
    semiotics conclusions on 110–12
Gap 104
Gardner, Howard 152
Gen Z 54, 114
Gift With Purchase (GWP) 175
Gillette 211
global and local 84–85, 151
    how to be global 85–86
    how to be local 86–88
    questions and answers 238–40
Google 202, 260
Google Images 227
gross merchandise value (GMV) 135, 136, 185
group effort 249–53
Guattari, Félix 258

H&M 90, 97, 98
Hamari, J 149
Happy Family Organics 234–35
Harari, Yuval Noah 165, 205, 206
Harris, Roman 260
Harvard School of Public Health 92
Hofstede Optick 239
Home Bargains 60
Home Depot 84
Home Shopping Network 135–36
Honest Tea 133–34
Hulu 108
HWKN architects 229–30

ideas, generating 242
    decoding stories 253–56
    everything is a group effort 249–53
    reality is in crisis 243–46
    reality is under construction 246–49
    tracking power 257–60
identity
    conspicuous consumption 119–20
    diversity and inclusivity 113–18
    and empowerment 116–17
    and feeling unique 123–24
    feelings outrank facts 111–12
    people love collections 122–23
    personal branding/self-construction 123
    and reality 112, 120–24
    showing customers how to envisage themselves 122
    stock market example 108–12
IKEA 133
inclusivity *see* diversity and inclusivity
influencers 58–59, 74, 120, 136, 145, 185–86, 193, 254

*Inside the Mind of the Shopper* (Sorensen) 18–19
inside-out approach to research 11–12
Instagram 54, 93, 119, 157

jam of death case study
  failed setup 4–5
  recommendations 6–7
  where have I seen this before question 5–6
JCDecaux 195
JD.com 134, 137, 139, 145
Jensen, Keld 133–34
Jinton, Jonna 74
Jobs, Steve 255
John Lewis Partnership 133
Joules 90, 97, 104

Katy Perry Collections 114–15
Kelly, Kevin 204, 207, 210, 245
Kevlar 78
key opinion leaders (KOLs) 136, 185
Kimberley-Clark 258
Kingston University 93
Kleenex 258

Li, Austin 185, 186, 187, 193
live streaming 135–37
  e-commerce 185–90
London South Bank University 93
L'Oreal 258
Loved Before 161, 162, 182
loyalty programmes 143
Lululemon 209
Lury, Celia 63
Lush body care 148

Ma, Jack 172–73, 177, 205
McClintock, Anne 113–14
McDonalds 202
McKinsey reports 72, 185
magic 133
Make a Wish Foundation 161
market research (methods, tools, theories) 11–12
marketing
  encouraging fantasy 61–62
  messages (efficiency, sustainability, harmony, social care) 201
  social media 74
  to specific cultures/regions 41–45
marketing (questions/answers)
  attention and attraction 220–21
  communicating brand architecture/range 233–35

communicating brand values 231–32
e-commerce 235–37
engagement 222–23
global marketing 238–40
in-store experience (including pleasure) 229–31
merchandising/category management 225–27
navigation 227–29
selling 223–25
mascots 160, 161
Maslow, Abraham 208
mass culture 160
materials 74, 76, 78, 81, 83
Mattel 255
'Me at 23' vs 'My parents at 23' memes 136–37
meaning creation 231
  authentic/traditional 75–77
  future-facing 77–79
  global/local 84–88
  introduction 68
  natural, healthy, sustainable 73–75
  power 82–84
  premium 68–70
  sensational/exciting 80–82
  value 70–72
Medium 144
merchandising 69, 73, 76, 79, 80, 82–83, 225–27
metaverse 203–04
Michigan University 152
Ministry of Defence (MoD) report (2021) 208, 212
mission 95–96
Morrisons 196
Mrs Hinch 58, 254
Musk, Elon 145, 164, 259
Mylar 78

National Institute for Health Research 152
natural, healthy, sustainable 73
  colours 73–74
  digital, e-commerce, social media marketing 74
  images/icons 74
  materials 74
  pack formats 73
  store furniture, category management, merchandising 73
  tone of voice 75
  typefaces 74
Natural History Museum (London) 178
needs 206, 208, 211
Netflix 93, 108, 130

networking  164
Niantic
    *Pokémon Go*  202
Nikčević, Ana  93
Nike  81–82
Nintendo  161
    *Animal Crossings: New Horizons*  159
    *Pokémon*  140
non-fungible tokens (NFTs)  140, 164, 166
non-human entities  159–60
Noom  252
normative  54
nostalgia  50, 155
    making adults feel like children  50–51
novelty  176–77

online vs offline  188
outrage economy  151
outside-in approach to research  11, 12

packaging  55–56, 57
    aesthetically pleasing  208
    e-commerce  184
    pack formats  69, 72, 73, 81, 83
    as precious objects  179
Paperchase  115–18
Patreon  144
Perry, Katy  114
Persil  245–46
Pikachu  161
Pillsbury Dough Boy  161
play-to-earn
    in depth  139–41
    exercise  143–44
    freemium games  140
    hallmarks of  140
    insights  143
    introduction  139
    retail marketers actions  142
    semiotic perspective  141–42
    subscription model  140
PlayStation  61, 93
pleasure/satisfaction  49, 64
    animation  57
    choice/variety  56
    colours  56–57
    communicating  25
    fragrance  57
    gifts/samples  57
    glitter/metallics  56
    immediate/real  56, 58–59, 60, 65
    in-store experience  229–31
    items that are charming/cute  58
    many items for not much money  57
    packaging satisfying to open  57
    something to celebrate  58
poverty (pain of unaffordability)  54–55
power  82
    colours  84
    materials  83
    pack formats  83
    store furniture, category management, merchandising  82–83
    tracking  257–60
    typefaces  83
premium
    colour  70
    pack formats  69
    Signs of Care  68–70
    store furniture, category management, merchandising  69
    typefaces  70
premium brands/lifestyle products & services  61
    build up anticipation  61
    maximalism  61
    stock limited supplies  61
    tertiary colours  61
    use past, future or exotic  61–62
Pringles  57
projection  51–52
promotions  55
prompt questions  9–10, 15–16

QR codes  176, 178, 227

*Ready Player One* (film, 2018)  154, 204
reality  111
    company vs customer version  111
    consensus  249–53
    in crisis  243–46
    escape back to  166
    feelings outrank facts  111–12
    moulding/shaping  132
    reality-enhancing experiences/products  150–51
    representations of  120–24
    retail marketing ideas  122–24
    unable to recognize  156
    under construction  246–49
Reddit  109–10, 112–13, 252
replenishment shopping  173–74
*Resurrecting Retail* (Stephens)  189
retail *see* marketing; shopping experience
retail marketers actions  68
    control, comfort, rewards  94–95
    creator/decentralized economies  147–48
    digital ecosystem  174–75

digital presence 182–84
future humans 208–10
integrated/innovative customer experience 188–89
objects of desire 166–67
play-to-earn 142
relationships 160–62
shopper mission 98–99
sickness of consumer culture 154–56
smart cities 200–201
stories 101, 102, 103, 104, 105
talent 195–97
tradition/physical stores 178–79
rewards 64–65, 91–95, 148
Roberts, Philippa 120
Robinhood mobile app 112
Roblox Corporation 206
Robocop 199–200
*The Romantic Ethic and the Spirit of Modern Consumerism* (Campbell) 58–59

Save the Children 133
Schwab, Klaus 193
Selfridges (Birmingham) 50–51
semiotic
    challenge 10
    perspective 4
    questions 9–10, 15–16
    signs and symbols 5–9, 13, 220, 238–39
semiotics 3–4
    overall approach 10–16
    in retail marketing 16–17
    there is nothing outside the text 244
    unique perspectives 131–32, 136–37, 141, 153–54, 159–60, 173–74, 186–88, 194–95, 199–200
    usefulness in designing customer experiences 17–18
*Semiotics, Marketing and Communication* (Floch) 19
sensational and exciting 80
    colours 81
    digital 81–82
    materials 81
    pack formats 81
    store furniture, category management, merchandising 80
Shop Now button 182
Shopify 182
shopper anxiety-shopping-anxiety feedback loop 94
shopper needs/behaviour 89
    control, comfort, rewards 91–95

mission 91, 95–96
need 96–99
personal example 89–91, 97–98
retail marketers actions 94–95, 98–99
shopping experience
    after purchase 63–64, 68
    collaborative not passive activities 181
    good/not good 196–97
    humour 221
    managing 64
    navigation 225–27
    own brand benefits 221
    rewards 64–65
    signs of happiness 220
    in store 62, 178–79, 229–31
Signs of Care 68–70
Singles Day 72, 134, 135, 193
singularity 204–06
Siri 159
Skinner, B F 131
Sky News 114
smart cities
    benefits/cultural differences 199–200
    democratic ideas 203
    in depth 197–98
    exotic/everyday 197–98
    introduction 197
    local meaning of 'better for society' 201
    making shopping easier 200–201
    pair ideas/see how they fit 201
    physical space/bricks-and-mortar part of solution 202
    practical exercise 202–03
    problems 199
    retail marketers actions 200–201
    semiotics perspective 199–200
    vending machines 202
smart devices 164
smartcitiesworld.net 198
social anxiety 159–60, 161
*The Social Dilemma* (docudrama, 2020) 130
social media 53, 54, 74, 75, 93, 144, 146–47, 157, 184, 251
society 12
Sorensen, Herb 18, 62, 130, 194–95
Spada, Marcantonio 93
Spielberg, Steven 154, 204, 206
Spotify 145
Sprint 202
staff (talent)
    attracting, retaining, compensating 194
    as brand ambassadors 193
    challenges 194
    dehumanization of retail 194–95

staff (talent) (*Continued*)
    in depth 193–94
    good/not good experiences 196–97
    introduction 192–93
    practical exercise 197
    retail marketers actions 195–97
    security issues 195
    semiotics perspective 194–95
Starbucks 202
Steen, Mats 158–59, 160
Stephens, Doug 189, 193, 194
store furniture 69, 73, 76, 79, 80, 82–83, 179, 208
stories
    about future events 102–03
    about past events 103–04
    about relationships 101
    about self 100–101
    decoding 253–56
    e-commerce sites 181–82
    hidden 254–55
    importance of 100
    as myth 254
    rags-to-riches 255–56
    recount shopping trips, after the fact 104–05
    shared/circulated 102
street art 87
Super Bowl 136
Swift, Taylor 135

Taobao Live 185–86
Teams 93
*The Telegraph* newspaper 93
teleology 205–06
Tencent Holdings Ltd 139, 145
Tide washing powder 84
TikTok 54, 93, 144, 146
Tinder 164
Titan Outdoor Advertising 195
Tmall 72, 147, 173, 184
tone of voice
    healthy 75
    natural 75
    sustainability 75
    wellbeing 75
top-down analysis 14–15, 242
Toyota Woven City (Japan) 198
traditional stores
    in depth 176–77
    exteriors/entrances 178
    furniture 179
    introduction 176
    novelty 176–77
    packaging/shopping bags 179
    practical exercise 179
    semiotics perspective 177–78
    service counters 178
    shopping experience 177–78
    supermarket trolleys 178
    very small spaces 179
    zones, aisles, in-store signs 178–79
transformative experiences 124
True to Size tag 183
truisms 245–46
trust and honour system 133–34
Turkle, Sherry 153–54, 196
Twinings Assam 173, 174
Twitch 144
Twitter 75, 117, 259
typeface 70, 74, 77, 79, 83

UNICEF 133
Unilever 33–34
Unilever (use of semiotics) 23
    application 25–27
    business practice 27–28
    category management, navigation, fixtures 31–33
    e-commerce 33–37
    global design/marketing 28–31
    introduction 24–27
    magic of semiotics 37–41
    marketing to specific cultures/regions 41–45
unique perspectives
    creator/decentralized economies 146–47
    digital ecosystems 173–74
    digital presence 181–82
    Double II festival 136–37
    future of business 131–32
    future humans 206–08
    integrated/innovative customer experience 186–88
    objects of desire 165–66
    play-to-earn 141–42
    relationships 159–60
    sickness of consumer culture 153–54
    smart cities 199–200
    talent 194–95
    traditional/physical store 177–78
unique selling point (USP) 174
University of California 152
user experience 17
*Using Semiotics in Marketing* (Lawes) 4, 19, 223, 245

Vahlo, J 149

value for money (VFM) 70–71, 72
  closing down sale example 71
  colours 72
  fixtures 72
  pack formats 72
  signage, price notifications, words and text 72
Verge podcast 204
videos 36, 184
  influencer 57, 59, 60, 185–86
  shopping-haul 57, 59–60, 186
  unboxing 186
  *see also* YouTube
virtue 162–63

Waitrose 69, 119, 133
Walgren Boots Alliance 239
Wall Street Bets (WSB) 60, 109–10, 111–13
Wannabe Toys 237
wants (future objects of desire) 206, 208–09, 211
  attract desirable things 165
  in depth 163–65
  escape (back) to reality 166
  escape from the body 166–67
  exclusive access 164
  exercise 168
  fly to the future 167
  fly to a new Eden 167
  frustrations 163
  improving digital self/life online 164
  introduction 163
  life-extending/life-preserving services 165
  living in desirable areas 164
  luxury/moral purity 163
  meeting people (networking) 164
  precious objects 164
  privacy/anonymity 164
  reach for freedom 166
  retail marketers actions 166–67
  self-improvement 165
  semiotics perspective 165–66
  smart devices 164
  things never seen before 164
Wegmans 228–29
where have I heard this before 8–9
where have I seen this before 245
  activity 7–8
  jam and death case study 5–6
  suggested answers 8–9
Wholesome Games (WG) 155–56
WHOO beauty brand 135
WHSmith 133–34
*Why We Buy* (Underhill) 18–19
Willis, Susan 113
Wilmot, Jack 152
*Wired* magazine 207
women 84
Workopolis 92
World Economic Forum 193
World Health Organization (WHO) 92, 152
*World of Warcraft* (game) 251
YouTube 57, 93, 144, 152, 164, 176, 177, 182, 186
  *see also* videos

Zakkour, A G 181, 200, 201
Zoflora 52
Zoom 92, 93, 97, 101, 102
Zuboff, Shoshanna 130, 158, 202–03, 206
Zuckerberg, Mark 92, 94, 100, 204